D1203092

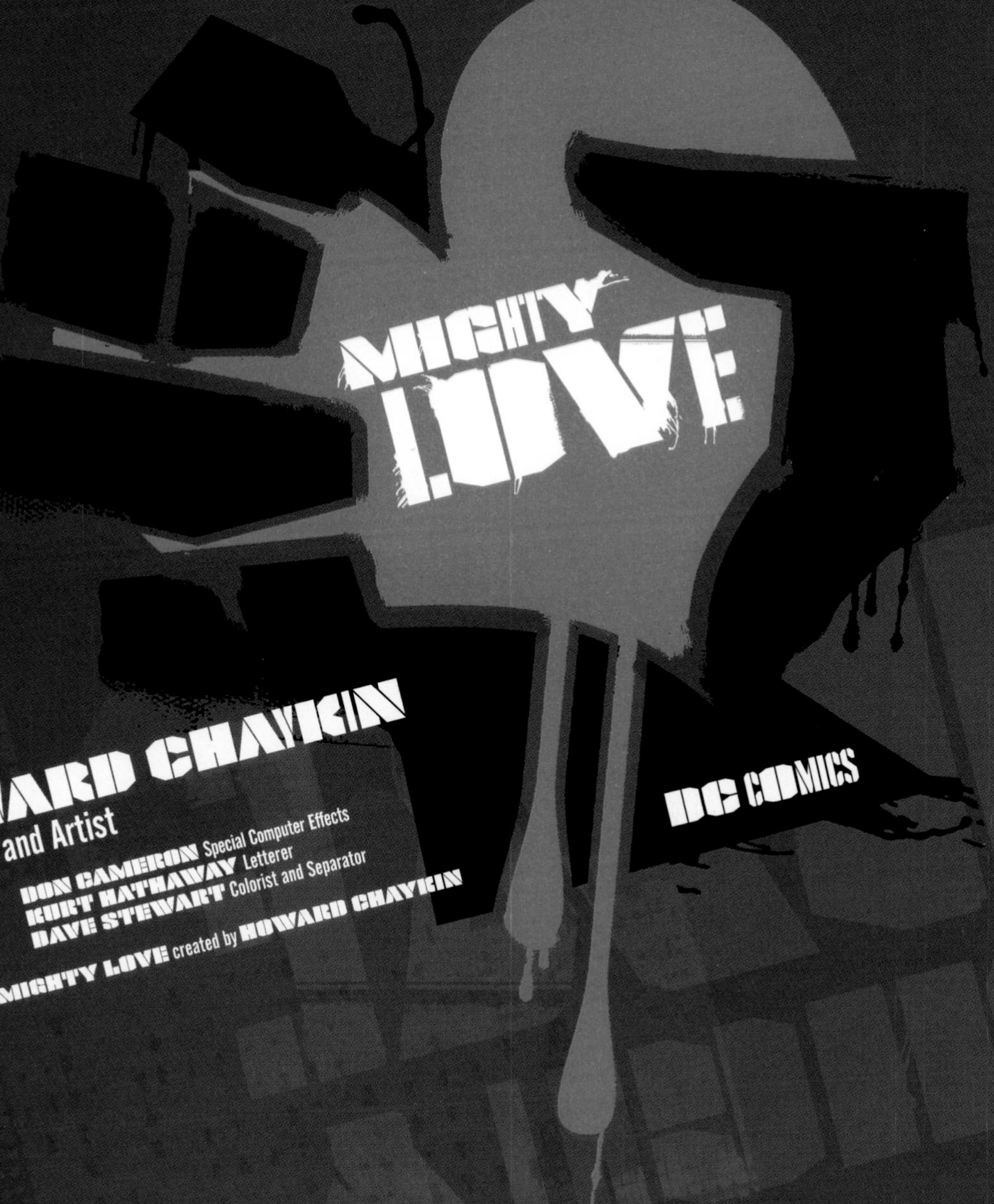

MIGHTY LOVE

HOWARD CHAYKIN

HOWARD CHAYKIN
Writer and Artist

DON CAMERON Special Computer Effects
KURT HATHAWAY Letterer
DAVE STEWART Colorist and Separator

MIGHTY LOVE created by HOWARD CHAYKIN

DC COMICS

MIGHTY LOVE
...published by DC Comics, 1700 Broadway, New York, NY 10019.

DC Comics. A Warner Bros. Entertainment Company
HC ISBN: 1-56389-930-2
SC ISBN: 1-56389-931-0

Cover Artist: Howard Chaykin
Cover Colorist and Separator: Dave Stewart
Publication Design: Rian Hughes

DC COMICS
Dan DiDio: VP - Editorial
Joey Cavalieri: Editor
Amie Brockway-Metcalf: Art Director
Paul Levitz: President & Publisher
Georg Brewer: VP - Design & Retail Product Development
Richard Bruning: Senior VP - Creative Director
Patrick Caldon: Senior VP - Finance & Operations
Chris Caramalis: VP - Finance
Terri Cunningham: VP - Managing Editor
Alison Gill: VP - Manufacturing
Lillian Laserson: Senior VP & General Counsel
Jim Lee: Editorial Director - WildStorm
David McKillips: VP - Advertising & Custom Publishing
John Nee: VP - Business Development
Cheryl Rubin: VP - Brand Management
Bob Wayne: VP - Sales & Marketing

For Laurel...
who thought of it first.
-HVC

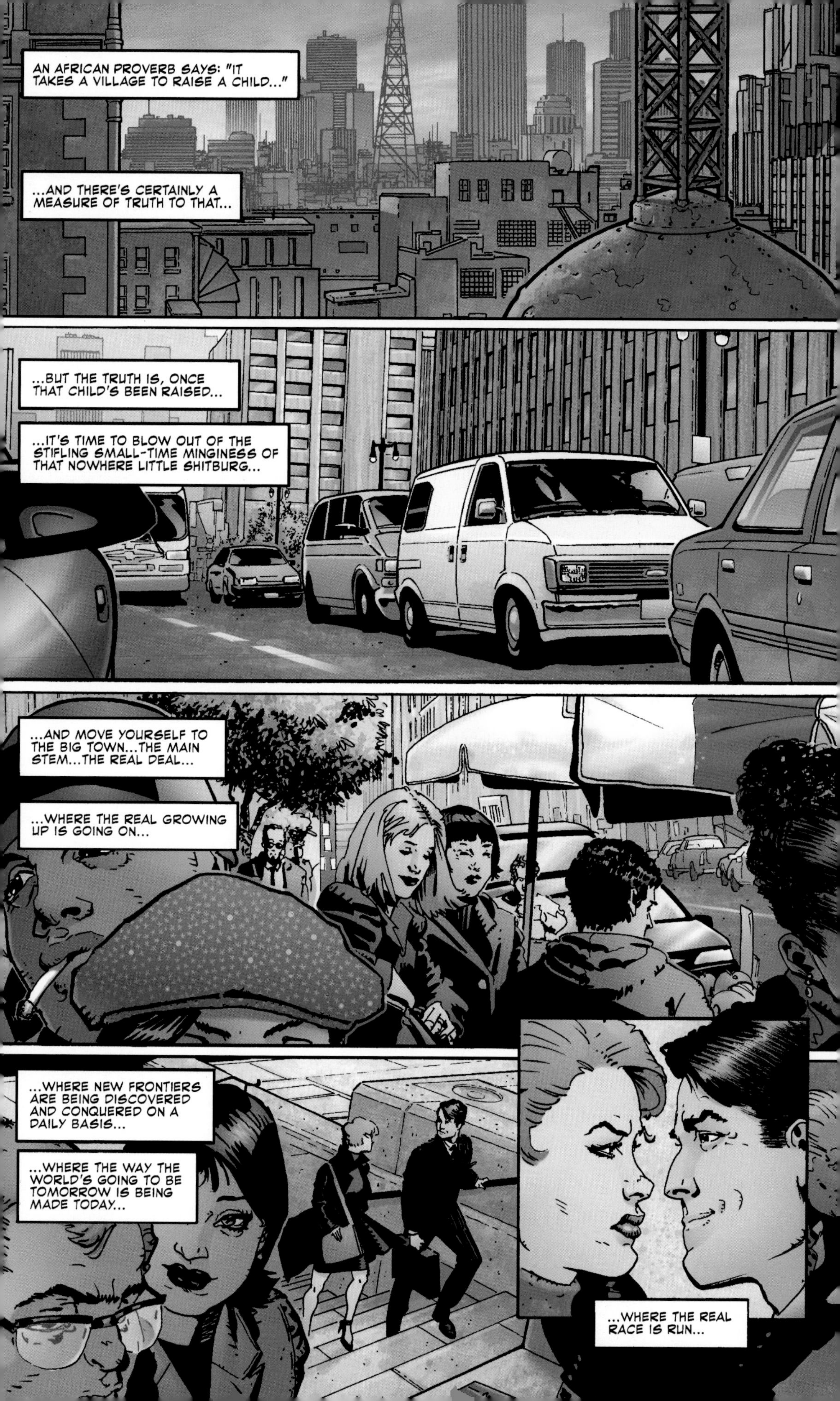

AN AFRICAN PROVERB SAYS: "IT TAKES A VILLAGE TO RAISE A CHILD..."
...AND THERE'S CERTAINLY A MEASURE OF TRUTH TO THAT...
...BUT THE TRUTH IS, ONCE THAT CHILD'S BEEN RAISED...
...IT'S TIME TO BLOW OUT OF THE STIFLING SMALL-TIME MINGINESS OF THAT NOWHERE LITTLE SHITBURG...
...AND MOVE YOURSELF TO THE BIG TOWN...THE MAIN STEM...THE REAL DEAL...
...WHERE THE REAL GROWING UP IS GOING ON...
...WHERE NEW FRONTIERS ARE BEING DISCOVERED AND CONQUERED ON A DAILY BASIS...
...WHERE THE WAY THE WORLD'S GOING TO BE TOMORROW IS BEING MADE TODAY...
...WHERE THE REAL RACE IS RUN...

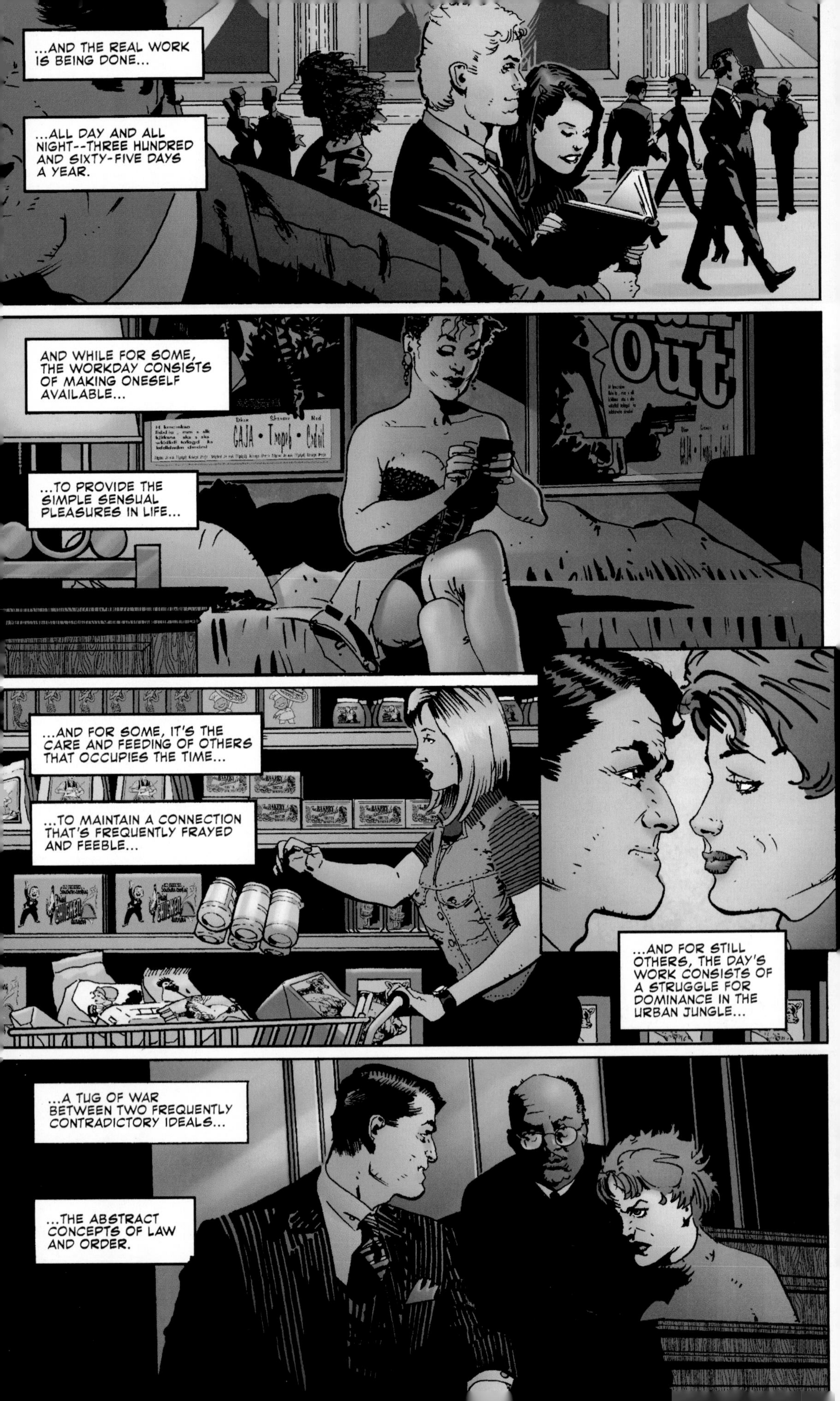
...AND THE REAL WORK IS BEING DONE...
...ALL DAY AND ALL NIGHT--THREE HUNDRED AND SIXTY-FIVE DAYS A YEAR.
AND WHILE FOR SOME, THE WORKDAY CONSISTS OF MAKING ONESELF AVAILABLE...
Out
...TO PROVIDE THE SIMPLE SENSUAL PLEASURES IN LIFE...
...AND FOR SOME, IT'S THE CARE AND FEEDING OF OTHERS THAT OCCUPIES THE TIME...
...TO MAINTAIN A CONNECTION THAT'S FREQUENTLY FRAYED AND FEEBLE...
...AND FOR STILL OTHERS, THE DAY'S WORK CONSISTS OF A STRUGGLE FOR DOMINANCE IN THE URBAN JUNGLE...
...A TUG OF WAR BETWEEN TWO FREQUENTLY CONTRADICTORY IDEALS...
...THE ABSTRACT CONCEPTS OF LAW AND ORDER.

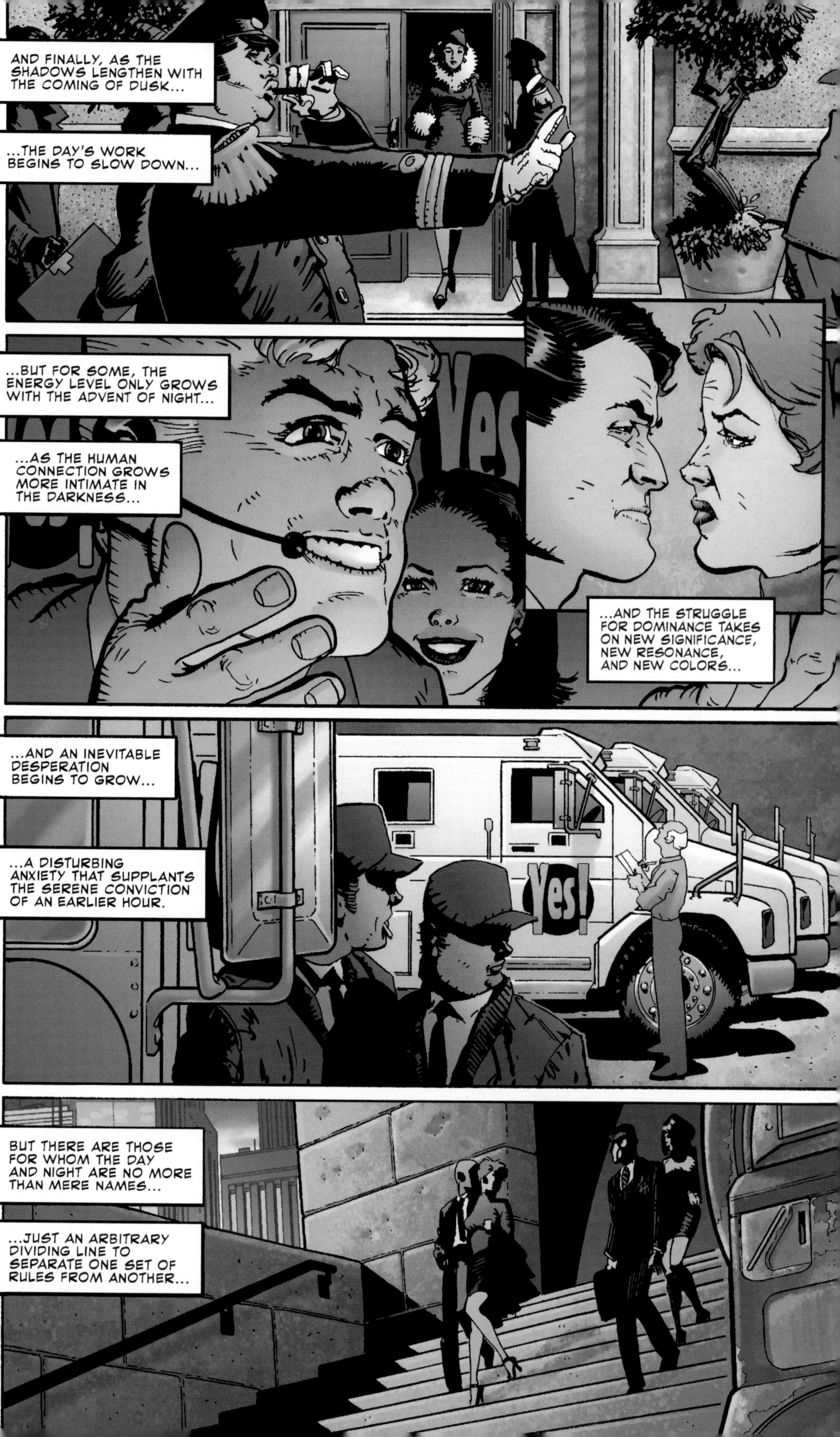
AND FINALLY, AS THE SHADOWS LENGTHEN WITH THE COMING OF DUSK...
...THE DAY'S WORK BEGINS TO SLOW DOWN...
...BUT FOR SOME, THE ENERGY LEVEL ONLY GROWS WITH THE ADVENT OF NIGHT...
...AS THE HUMAN CONNECTION GROWS MORE INTIMATE IN THE DARKNESS...
...AND THE STRUGGLE FOR DOMINANCE TAKES ON NEW SIGNIFICANCE, NEW RESONANCE, AND NEW COLORS...
...AND AN INEVITABLE DESPERATION BEGINS TO GROW...
...A DISTURBING ANXIETY THAT SUPPLANTS THE SERENE CONVICTION OF AN EARLIER HOUR.
Yes!
BUT THERE ARE THOSE FOR WHOM THE DAY AND NIGHT ARE NO MORE THAN MERE NAMES...
...JUST AN ARBITRARY DIVIDING LINE TO SEPARATE ONE SET OF RULES FROM ANOTHER...

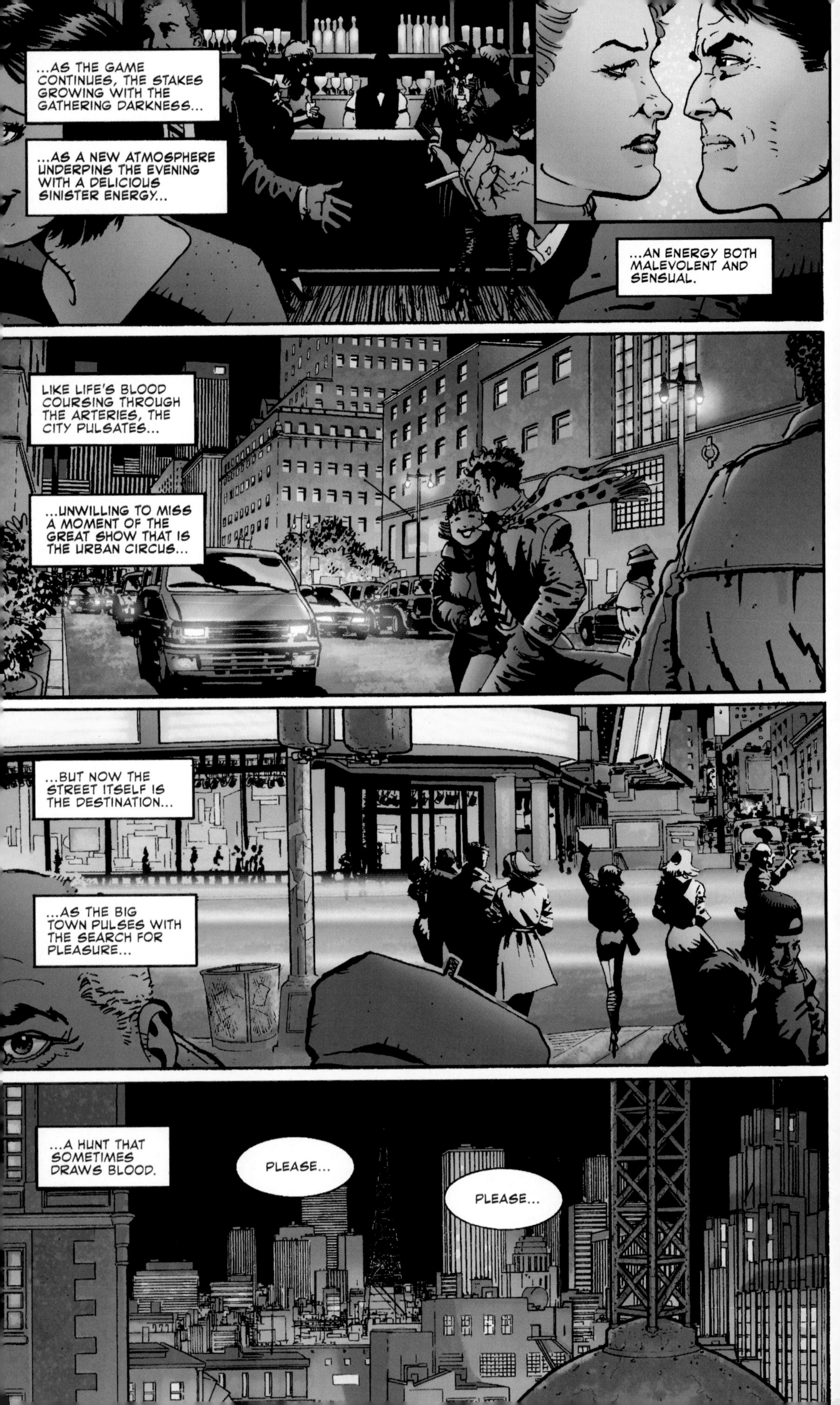
...AS THE GAME CONTINUES, THE STAKES GROWING WITH THE GATHERING DARKNESS...
...AS A NEW ATMOSPHERE UNDERPINS THE EVENING WITH A DELICIOUS SINISTER ENERGY...
...AN ENERGY BOTH MALEVOLENT AND SENSUAL.
LIKE LIFE'S BLOOD COURSING THROUGH THE ARTERIES, THE CITY PULSATES...
...UNWILLING TO MISS A MOMENT OF THE GREAT SHOW THAT IS THE URBAN CIRCUS...
...BUT NOW THE STREET ITSELF IS THE DESTINATION...
...AS THE BIG TOWN PULSES WITH THE SEARCH FOR PLEASURE...
...A HUNT THAT SOMETIMES DRAWS BLOOD.
PLEASE...
PLEASE...

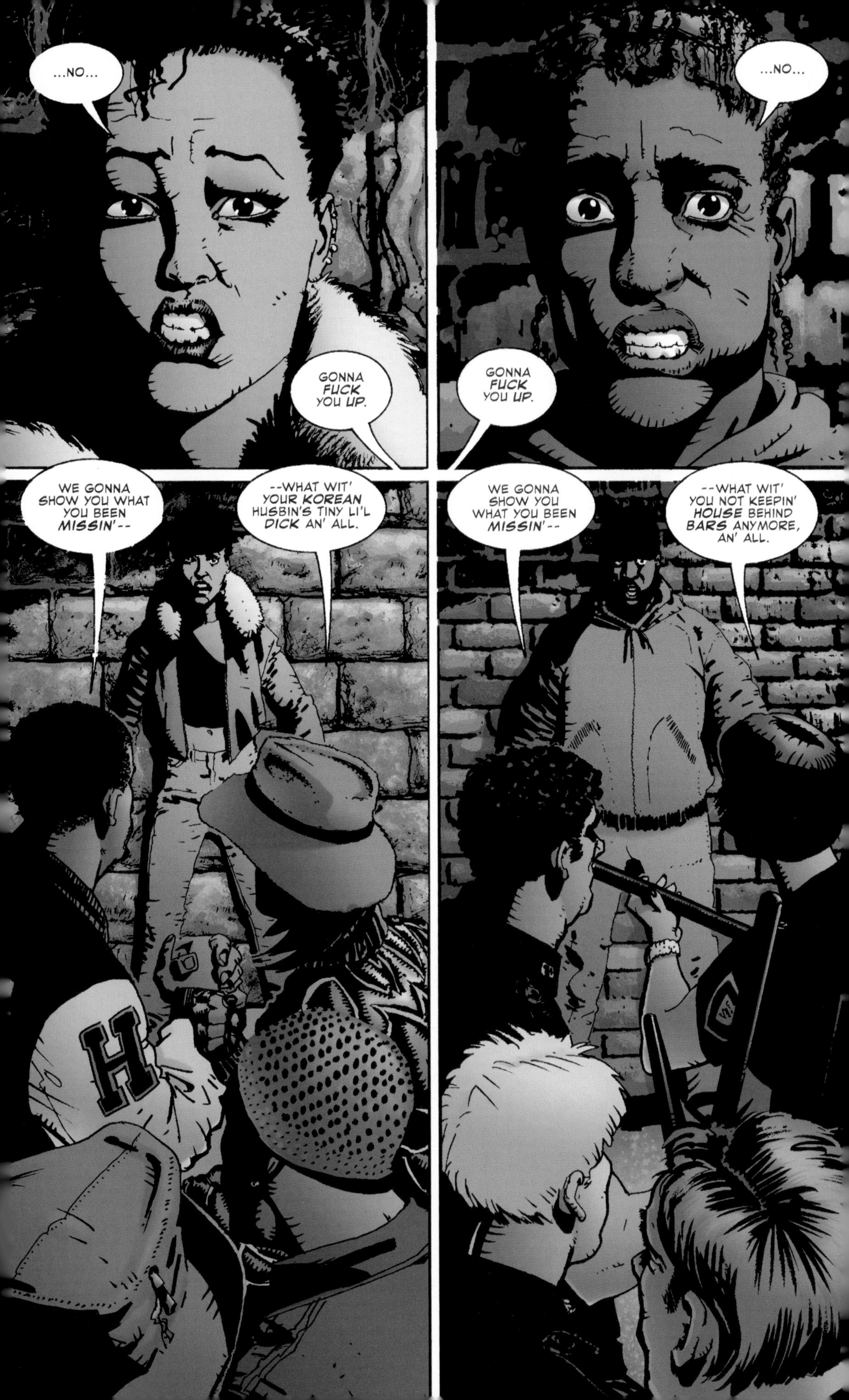
...NO...
GONNA FUCK YOU UP.
...NO...
GONNA FUCK YOU UP.
WE GONNA SHOW YOU WHAT YOU BEEN MISSIN'--
--WHAT WIT' YOUR KOREAN HUSBIN'S TINY LI'L DICK AN' ALL.
WE GONNA SHOW YOU WHAT YOU BEEN MISSIN'--
--WHAT WIT' YOU NOT KEEPIN' HOUSE BEHIND BARS ANYMORE, AN' ALL.

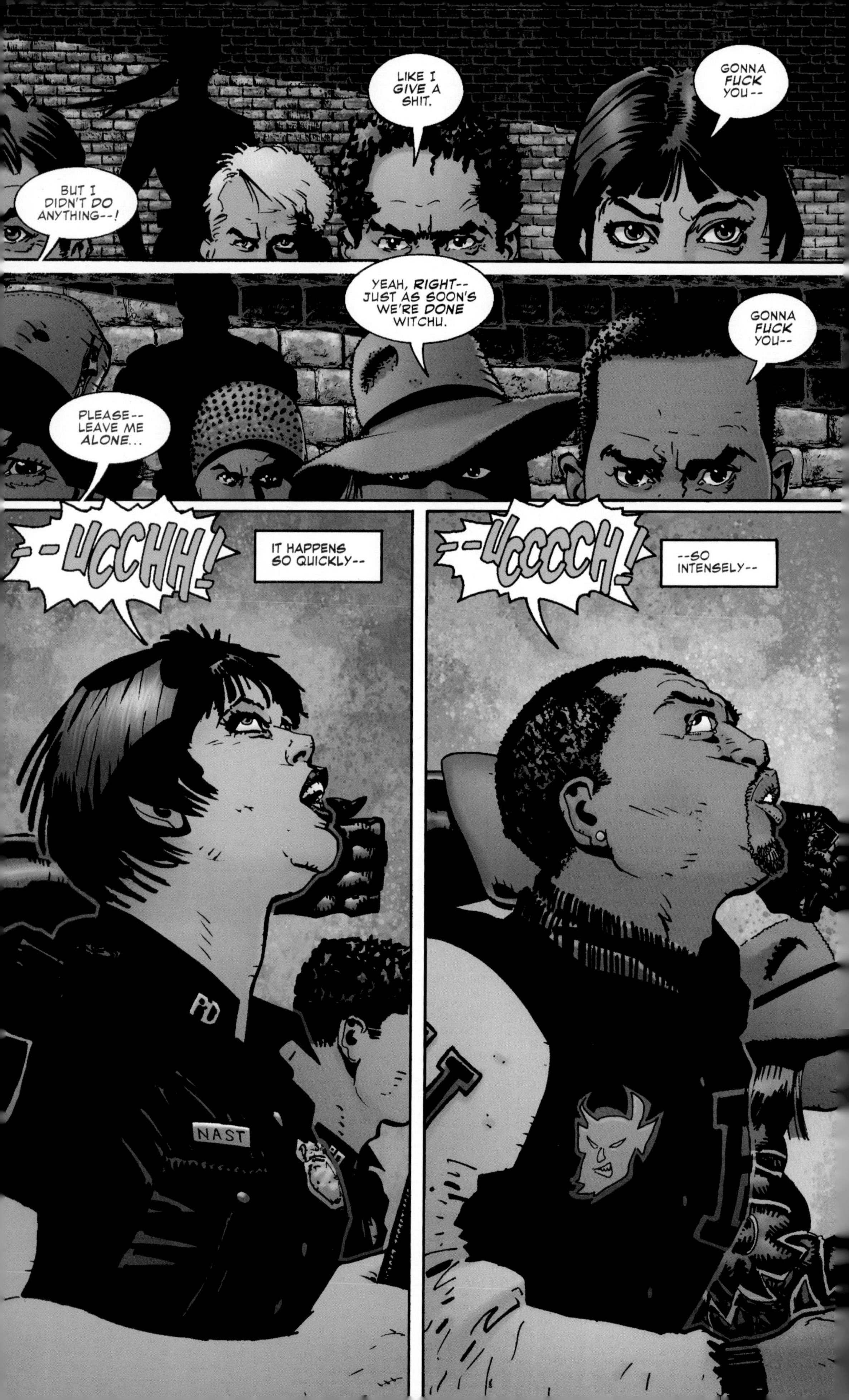
BUT I DIDN'T DO ANYTHING--!
LIKE I GIVE A SHIT.
GONNA FUCK YOU--
PLEASE-- LEAVE ME ALONE...
YEAH, RIGHT-- JUST AS SOON'S WE'RE DONE WITCHU.
GONNA FUCK YOU--
--UCCHH!
IT HAPPENS SO QUICKLY--
PD
NAST
--UCCCCH!
--SO INTENSELY--

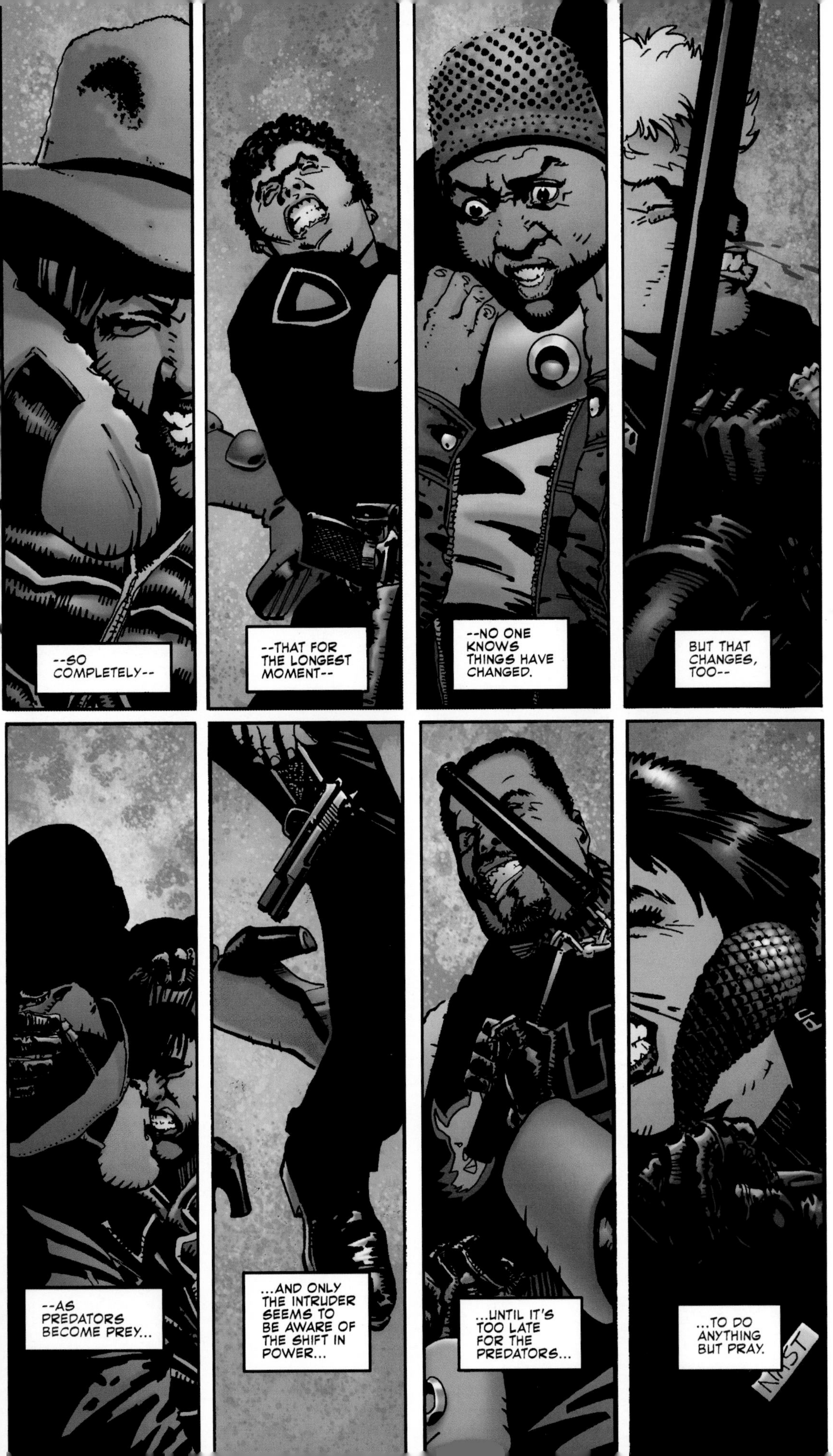
--SO COMPLETELY--
--THAT FOR THE LONGEST MOMENT--
--NO ONE KNOWS THINGS HAVE CHANGED.
BUT THAT CHANGES, TOO--
--AS PREDATORS BECOME PREY...
...AND ONLY THE INTRUDER SEEMS TO BE AWARE OF THE SHIFT IN POWER...
...UNTIL IT'S TOO LATE FOR THE PREDATORS...
...TO DO ANYTHING BUT PRAY.
NMST

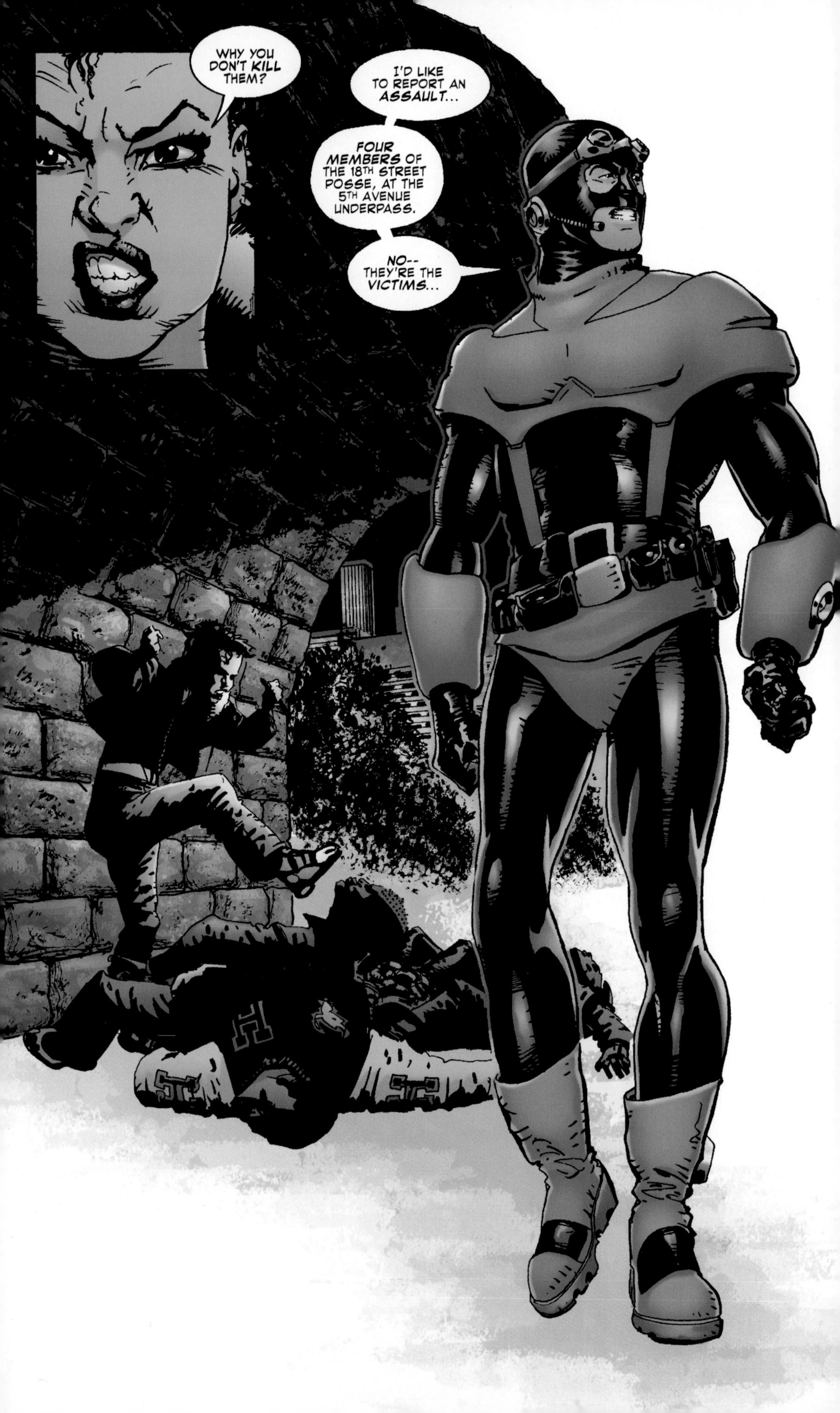
WHY YOU DON'T KILL THEM?
I'D LIKE TO REPORT AN ASSAULT...
FOUR MEMBERS OF THE 18TH STREET POSSE, AT THE 5TH AVENUE UNDERPASS.
NO-- THEY'RE THE VICTIMS...

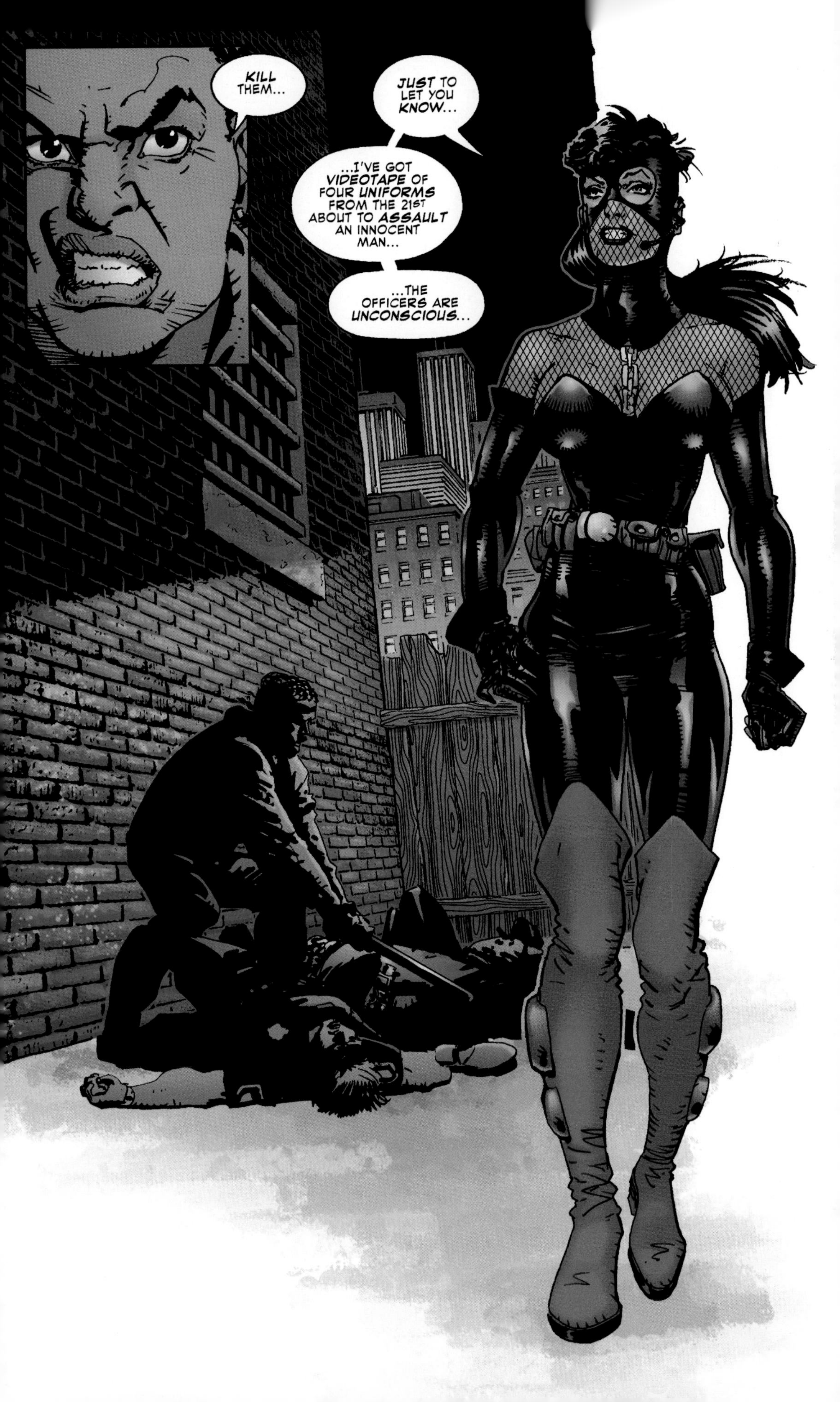
KILL THEM...
JUST TO LET YOU KNOW...
...I'VE GOT VIDEOTAPE OF FOUR UNIFORMS FROM THE 21ST ABOUT TO ASSAULT AN INNOCENT MAN...
...THE OFFICERS ARE UNCONSCIOUS...

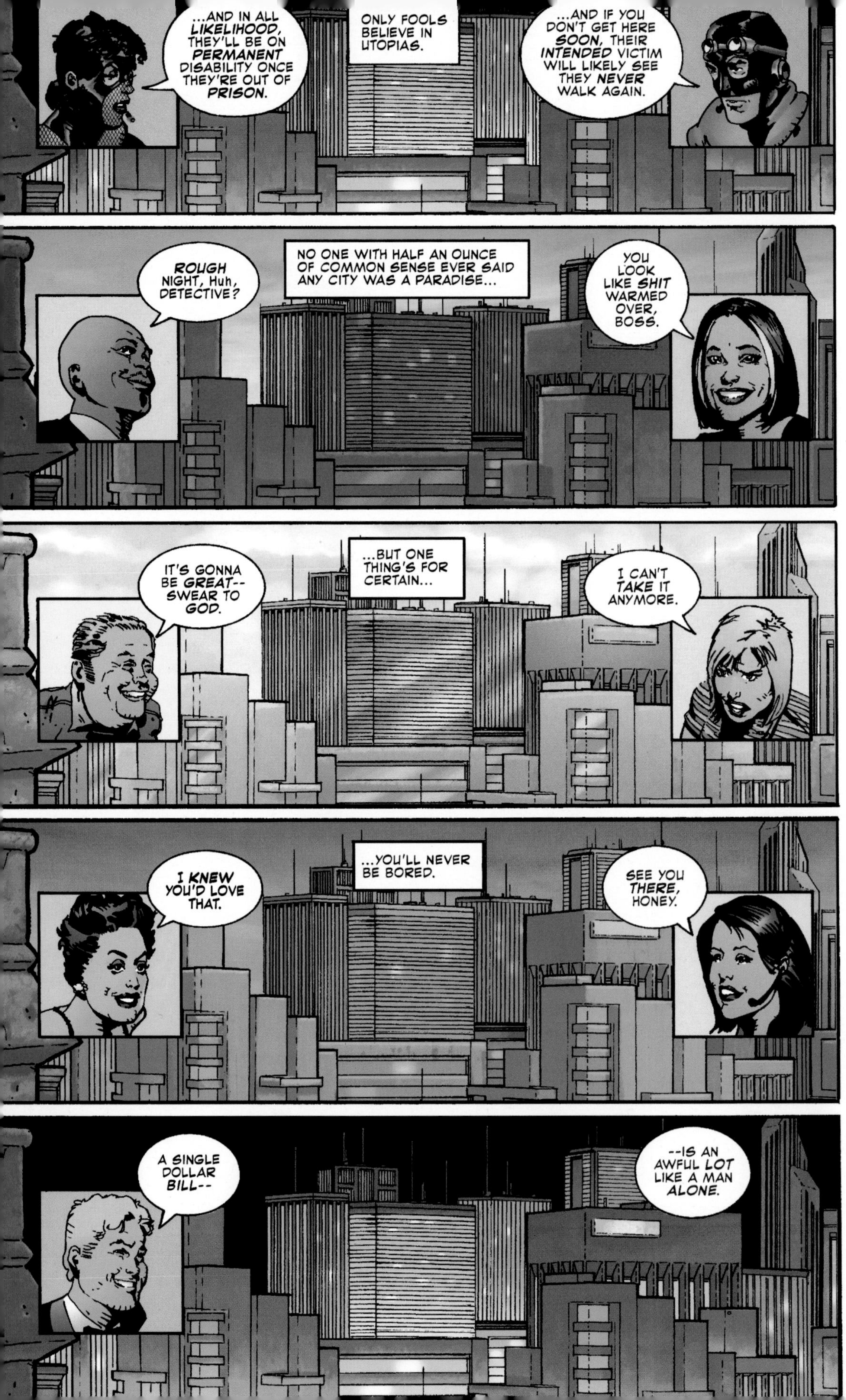

...AND IN ALL LIKELIHOOD, THEY'LL BE ON PERMANENT DISABILITY ONCE THEY'RE OUT OF PRISON.
ONLY FOOLS BELIEVE IN UTOPIAS.
...AND IF YOU DON'T GET HERE SOON, THEIR INTENDED VICTIM WILL LIKELY SEE THEY NEVER WALK AGAIN.
ROUGH NIGHT, Huh, DETECTIVE?
NO ONE WITH HALF AN OUNCE OF COMMON SENSE EVER SAID ANY CITY WAS A PARADISE...
YOU LOOK LIKE SHIT WARMED OVER, BOSS.
IT'S GONNA BE GREAT-- SWEAR TO GOD.
...BUT ONE THING'S FOR CERTAIN...
I CAN'T TAKE IT ANYMORE.
I KNEW YOU'D LOVE THAT.
...YOU'LL NEVER BE BORED.
SEE YOU THERE, HONEY.
A SINGLE DOLLAR BILL--
--IS AN AWFUL LOT LIKE A MAN ALONE.

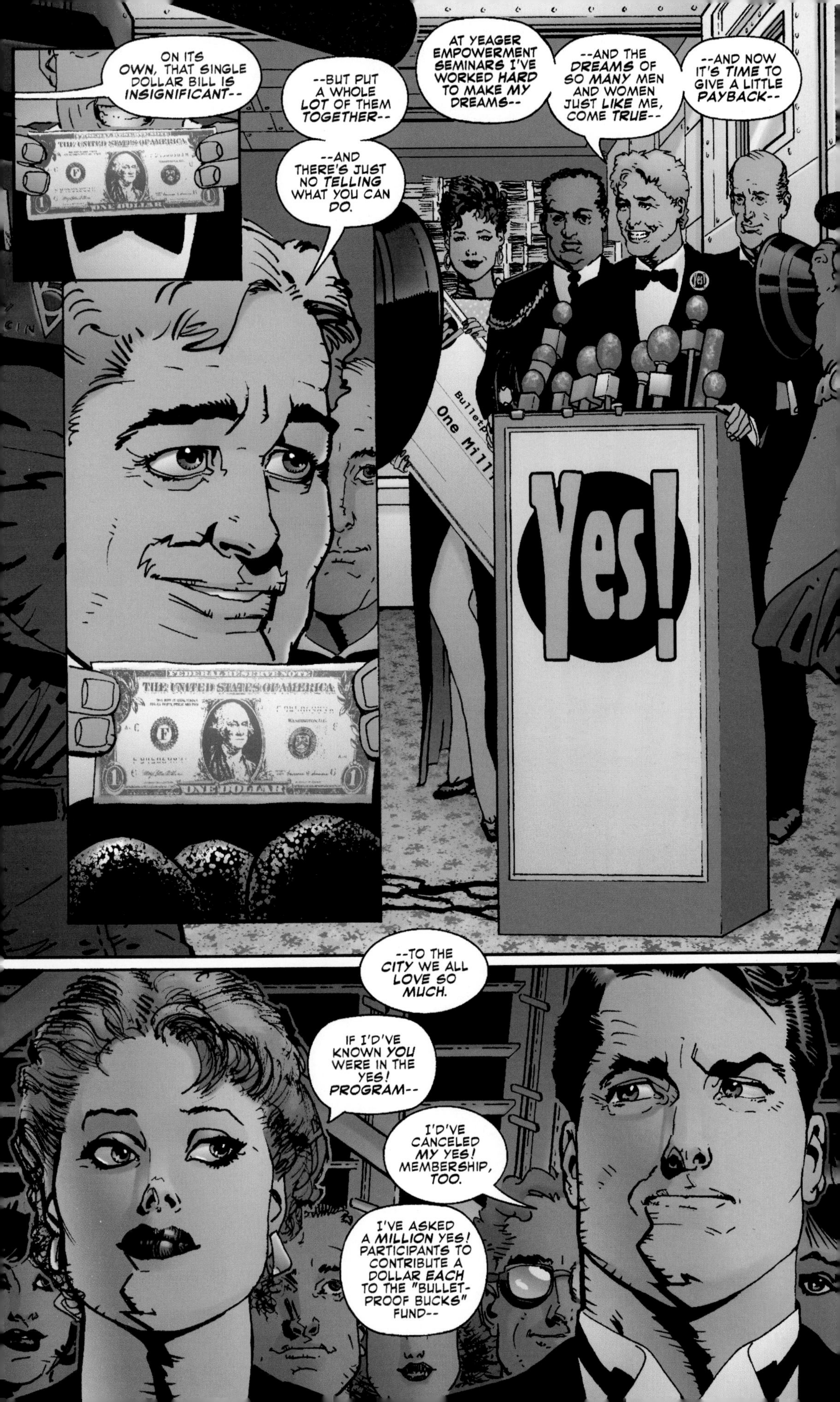

ON ITS OWN, THAT SINGLE DOLLAR BILL IS INSIGNIFICANT--
--BUT PUT A WHOLE LOT OF THEM TOGETHER--
--AND THERE'S JUST NO TELLING WHAT YOU CAN DO.
AT YEAGER EMPOWERMENT SEMINARS I'VE WORKED HARD TO MAKE MY DREAMS--
--AND THE DREAMS OF SO MANY MEN AND WOMEN JUST LIKE ME, COME TRUE--
--AND NOW IT'S TIME TO GIVE A LITTLE PAYBACK--
Yes!
--TO THE CITY WE ALL LOVE SO MUCH.
IF I'D'VE KNOWN YOU WERE IN THE YES! PROGRAM--
I'D'VE CANCELED MY YES! MEMBERSHIP, TOO.
I'VE ASKED A MILLION YES! PARTICIPANTS TO CONTRIBUTE A DOLLAR EACH TO THE "BULLET-PROOF BUCKS" FUND--

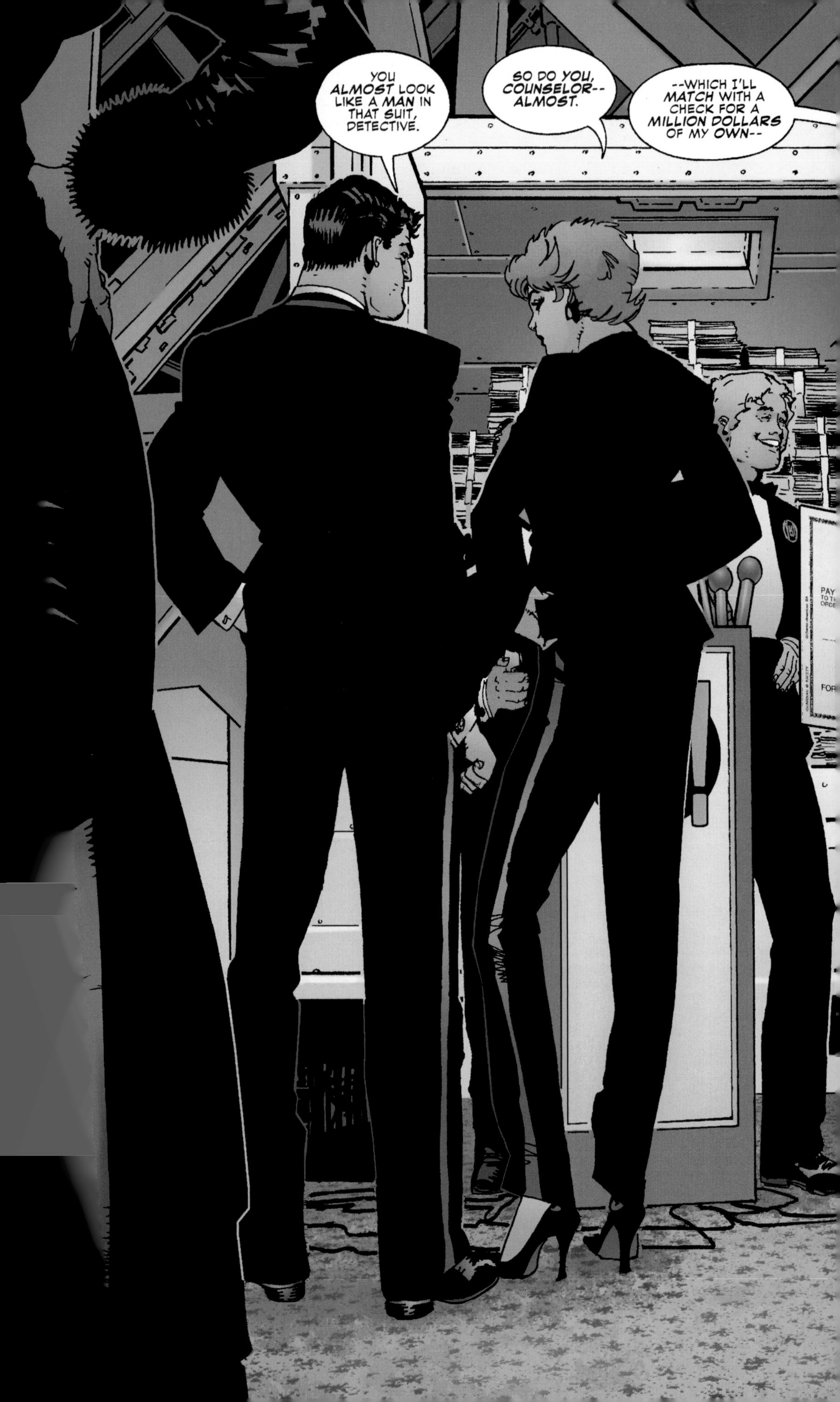
YOU ALMOST LOOK LIKE A MAN IN THAT SUIT, DETECTIVE.
SO DO YOU, COUNSELOR-- ALMOST.
--WHICH I'LL MATCH WITH A CHECK FOR A MILLION DOLLARS OF MY OWN--

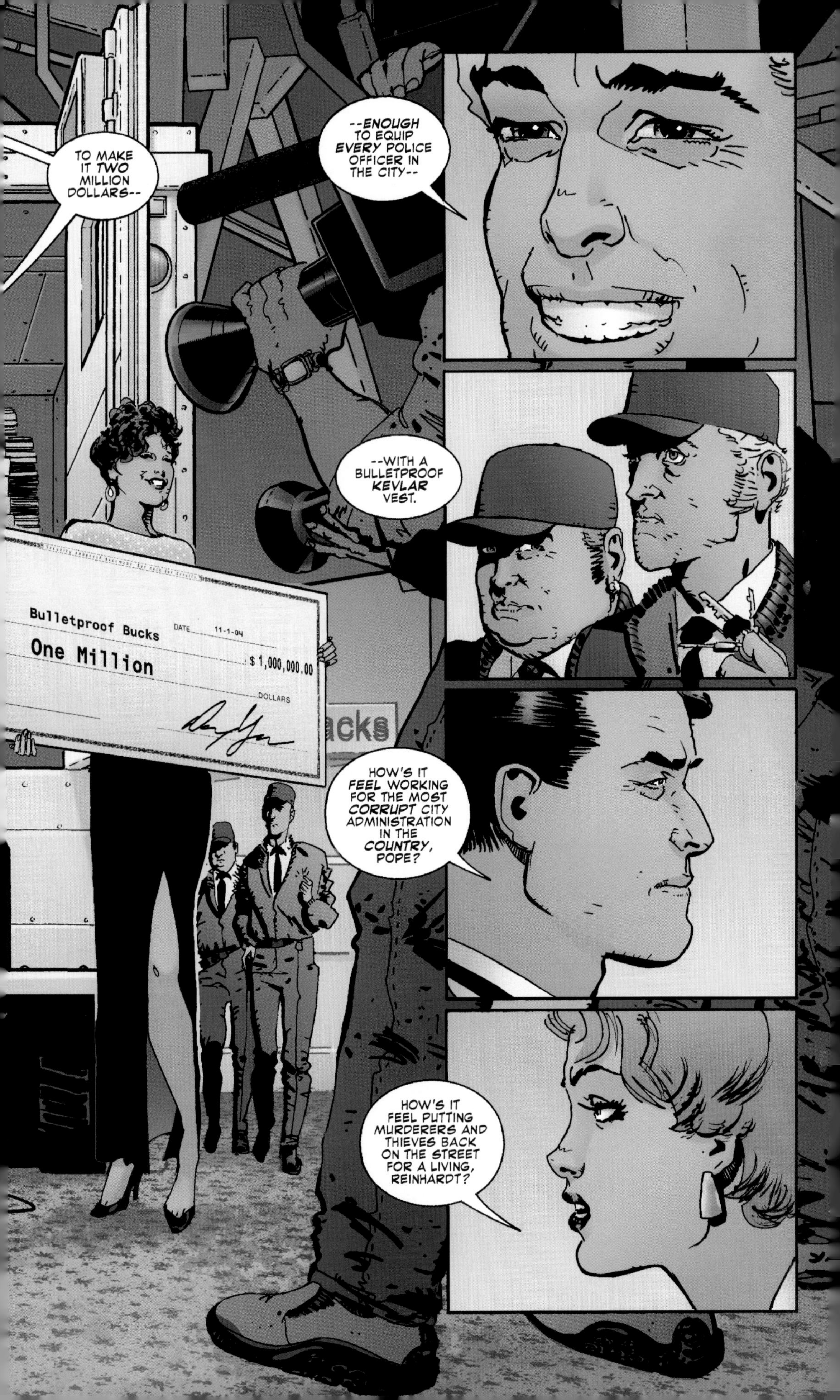
TO MAKE IT TWO MILLION DOLLARS--
--ENOUGH TO EQUIP EVERY POLICE OFFICER IN THE CITY--
--WITH A BULLETPROOF KEVLAR VEST.
Bulletproof Bucks
DATE 11-1-04
One Million
$ 1,000,000.00
DOLLARS
HOW'S IT FEEL WORKING FOR THE MOST CORRUPT CITY ADMINISTRATION IN THE COUNTRY, POPE?
HOW'S IT FEEL PUTTING MURDERERS AND THIEVES BACK ON THE STREET FOR A LIVING, REINHARDT?

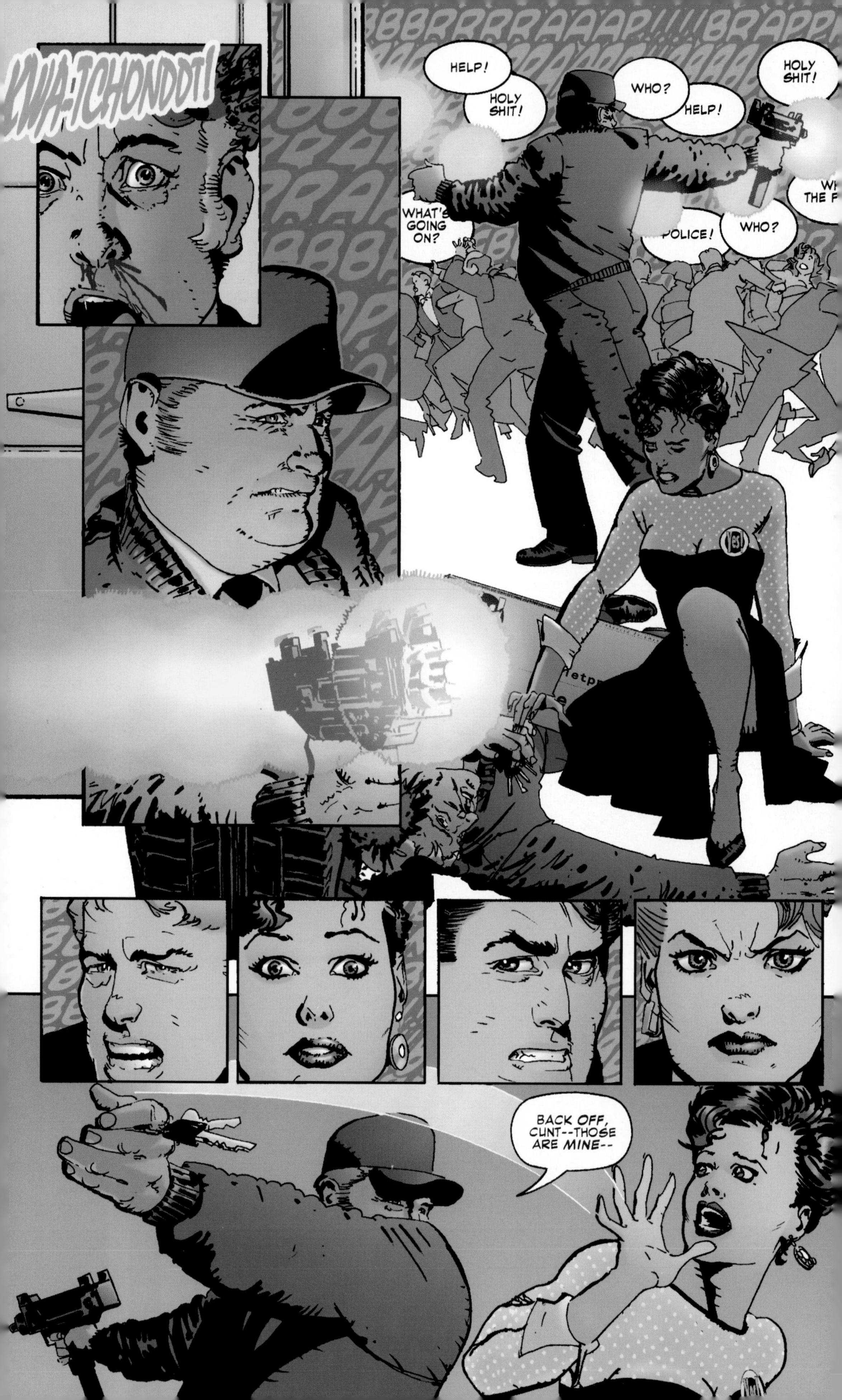
KWA-TCHONDDT!
BBRRRRRAAAP!!! BRAPP
HELP!
HOLY SHIT!
WHO?
HELP!
HOLY SHIT!
WHAT'S GOING ON?
POLICE!
WHO?
BACK OFF, CUNT--THOSE ARE MINE--

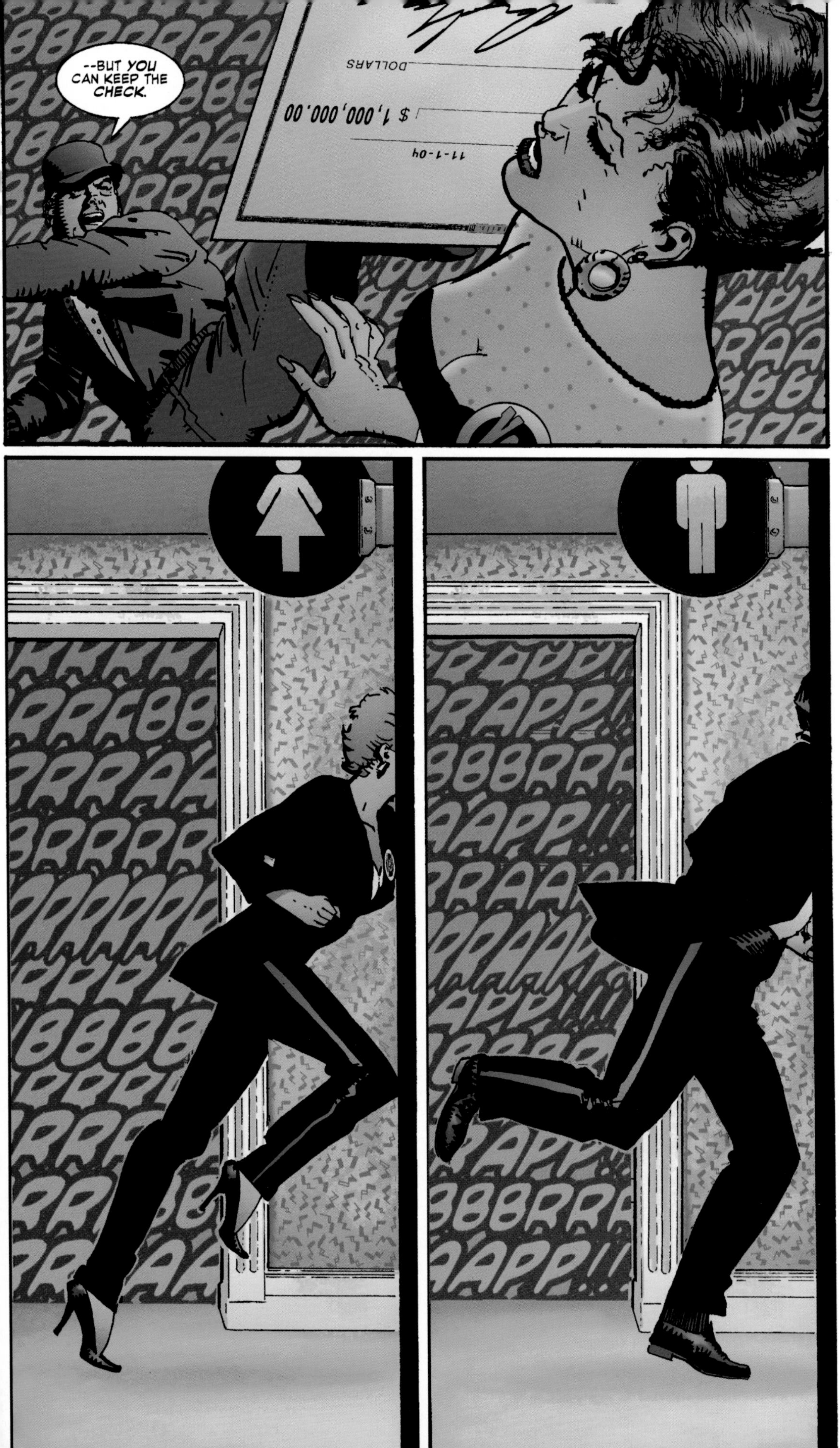
--BUT YOU CAN KEEP THE CHECK.
11-1-04
$ 1,000,000.00
DOLLARS

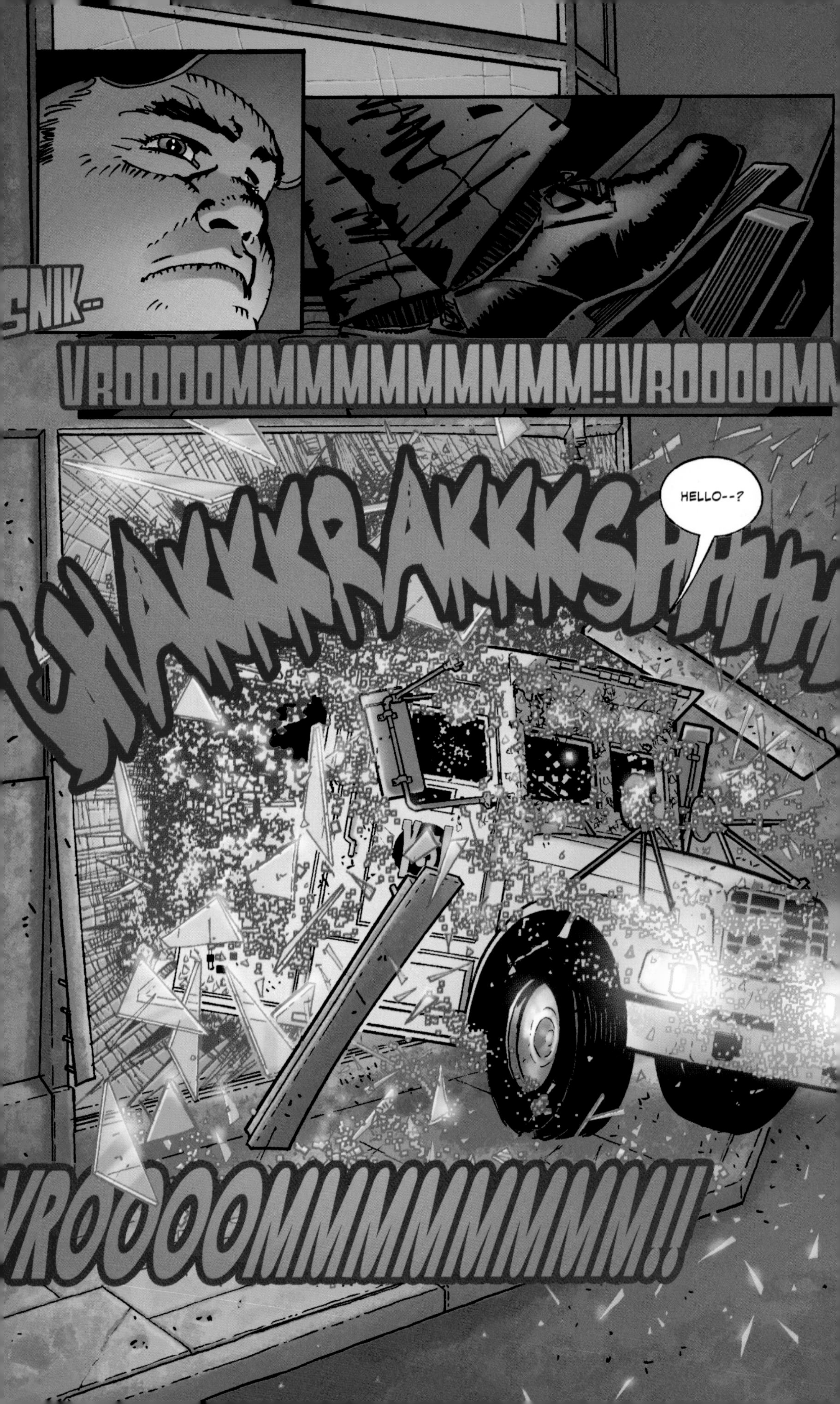
SNIK--
VROOOOMMMMMMMMMMMM!!VROOOOMM
HELLO--?
VROOOOMMMMMMMMMMM!!

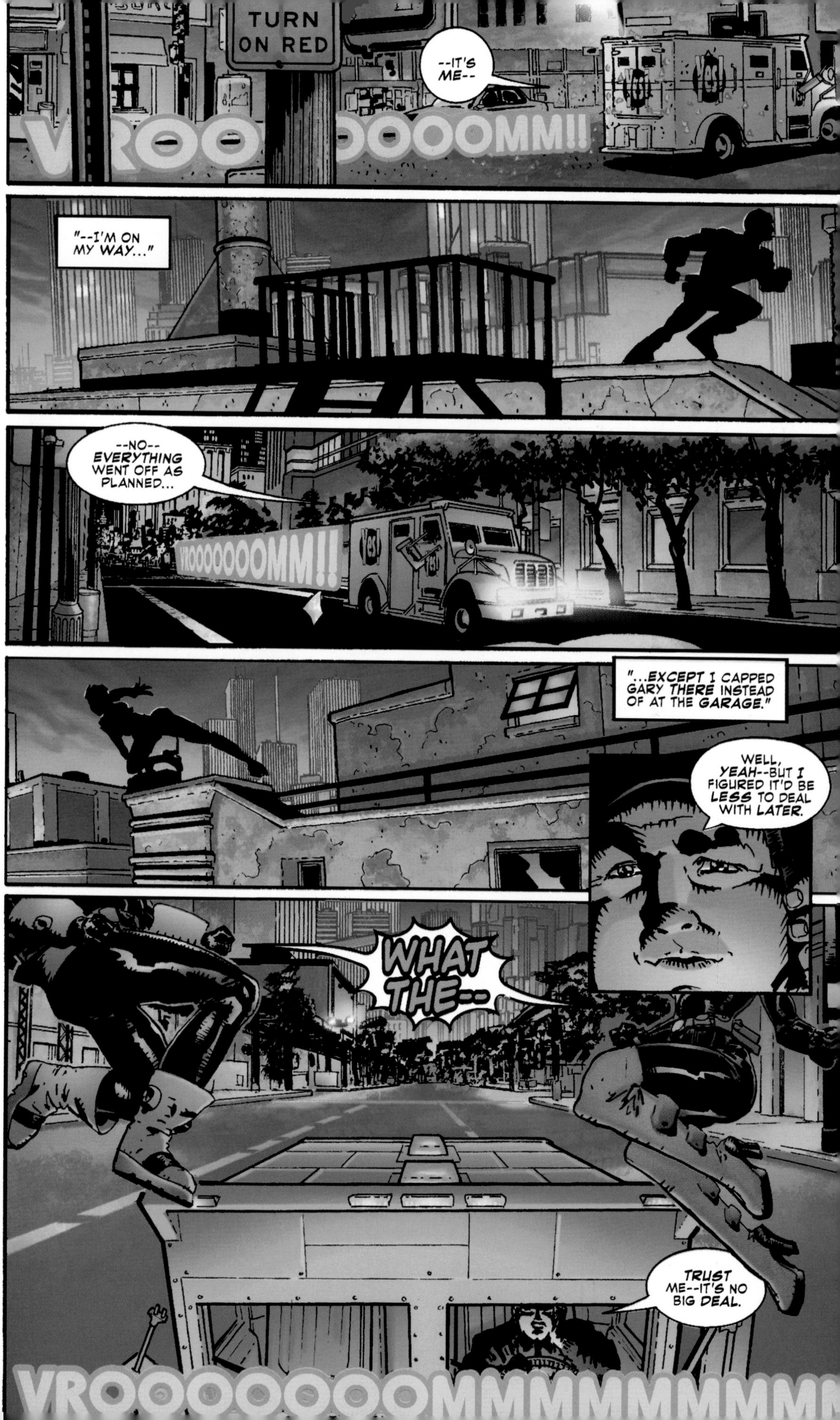

TURN ON RED
--IT'S ME--
VROOOOOOOOMM!!
"--I'M ON MY WAY..."
--NO-- EVERYTHING WENT OFF AS PLANNED...
VROOOOOOOMM!!
"...EXCEPT I CAPPED GARY THERE INSTEAD OF AT THE GARAGE."
WELL, YEAH--BUT I FIGURED IT'D BE LESS TO DEAL WITH LATER.
WHAT THE--
TRUST ME--IT'S NO BIG DEAL.
VROOOOOOOOMMMMMMMMMM

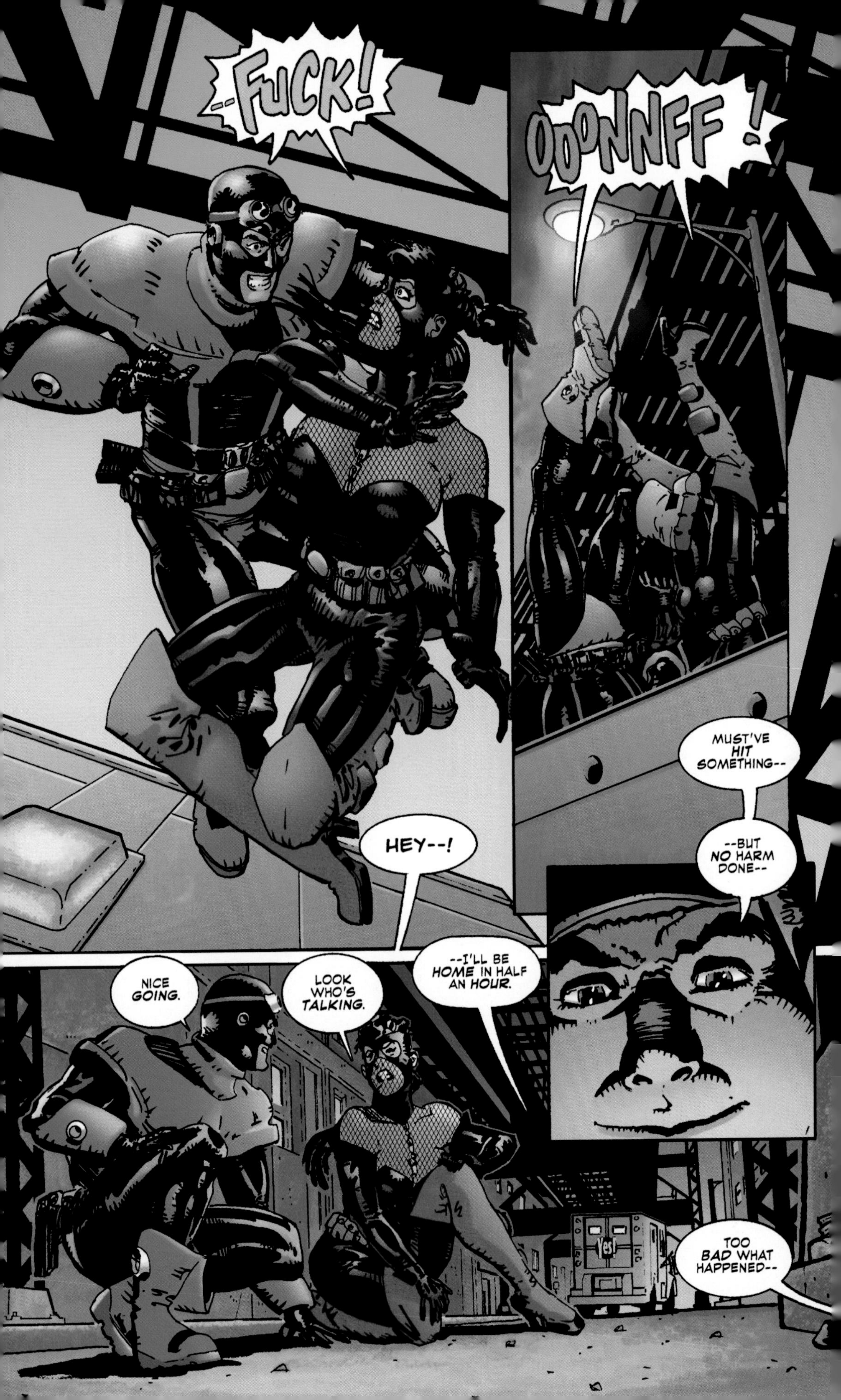
--FUCK!
OOONNFF !
HEY--!
MUST'VE HIT SOMETHING--
--BUT NO HARM DONE--
--I'LL BE HOME IN HALF AN HOUR.
NICE GOING.
LOOK WHO'S TALKING.
TOO BAD WHAT HAPPENED--

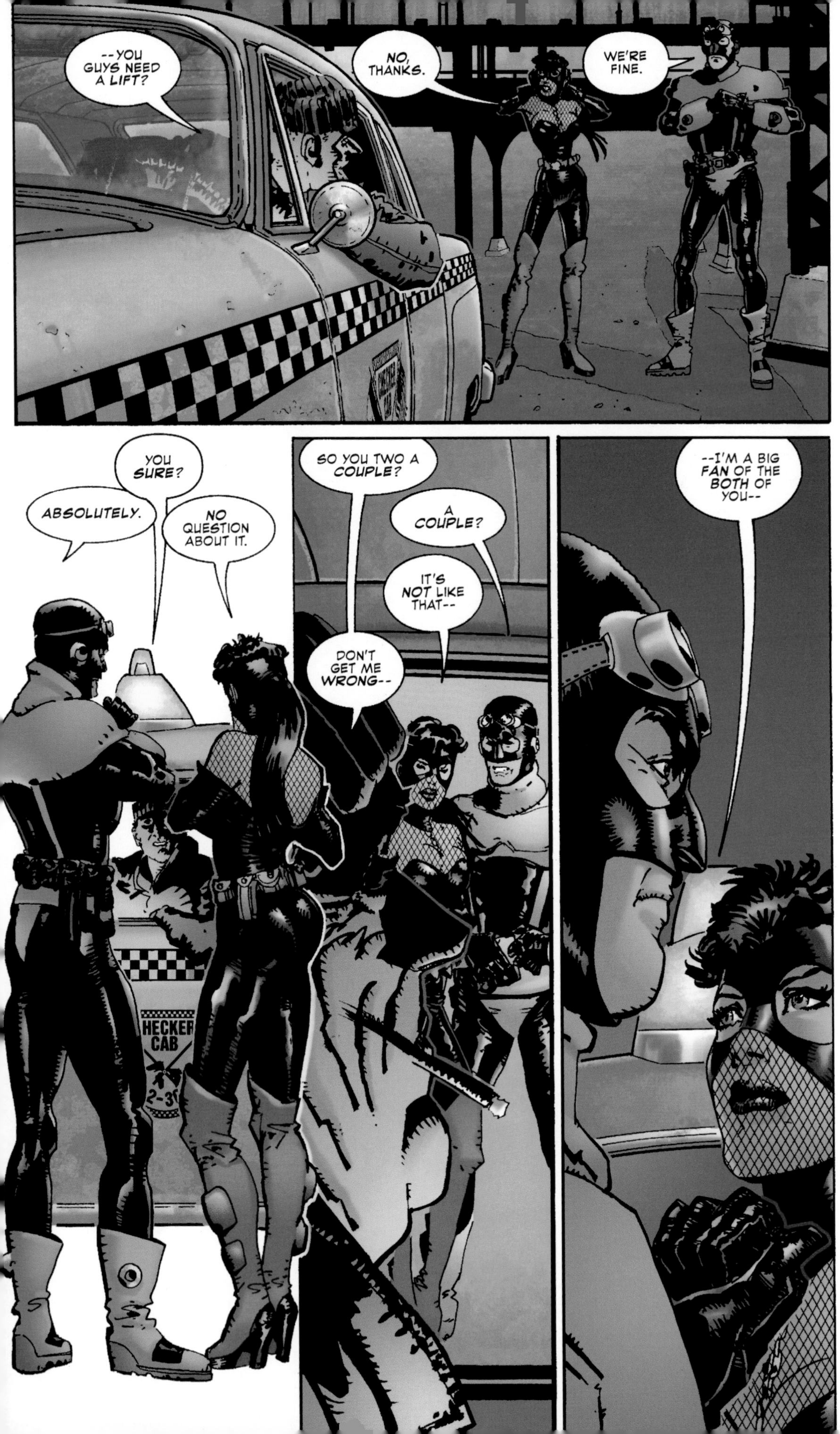
--YOU GUYS NEED A LIFT?
NO, THANKS.
WE'RE FINE.
YOU SURE?
ABSOLUTELY.
NO QUESTION ABOUT IT.
SO YOU TWO A COUPLE?
A COUPLE?
IT'S NOT LIKE THAT--
DON'T GET ME WRONG--
--I'M A BIG FAN OF THE BOTH OF YOU--

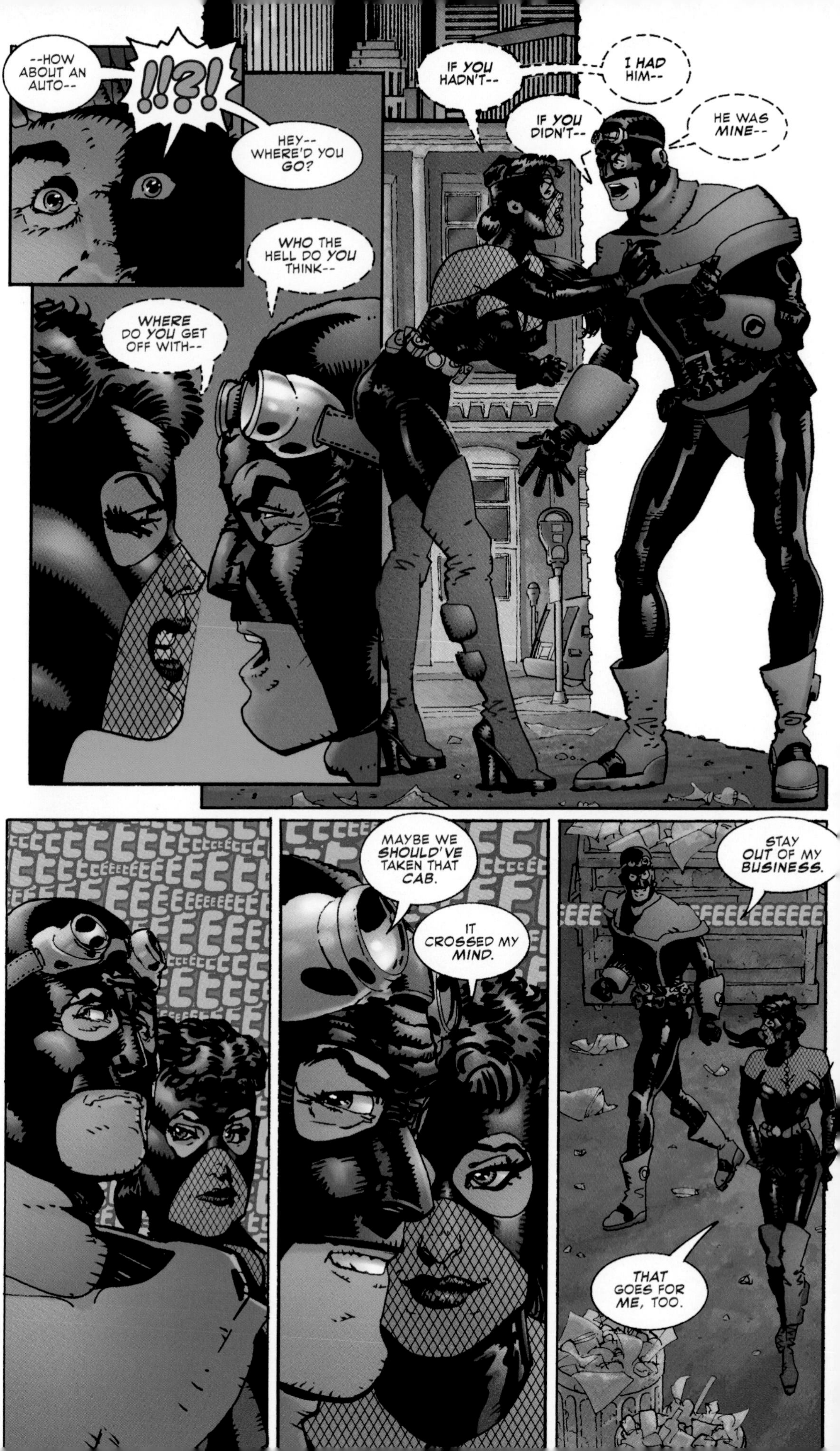
--HOW ABOUT AN AUTO--
!!?!
HEY-- WHERE'D YOU GO?
IF YOU HADN'T--
I HAD HIM--
IF YOU DIDN'T--
HE WAS MINE--
WHO THE HELL DO YOU THINK--
WHERE DO YOU GET OFF WITH--
MAYBE WE SHOULD'VE TAKEN THAT CAB.
IT CROSSED MY MIND.
STAY OUT OF MY BUSINESS.
THAT GOES FOR ME, TOO.

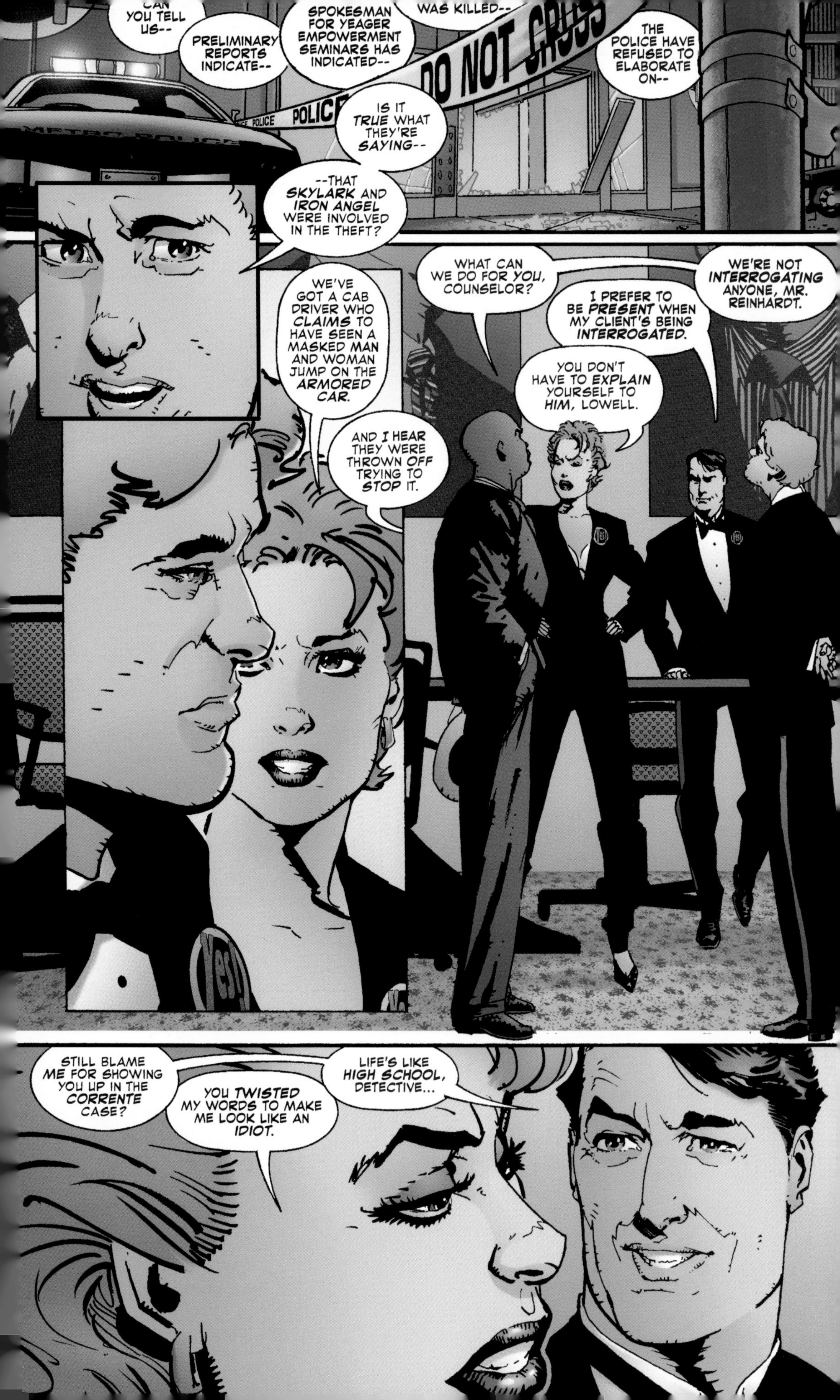

CAN YOU TELL US--
PRELIMINARY REPORTS INDICATE--
SPOKESMAN FOR YEAGER EMPOWERMENT SEMINARS HAS INDICATED--
WAS KILLED--
DO NOT CROSS
THE POLICE HAVE REFUSED TO ELABORATE ON--
POLICE
IS IT TRUE WHAT THEY'RE SAYING--
--THAT SKYLARK AND IRON ANGEL WERE INVOLVED IN THE THEFT?
WE'VE GOT A CAB DRIVER WHO CLAIMS TO HAVE SEEN A MASKED MAN AND WOMAN JUMP ON THE ARMORED CAR.
AND I HEAR THEY WERE THROWN OFF TRYING TO STOP IT.
WHAT CAN WE DO FOR YOU, COUNSELOR?
I PREFER TO BE PRESENT WHEN MY CLIENT'S BEING INTERROGATED.
WE'RE NOT INTERROGATING ANYONE, MR. REINHARDT.
YOU DON'T HAVE TO EXPLAIN YOURSELF TO HIM, LOWELL.
STILL BLAME ME FOR SHOWING YOU UP IN THE CORRENTE CASE?
YOU TWISTED MY WORDS TO MAKE ME LOOK LIKE AN IDIOT.
LIFE'S LIKE HIGH SCHOOL, DETECTIVE...

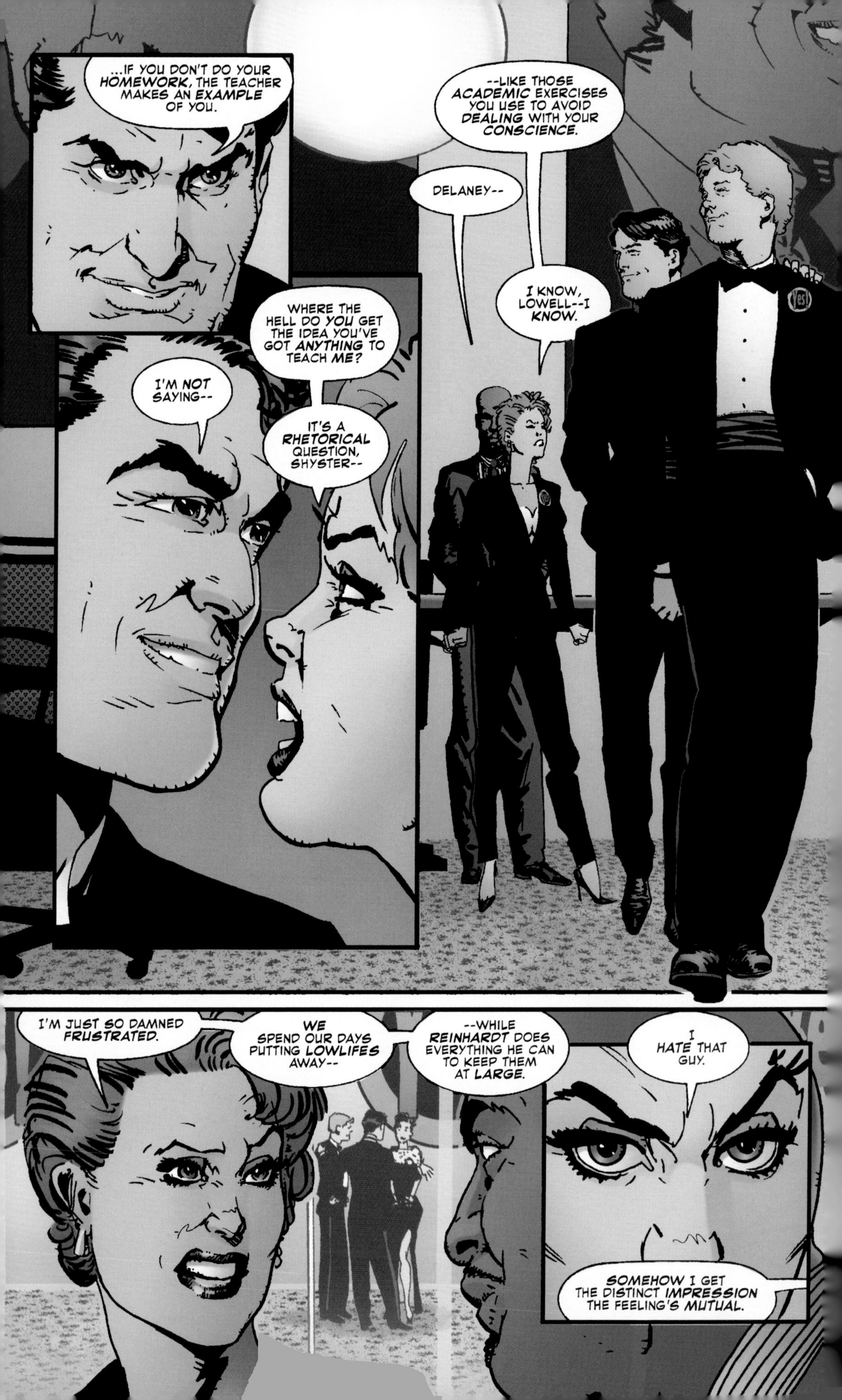
...IF YOU DON'T DO YOUR HOMEWORK, THE TEACHER MAKES AN EXAMPLE OF YOU.
WHERE THE HELL DO YOU GET THE IDEA YOU'VE GOT ANYTHING TO TEACH ME?
I'M NOT SAYING--
IT'S A RHETORICAL QUESTION, SHYSTER--
--LIKE THOSE ACADEMIC EXERCISES YOU USE TO AVOID DEALING WITH YOUR CONSCIENCE.
DELANEY--
I KNOW, LOWELL--I KNOW.
YES!
I'M JUST SO DAMNED FRUSTRATED.
WE SPEND OUR DAYS PUTTING LOWLIFES AWAY--
--WHILE REINHARDT DOES EVERYTHING HE CAN TO KEEP THEM AT LARGE.
I HATE THAT GUY.
SOMEHOW I GET THE DISTINCT IMPRESSION THE FEELING'S MUTUAL.

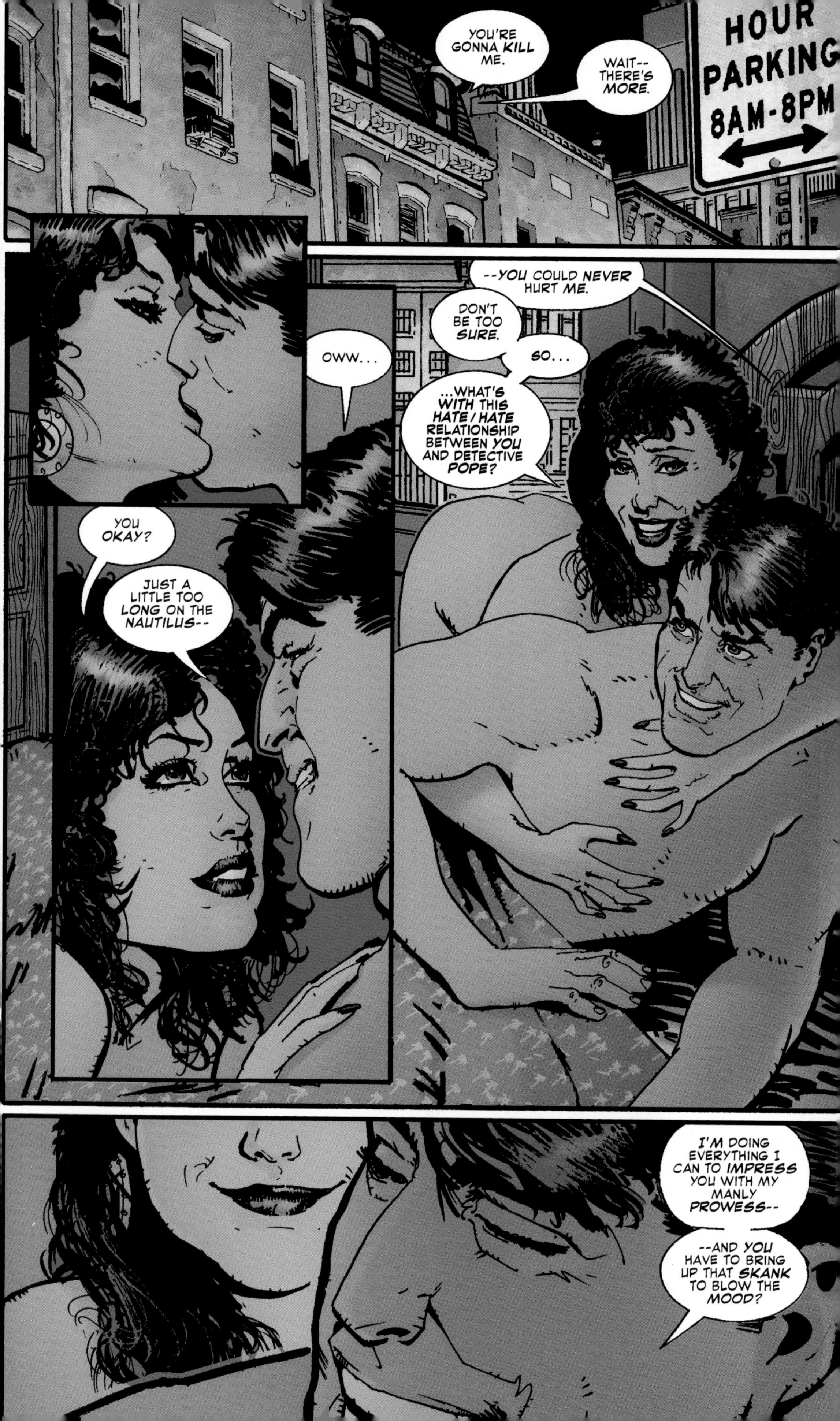
HOUR PARKING 8AM-8PM
YOU'RE GONNA KILL ME.
WAIT-- THERE'S MORE.
OWW...
YOU OKAY?
JUST A LITTLE TOO LONG ON THE NAUTILUS--
--YOU COULD NEVER HURT ME.
DON'T BE TOO SURE.
SO...
...WHAT'S WITH THIS HATE / HATE RELATIONSHIP BETWEEN YOU AND DETECTIVE POPE?
I'M DOING EVERYTHING I CAN TO IMPRESS YOU WITH MY MANLY PROWESS--
--AND YOU HAVE TO BRING UP THAT SKANK TO BLOW THE MOOD?

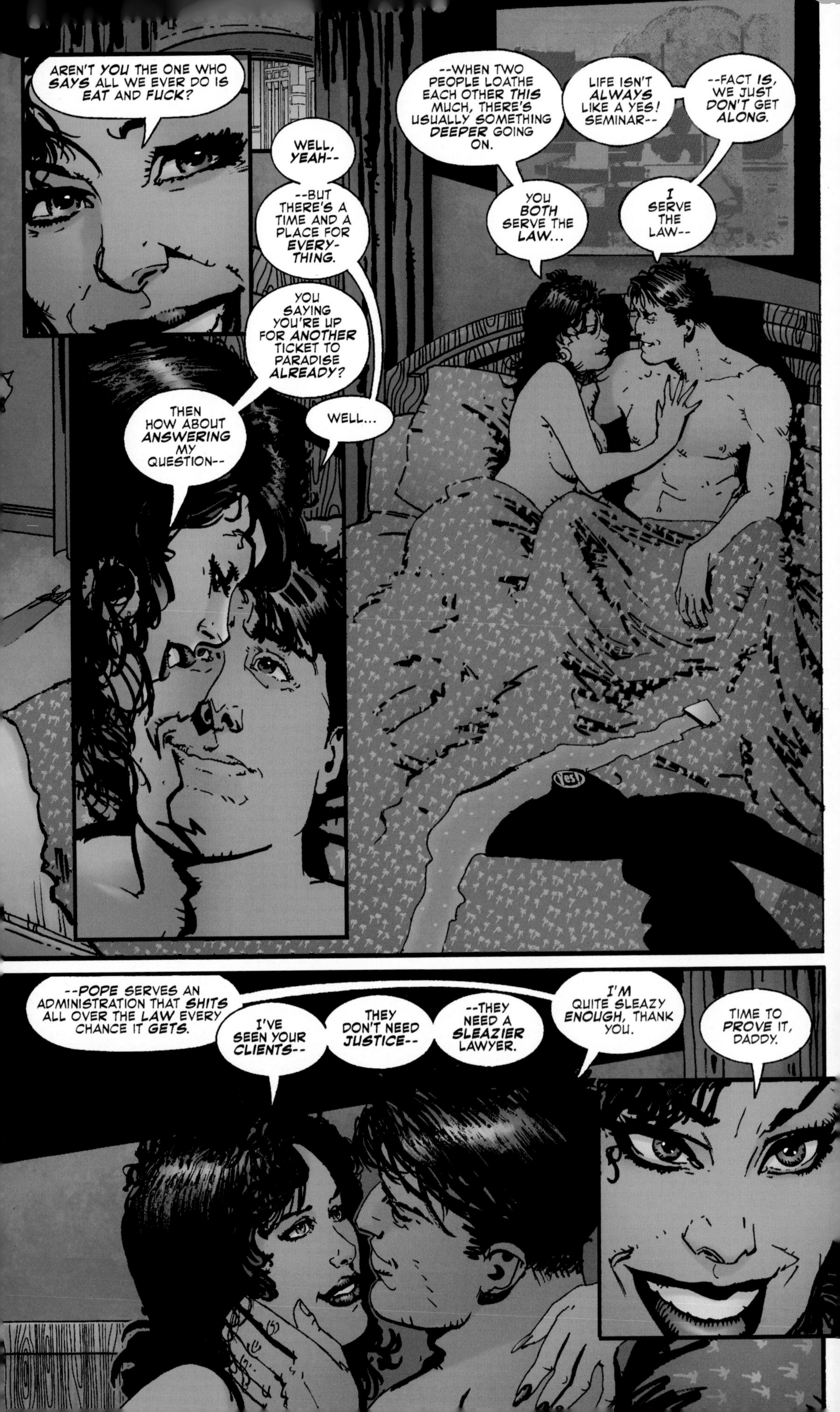
AREN'T YOU THE ONE WHO SAYS ALL WE EVER DO IS EAT AND FUCK?
WELL, YEAH--
--BUT THERE'S A TIME AND A PLACE FOR EVERY-THING.
YOU SAYING YOU'RE UP FOR ANOTHER TICKET TO PARADISE ALREADY?
THEN HOW ABOUT ANSWERING MY QUESTION--
WELL...
--WHEN TWO PEOPLE LOATHE EACH OTHER THIS MUCH, THERE'S USUALLY SOMETHING DEEPER GOING ON.
YOU BOTH SERVE THE LAW...
LIFE ISN'T ALWAYS LIKE A YES! SEMINAR--
--FACT IS, WE JUST DON'T GET ALONG.
I SERVE THE LAW--
--POPE SERVES AN ADMINISTRATION THAT SHITS ALL OVER THE LAW EVERY CHANCE IT GETS.
I'VE SEEN YOUR CLIENTS--
THEY DON'T NEED JUSTICE--
--THEY NEED A SLEAZIER LAWYER.
I'M QUITE SLEAZY ENOUGH, THANK YOU.
TIME TO PROVE IT, DADDY.

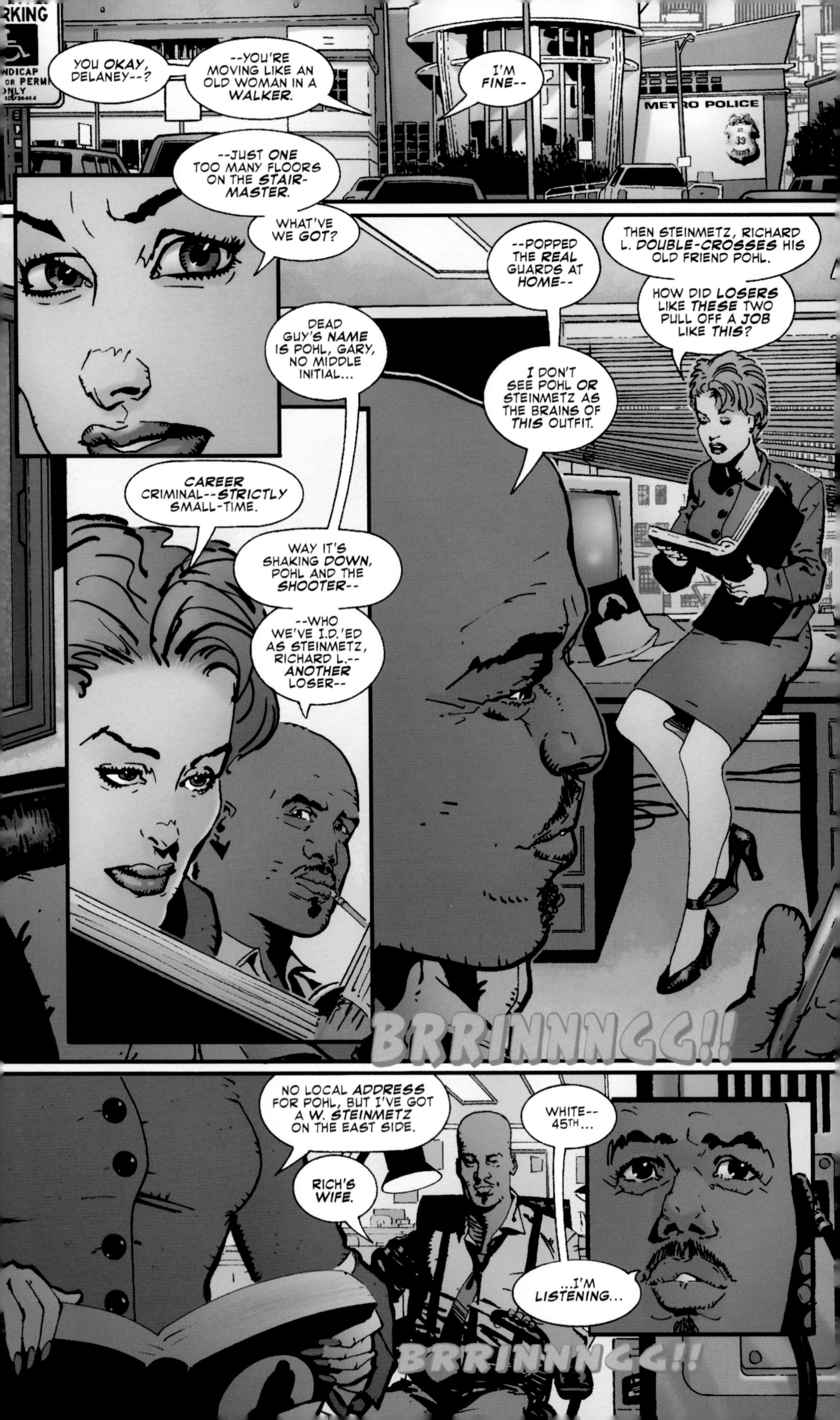
RKING
NDICAP
OR PERM
ONLY
YOU OKAY, DELANEY--?
--YOU'RE MOVING LIKE AN OLD WOMAN IN A WALKER.
I'M FINE--
METRO POLICE
--JUST ONE TOO MANY FLOORS ON THE STAIR-MASTER.
WHAT'VE WE GOT?
DEAD GUY'S NAME IS POHL, GARY, NO MIDDLE INITIAL...
CAREER CRIMINAL--STRICTLY SMALL-TIME.
WAY IT'S SHAKING DOWN, POHL AND THE SHOOTER--
--WHO WE'VE I.D.'ED AS STEINMETZ, RICHARD L.--ANOTHER LOSER--
--POPPED THE REAL GUARDS AT HOME--
THEN STEINMETZ, RICHARD L. DOUBLE-CROSSES HIS OLD FRIEND POHL.
HOW DID LOSERS LIKE THESE TWO PULL OFF A JOB LIKE THIS?
I DON'T SEE POHL OR STEINMETZ AS THE BRAINS OF THIS OUTFIT.
BRRINNNGG!!
NO LOCAL ADDRESS FOR POHL, BUT I'VE GOT A W. STEINMETZ ON THE EAST SIDE.
RICH'S WIFE.
WHITE--45TH...
...I'M LISTENING...
BRRINNNGG!!

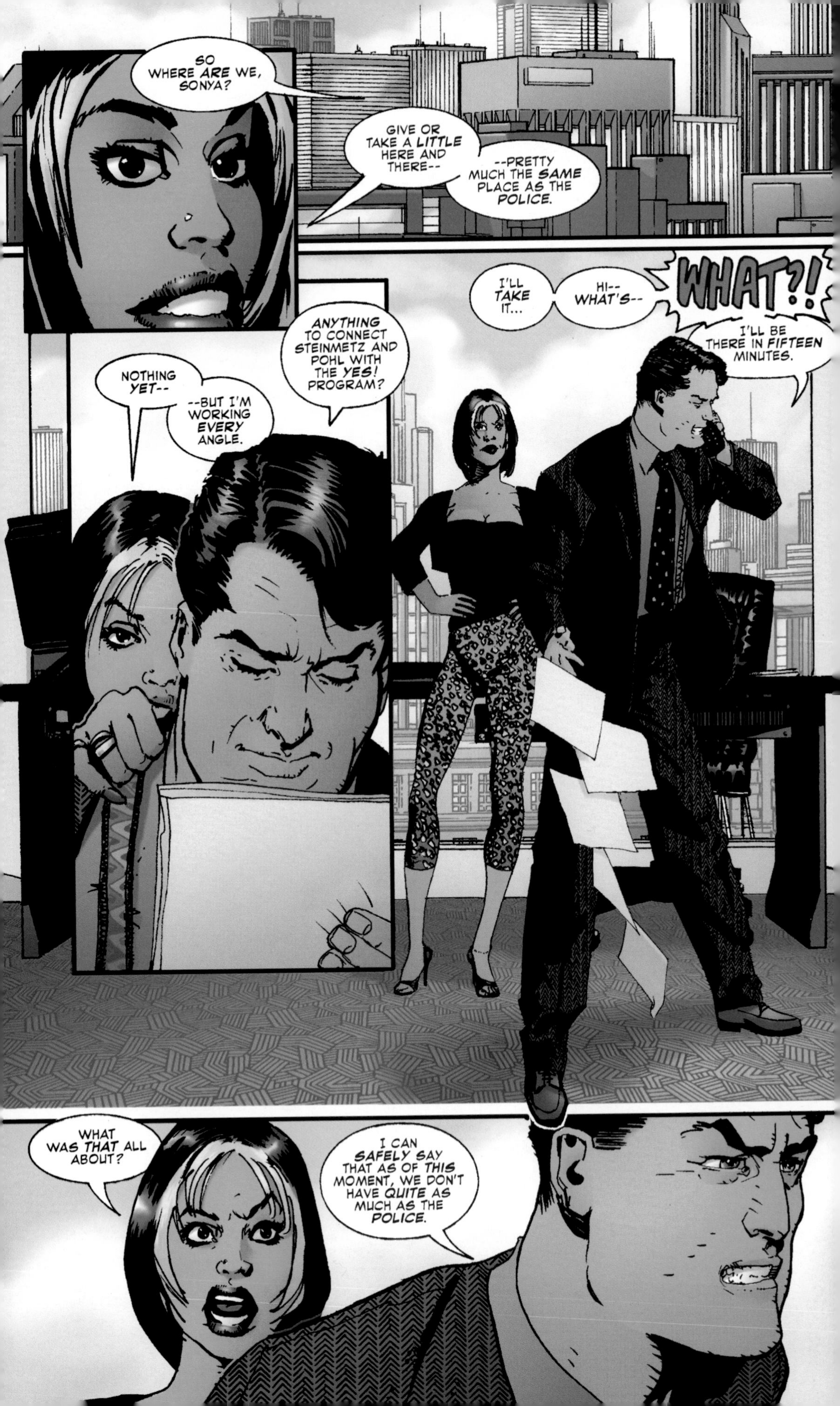
SO WHERE ARE WE, SONYA?
GIVE OR TAKE A LITTLE HERE AND THERE--
--PRETTY MUCH THE SAME PLACE AS THE POLICE.
NOTHING YET--
--BUT I'M WORKING EVERY ANGLE.
ANYTHING TO CONNECT STEINMETZ AND POHL WITH THE YES! PROGRAM?
I'LL TAKE IT...
HI-- WHAT'S--
WHAT?!
I'LL BE THERE IN FIFTEEN MINUTES.
WHAT WAS THAT ALL ABOUT?
I CAN SAFELY SAY THAT AS OF THIS MOMENT, WE DON'T HAVE QUITE AS MUCH AS THE POLICE.

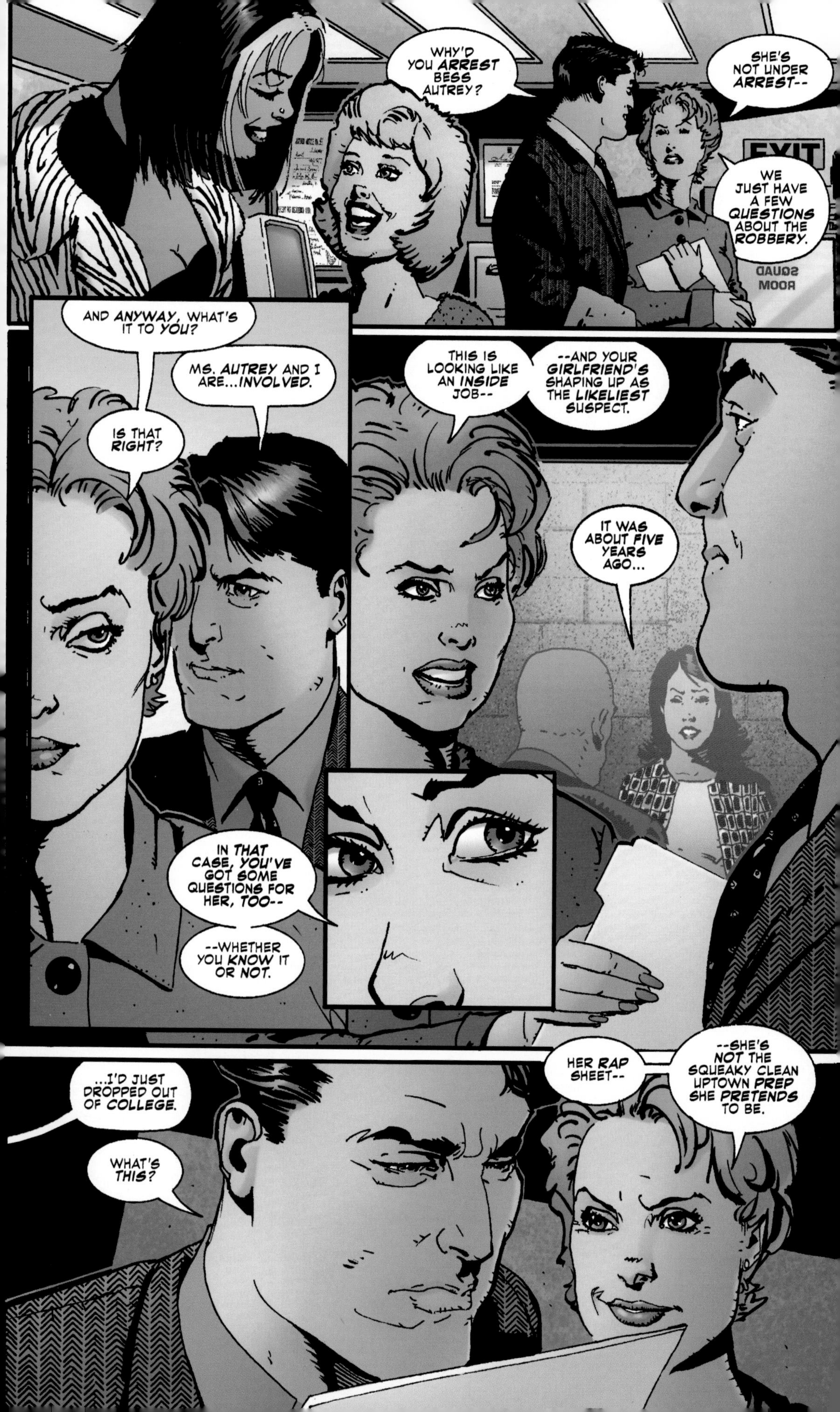

WHY'D YOU ARREST BESS AUTREY?
SHE'S NOT UNDER ARREST--
WE JUST HAVE A FEW QUESTIONS ABOUT THE ROBBERY.
SQUAD ROOM
EXIT
AND ANYWAY, WHAT'S IT TO YOU?
MS. AUTREY AND I ARE...INVOLVED.
IS THAT RIGHT?
THIS IS LOOKING LIKE AN INSIDE JOB--
--AND YOUR GIRLFRIEND'S SHAPING UP AS THE LIKELIEST SUSPECT.
IT WAS ABOUT FIVE YEARS AGO...
IN THAT CASE, YOU'VE GOT SOME QUESTIONS FOR HER, TOO--
--WHETHER YOU KNOW IT OR NOT.
...I'D JUST DROPPED OUT OF COLLEGE.
WHAT'S THIS?
HER RAP SHEET--
--SHE'S NOT THE SQUEAKY CLEAN UPTOWN PREP SHE PRETENDS TO BE.

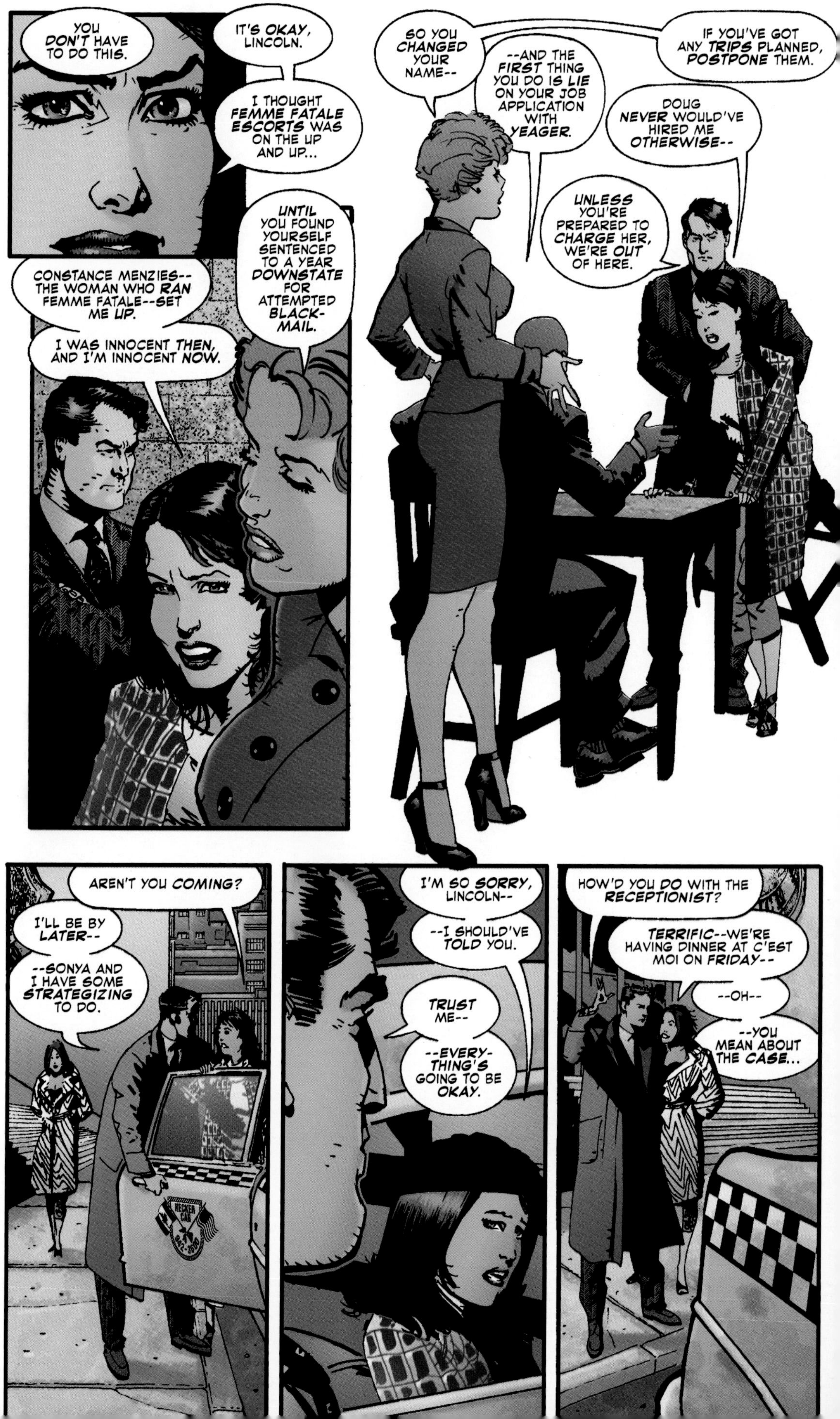
YOU DON'T HAVE TO DO THIS.
IT'S OKAY, LINCOLN.
I THOUGHT FEMME FATALE ESCORTS WAS ON THE UP AND UP...
UNTIL YOU FOUND YOURSELF SENTENCED TO A YEAR DOWNSTATE FOR ATTEMPTED BLACK-MAIL.
CONSTANCE MENZIES--THE WOMAN WHO RAN FEMME FATALE--SET ME UP.
I WAS INNOCENT THEN, AND I'M INNOCENT NOW.
SO YOU CHANGED YOUR NAME--
--AND THE FIRST THING YOU DO IS LIE ON YOUR JOB APPLICATION WITH YEAGER.
IF YOU'VE GOT ANY TRIPS PLANNED, POSTPONE THEM.
DOUG NEVER WOULD'VE HIRED ME OTHERWISE--
UNLESS YOU'RE PREPARED TO CHARGE HER, WE'RE OUT OF HERE.
AREN'T YOU COMING?
I'LL BE BY LATER--
--SONYA AND I HAVE SOME STRATEGIZING TO DO.
I'M SO SORRY, LINCOLN--
--I SHOULD'VE TOLD YOU.
TRUST ME--
--EVERY-THING'S GOING TO BE OKAY.
HOW'D YOU DO WITH THE RECEPTIONIST?
TERRIFIC--WE'RE HAVING DINNER AT C'EST MOI ON FRIDAY--
--OH--
--YOU MEAN ABOUT THE CASE...

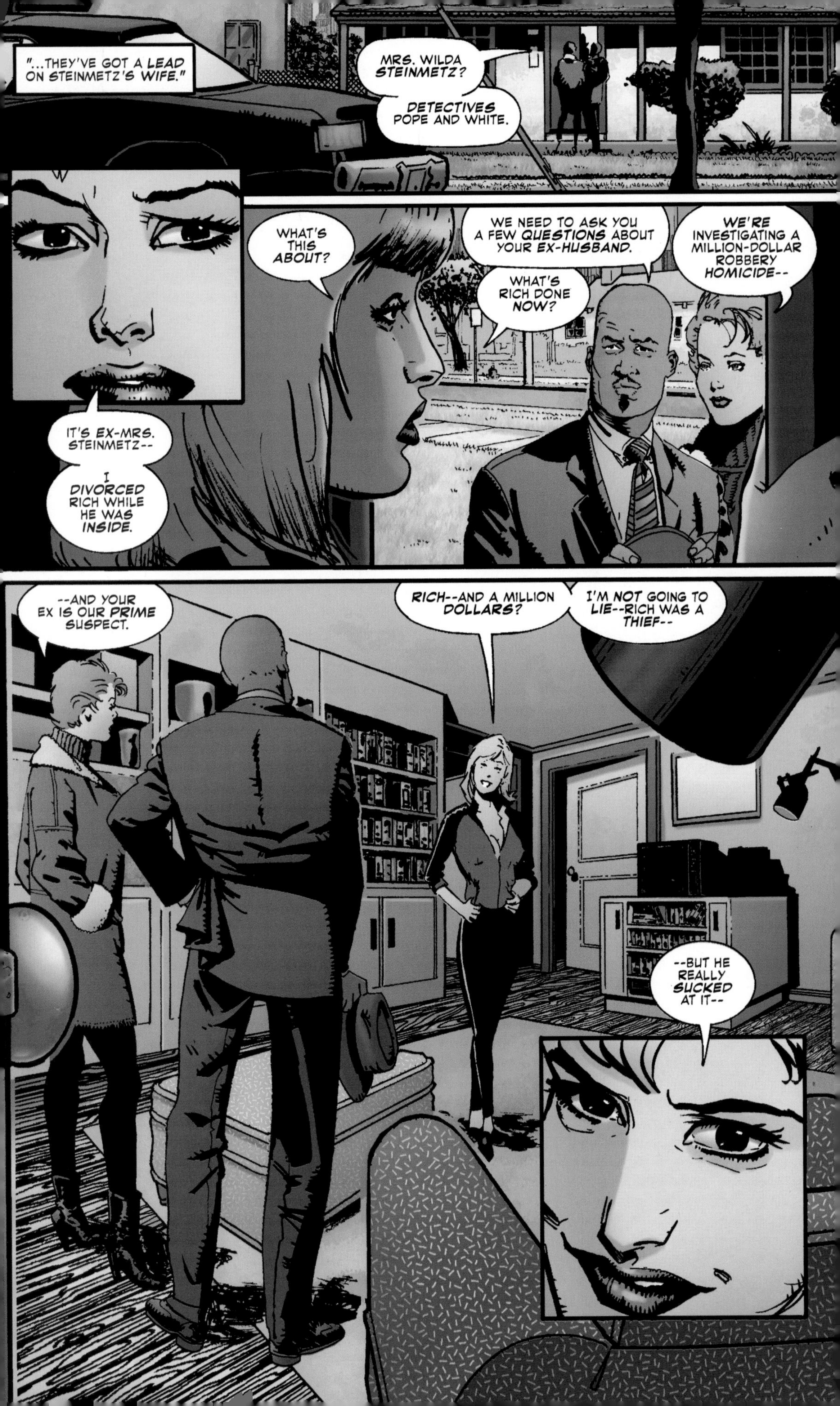
"...THEY'VE GOT A LEAD ON STEINMETZ'S WIFE."
MRS. WILDA STEINMETZ?
DETECTIVES POPE AND WHITE.
WHAT'S THIS ABOUT?
WE NEED TO ASK YOU A FEW QUESTIONS ABOUT YOUR EX-HUSBAND.
WHAT'S RICH DONE NOW?
WE'RE INVESTIGATING A MILLION-DOLLAR ROBBERY HOMICIDE--
IT'S EX-MRS. STEINMETZ--
I DIVORCED RICH WHILE HE WAS INSIDE.
--AND YOUR EX IS OUR PRIME SUSPECT.
RICH--AND A MILLION DOLLARS?
I'M NOT GOING TO LIE--RICH WAS A THIEF--
--BUT HE REALLY SUCKED AT IT--

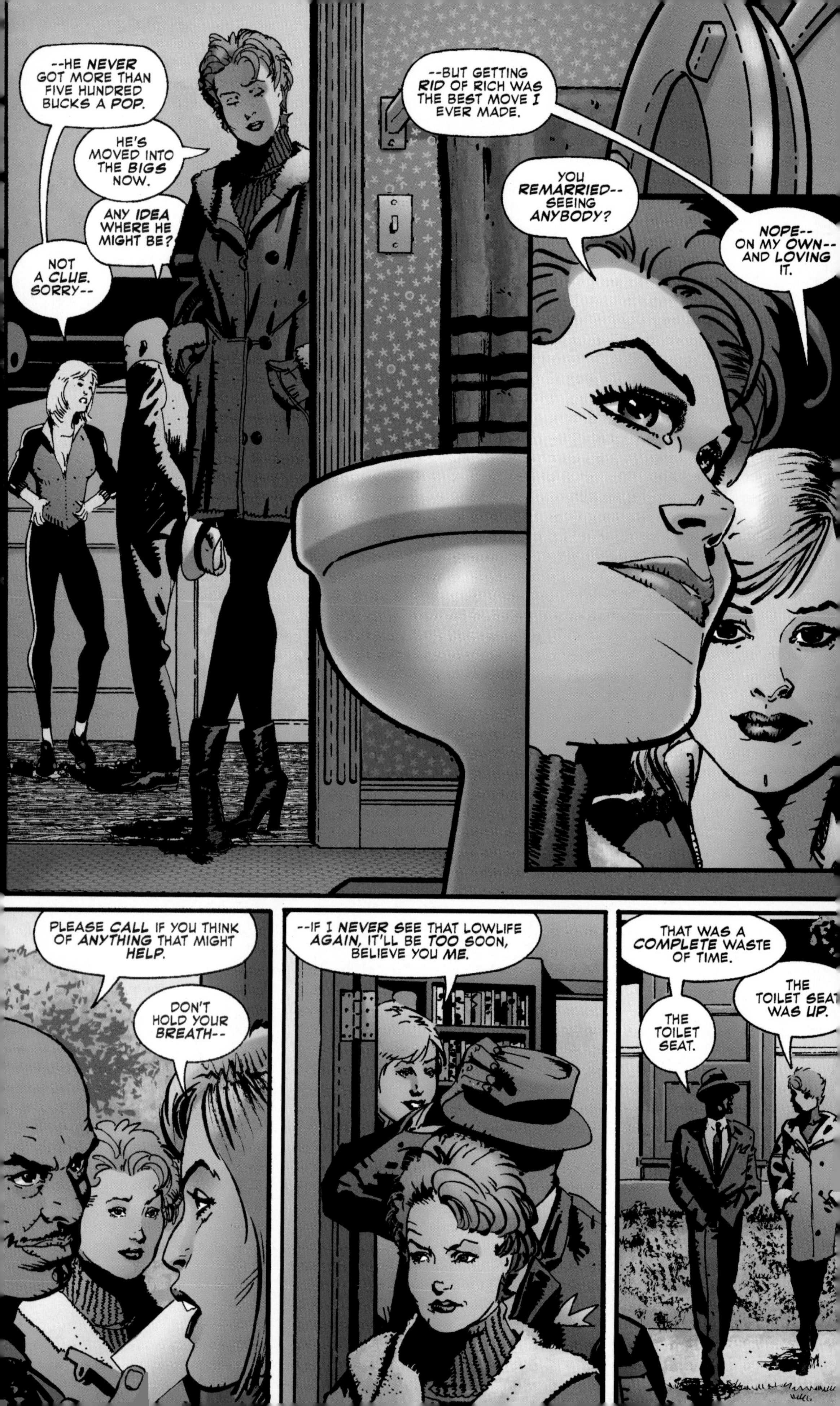
--HE NEVER GOT MORE THAN FIVE HUNDRED BUCKS A POP.
HE'S MOVED INTO THE BIGS NOW.
ANY IDEA WHERE HE MIGHT BE?
NOT A CLUE. SORRY--
--BUT GETTING RID OF RICH WAS THE BEST MOVE I EVER MADE.
YOU REMARRIED-- SEEING ANYBODY?
NOPE-- ON MY OWN-- AND LOVING IT.
PLEASE CALL IF YOU THINK OF ANYTHING THAT MIGHT HELP.
DON'T HOLD YOUR BREATH--
--IF I NEVER SEE THAT LOWLIFE AGAIN, IT'LL BE TOO SOON, BELIEVE YOU ME.
THAT WAS A COMPLETE WASTE OF TIME.
THE TOILET SEAT.
THE TOILET SEAT WAS UP.

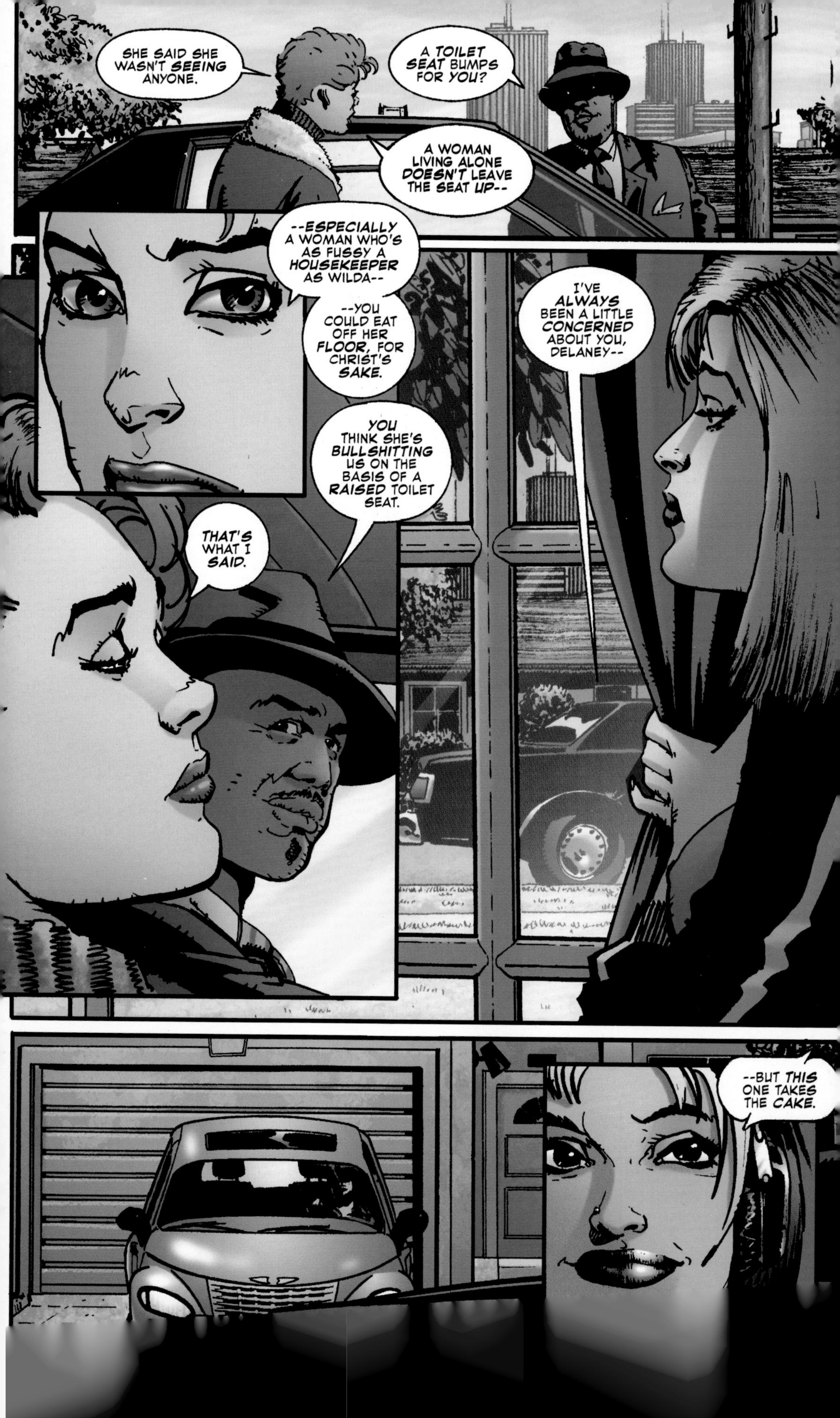
SHE SAID SHE WASN'T SEEING ANYONE.
A TOILET SEAT BUMPS FOR YOU?
A WOMAN LIVING ALONE DOESN'T LEAVE THE SEAT UP--
--ESPECIALLY A WOMAN WHO'S AS FUSSY A HOUSEKEEPER AS WILDA--
--YOU COULD EAT OFF HER FLOOR, FOR CHRIST'S SAKE.
YOU THINK SHE'S BULLSHITTING US ON THE BASIS OF A RAISED TOILET SEAT.
THAT'S WHAT I SAID.
I'VE ALWAYS BEEN A LITTLE CONCERNED ABOUT YOU, DELANEY--
--BUT THIS ONE TAKES THE CAKE.

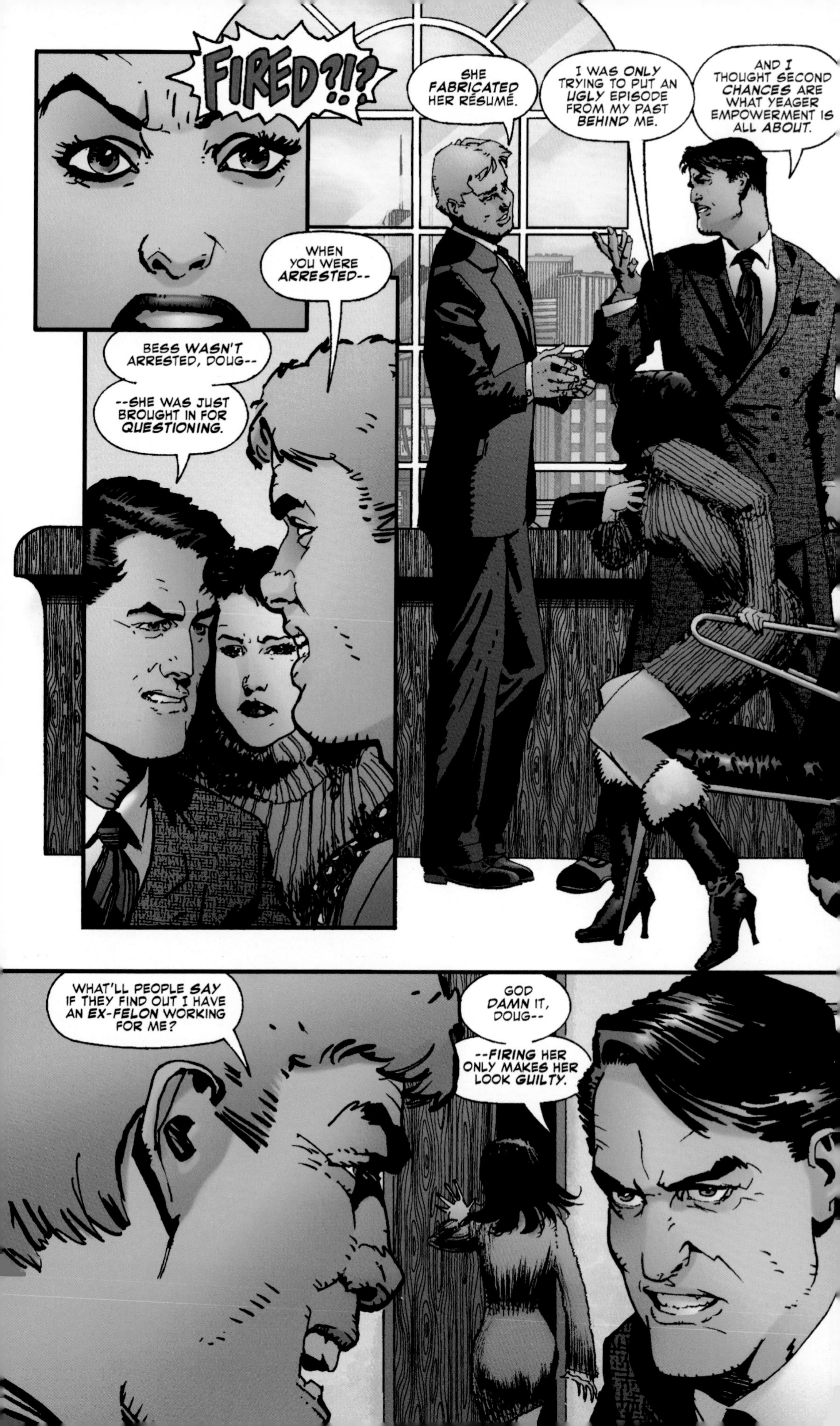
FIRED?!?
SHE FABRICATED HER RÉSUMÉ.
I WAS ONLY TRYING TO PUT AN UGLY EPISODE FROM MY PAST BEHIND ME.
AND I THOUGHT SECOND CHANCES ARE WHAT YEAGER EMPOWERMENT IS ALL ABOUT.
WHEN YOU WERE ARRESTED--
BESS WASN'T ARRESTED, DOUG--
--SHE WAS JUST BROUGHT IN FOR QUESTIONING.
WHAT'LL PEOPLE SAY IF THEY FIND OUT I HAVE AN EX-FELON WORKING FOR ME?
GOD DAMN IT, DOUG--
--FIRING HER ONLY MAKES HER LOOK GUILTY.

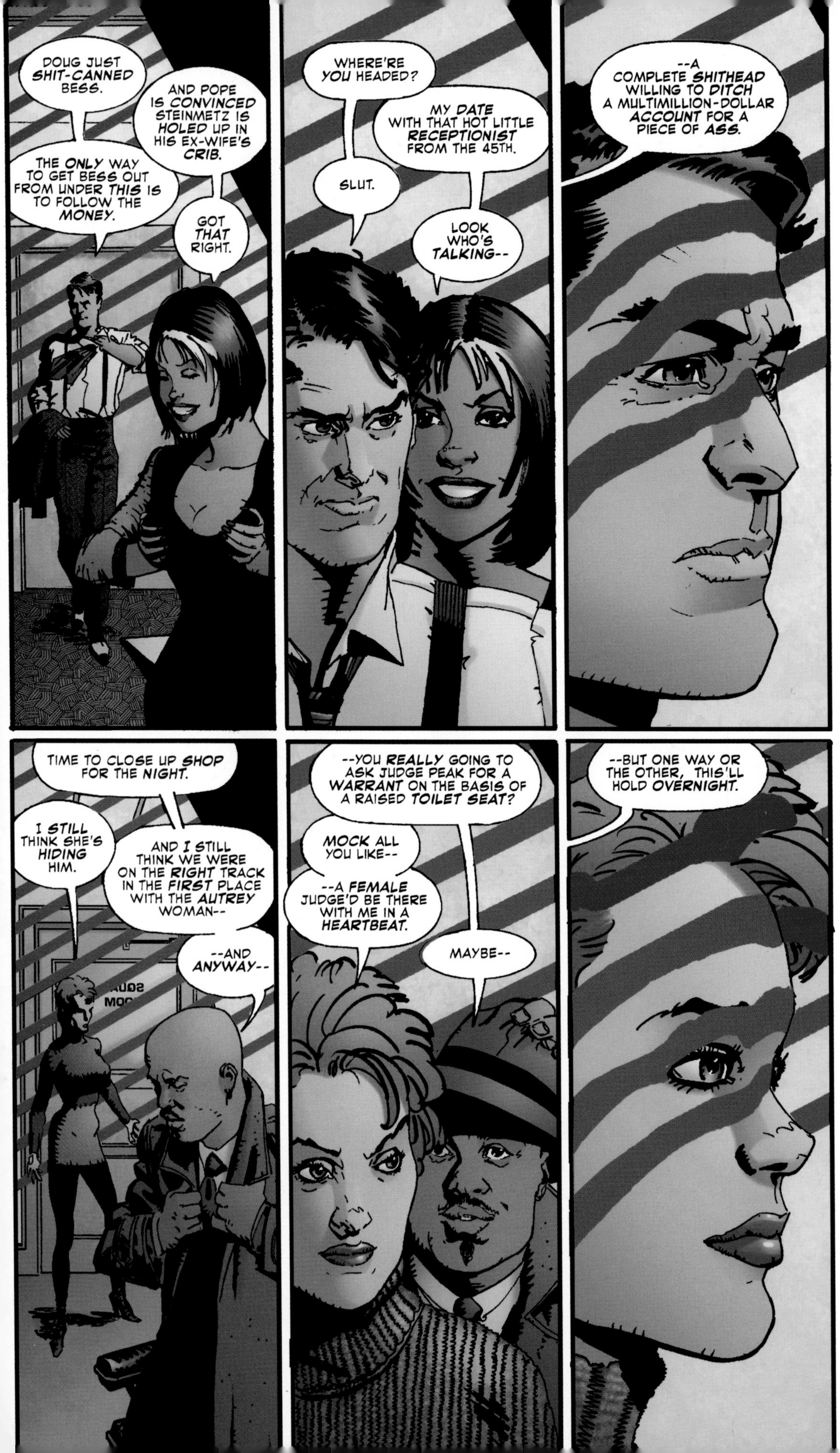
DOUG JUST SHIT-CANNED BESS.
AND POPE IS CONVINCED STEINMETZ IS HOLED UP IN HIS EX-WIFE'S CRIB.
THE ONLY WAY TO GET BESS OUT FROM UNDER THIS IS TO FOLLOW THE MONEY.
GOT THAT RIGHT.
WHERE'RE YOU HEADED?
MY DATE WITH THAT HOT LITTLE RECEPTIONIST FROM THE 45TH.
SLUT.
LOOK WHO'S TALKING--
--A COMPLETE SHITHEAD WILLING TO DITCH A MULTIMILLION-DOLLAR ACCOUNT FOR A PIECE OF ASS.
TIME TO CLOSE UP SHOP FOR THE NIGHT.
I STILL THINK SHE'S HIDING HIM.
AND I STILL THINK WE WERE ON THE RIGHT TRACK IN THE FIRST PLACE WITH THE AUTREY WOMAN--
--AND ANYWAY--
--YOU REALLY GOING TO ASK JUDGE PEAK FOR A WARRANT ON THE BASIS OF A RAISED TOILET SEAT?
MOCK ALL YOU LIKE--
--A FEMALE JUDGE'D BE THERE WITH ME IN A HEARTBEAT.
MAYBE--
--BUT ONE WAY OR THE OTHER, THIS'LL HOLD OVERNIGHT.

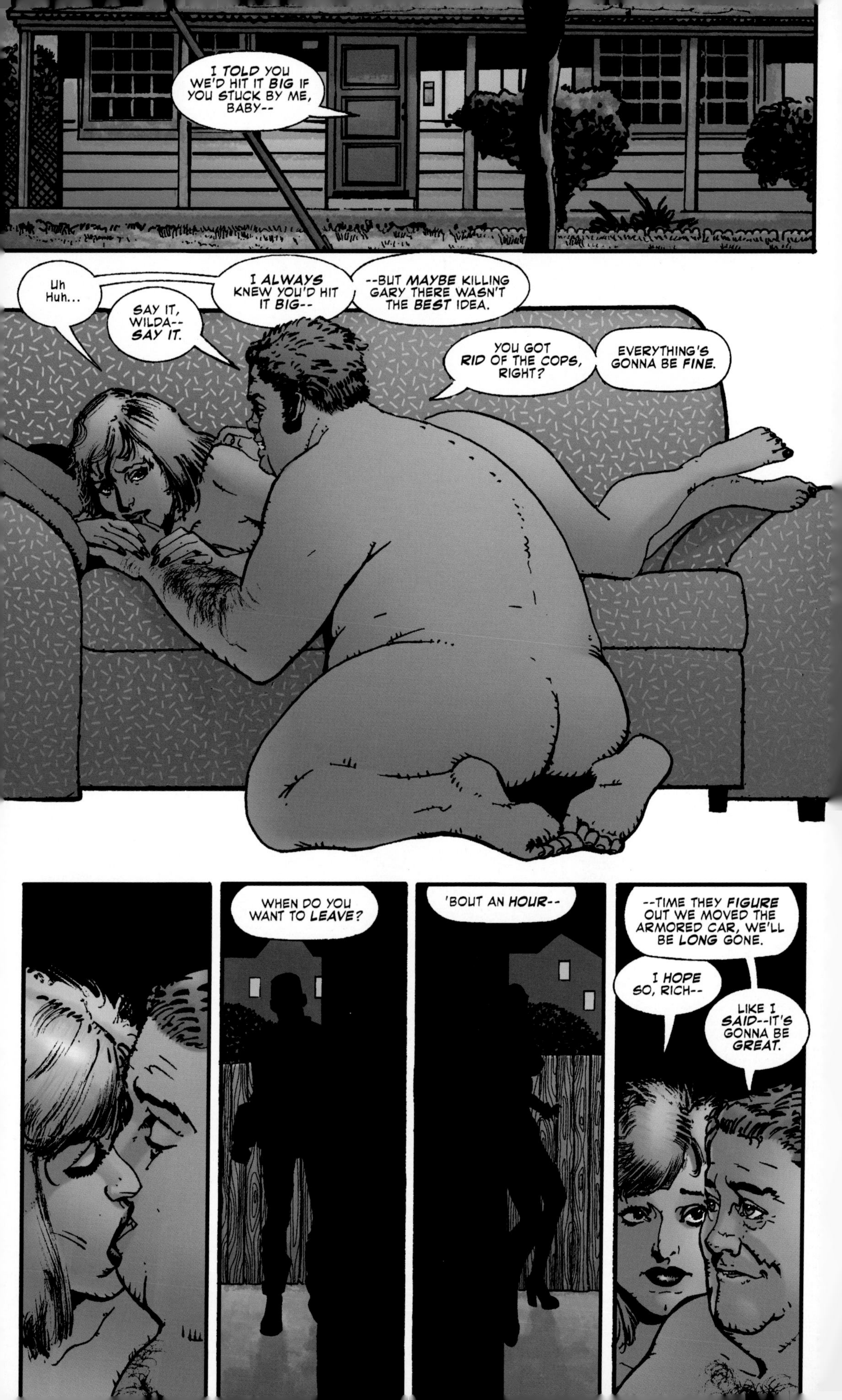

I TOLD YOU WE'D HIT IT BIG IF YOU STUCK BY ME, BABY--
Uh Huh...
SAY IT, WILDA-- SAY IT.
I ALWAYS KNEW YOU'D HIT IT BIG--
--BUT MAYBE KILLING GARY THERE WASN'T THE BEST IDEA.
YOU GOT RID OF THE COPS, RIGHT?
EVERYTHING'S GONNA BE FINE.
WHEN DO YOU WANT TO LEAVE?
'BOUT AN HOUR--
--TIME THEY FIGURE OUT WE MOVED THE ARMORED CAR, WE'LL BE LONG GONE.
I HOPE SO, RICH--
LIKE I SAID--IT'S GONNA BE GREAT.

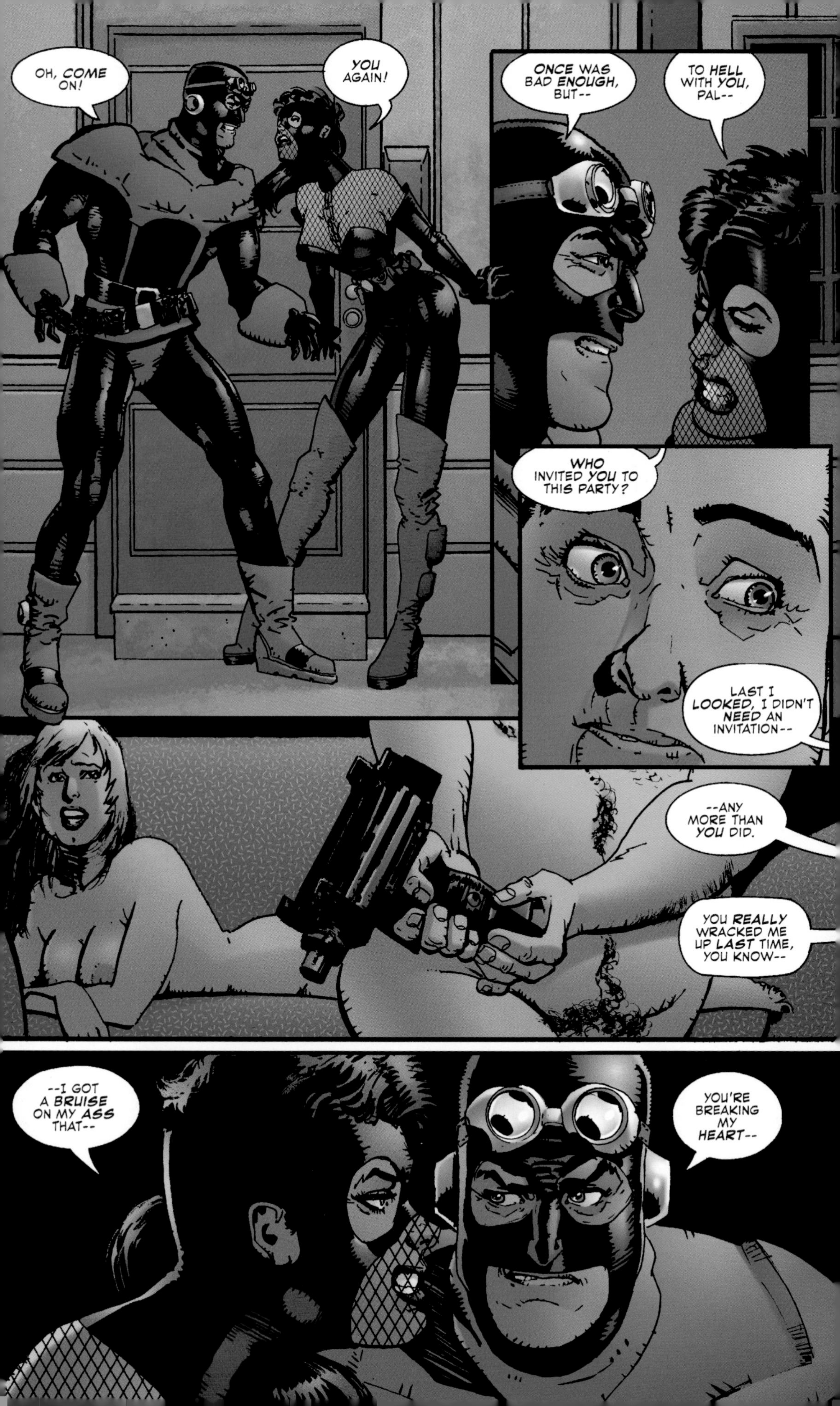
OH, COME ON!
YOU AGAIN!
ONCE WAS BAD ENOUGH, BUT--
TO HELL WITH YOU, PAL--
WHO INVITED YOU TO THIS PARTY?
LAST I LOOKED, I DIDN'T NEED AN INVITATION--
--ANY MORE THAN YOU DID.
YOU REALLY WRACKED ME UP LAST TIME, YOU KNOW--
--I GOT A BRUISE ON MY ASS THAT--
YOU'RE BREAKING MY HEART--

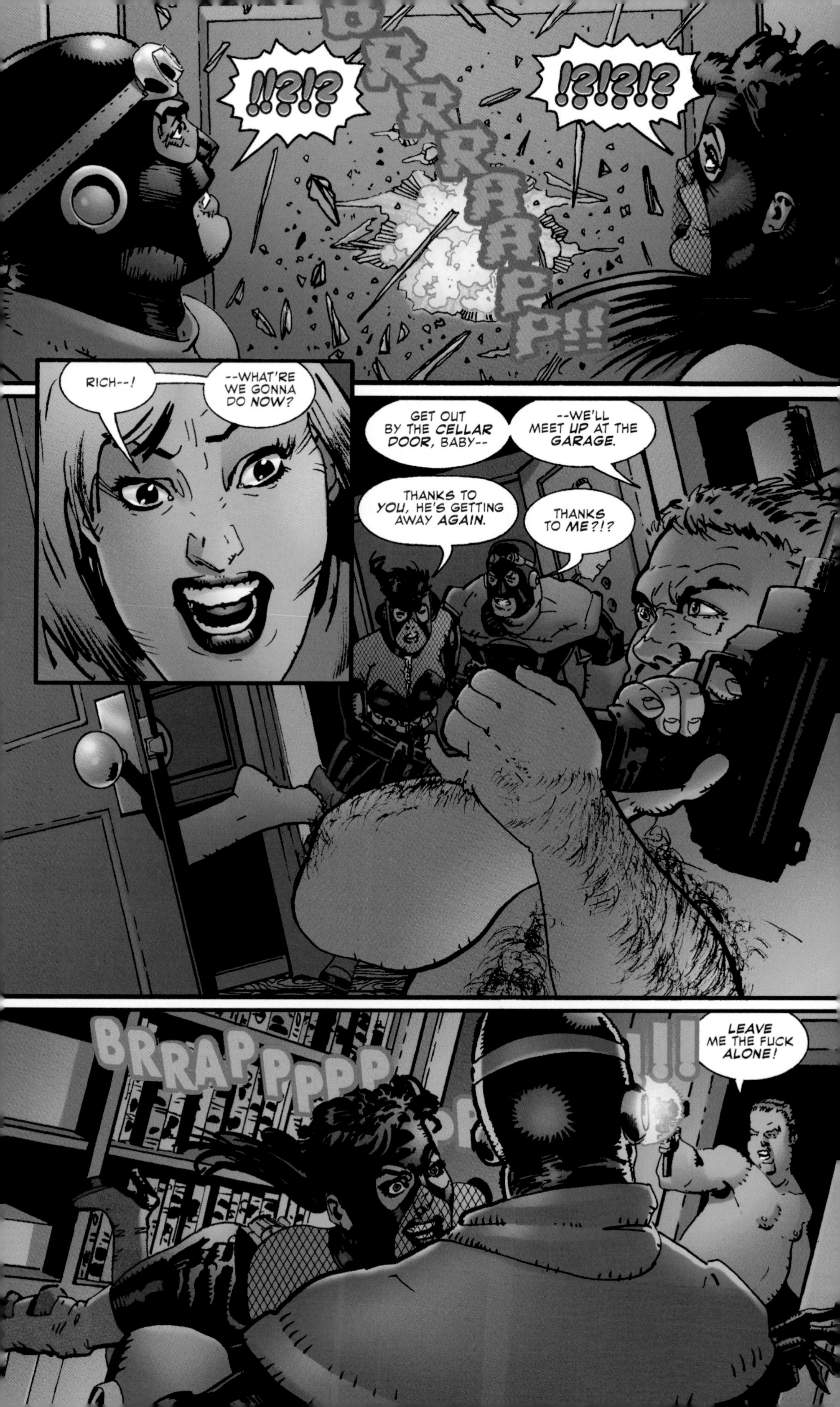

!!?!?
BRRRAAPP!!
!?!?!?
RICH--!
--WHAT'RE WE GONNA DO NOW?
GET OUT BY THE CELLAR DOOR, BABY--
--WE'LL MEET UP AT THE GARAGE.
THANKS TO YOU, HE'S GETTING AWAY AGAIN.
THANKS TO ME?!?
BRRAPPPPP
LEAVE ME THE FUCK ALONE!

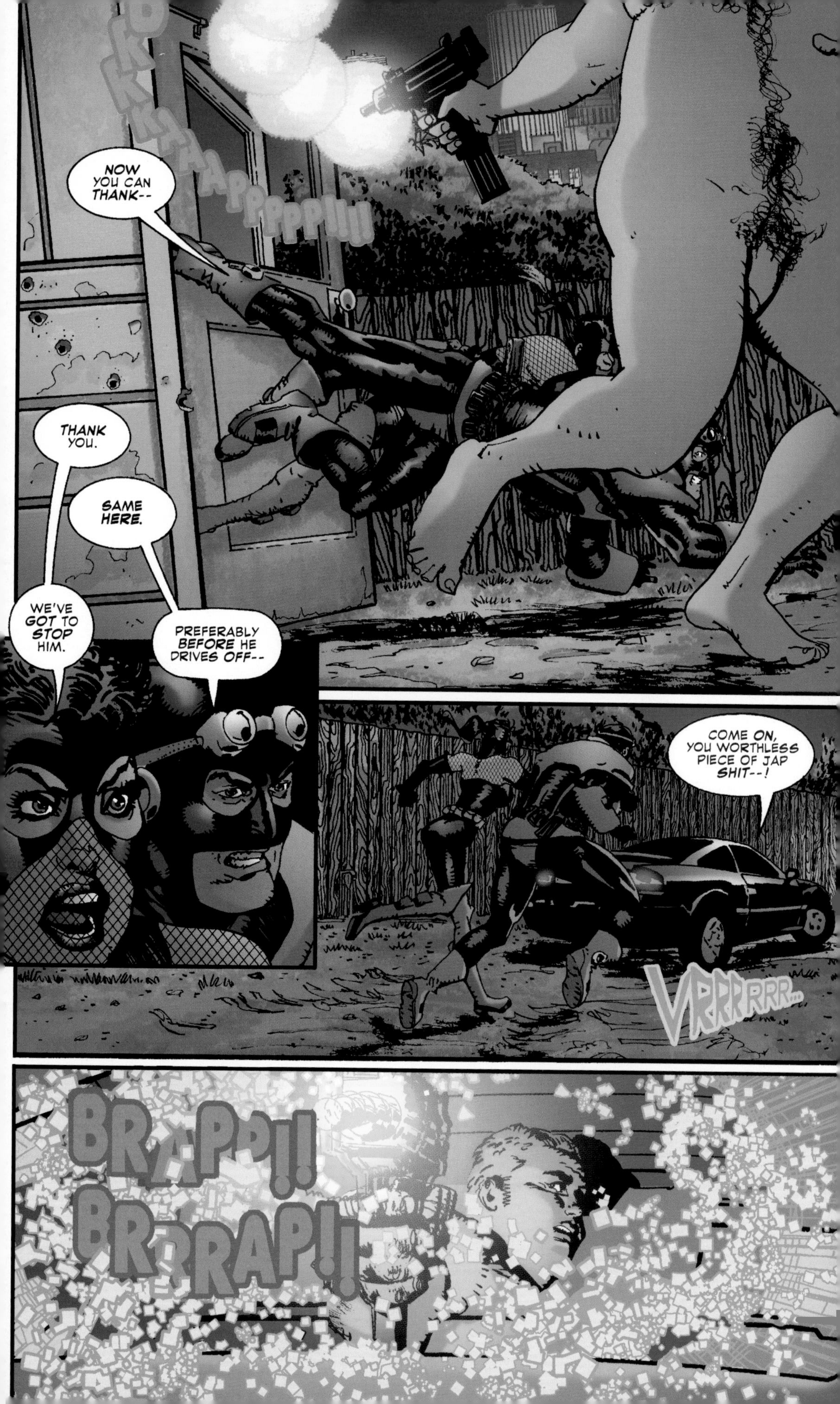

RRKKAAAAPPPPP!!!
NOW YOU CAN THANK--
THANK YOU.
SAME HERE.
WE'VE GOT TO STOP HIM.
PREFERABLY BEFORE HE DRIVES OFF--
COME ON, YOU WORTHLESS PIECE OF JAP SHIT--!
VRRRRRR...
BRAPP!!
BRRRAP!!

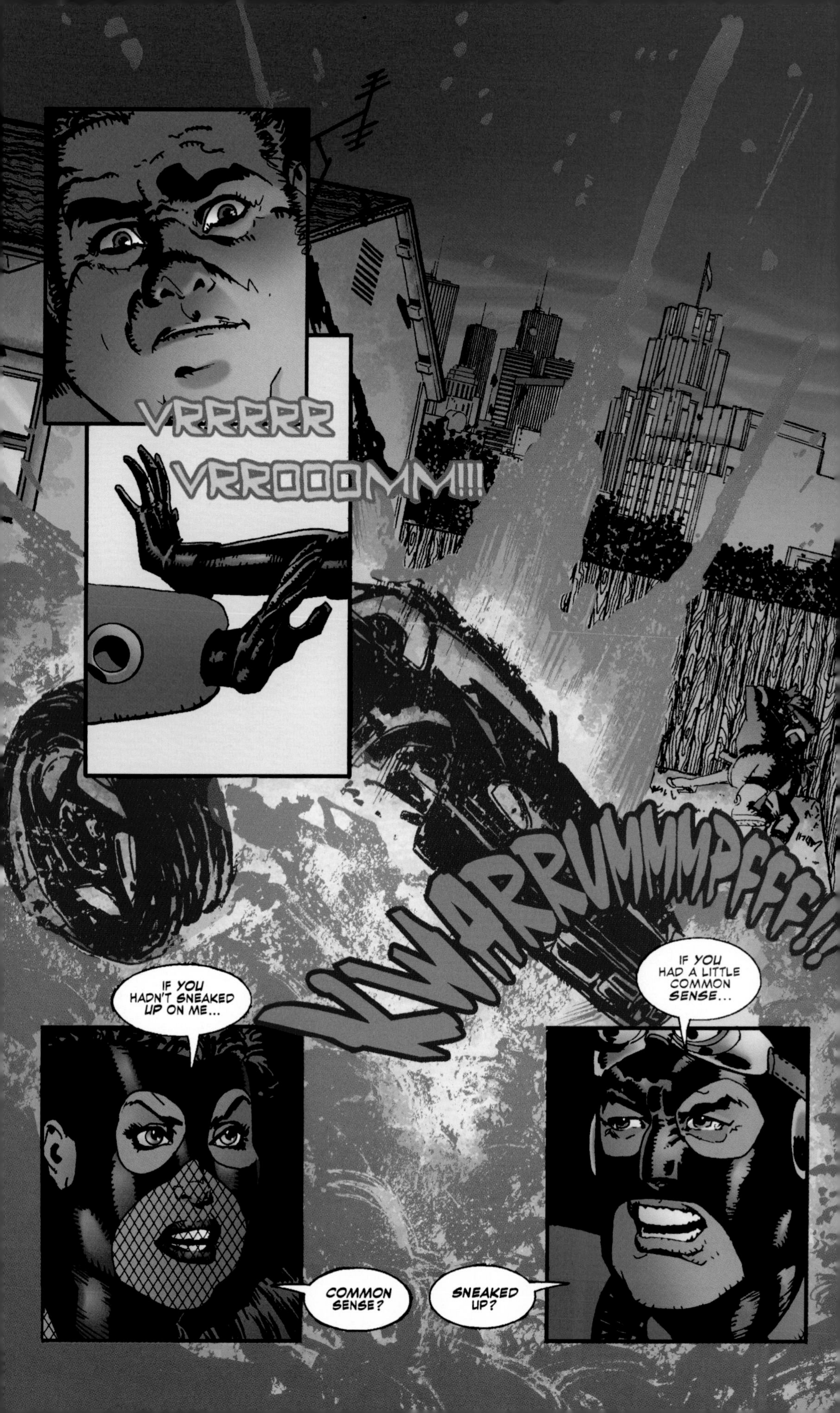
VRRRRR
VRROOOMM!!!
VWARRUMMMPFFF!!
IF YOU HADN'T SNEAKED UP ON ME...
IF YOU HAD A LITTLE COMMON SENSE...
COMMON SENSE?
SNEAKED UP?

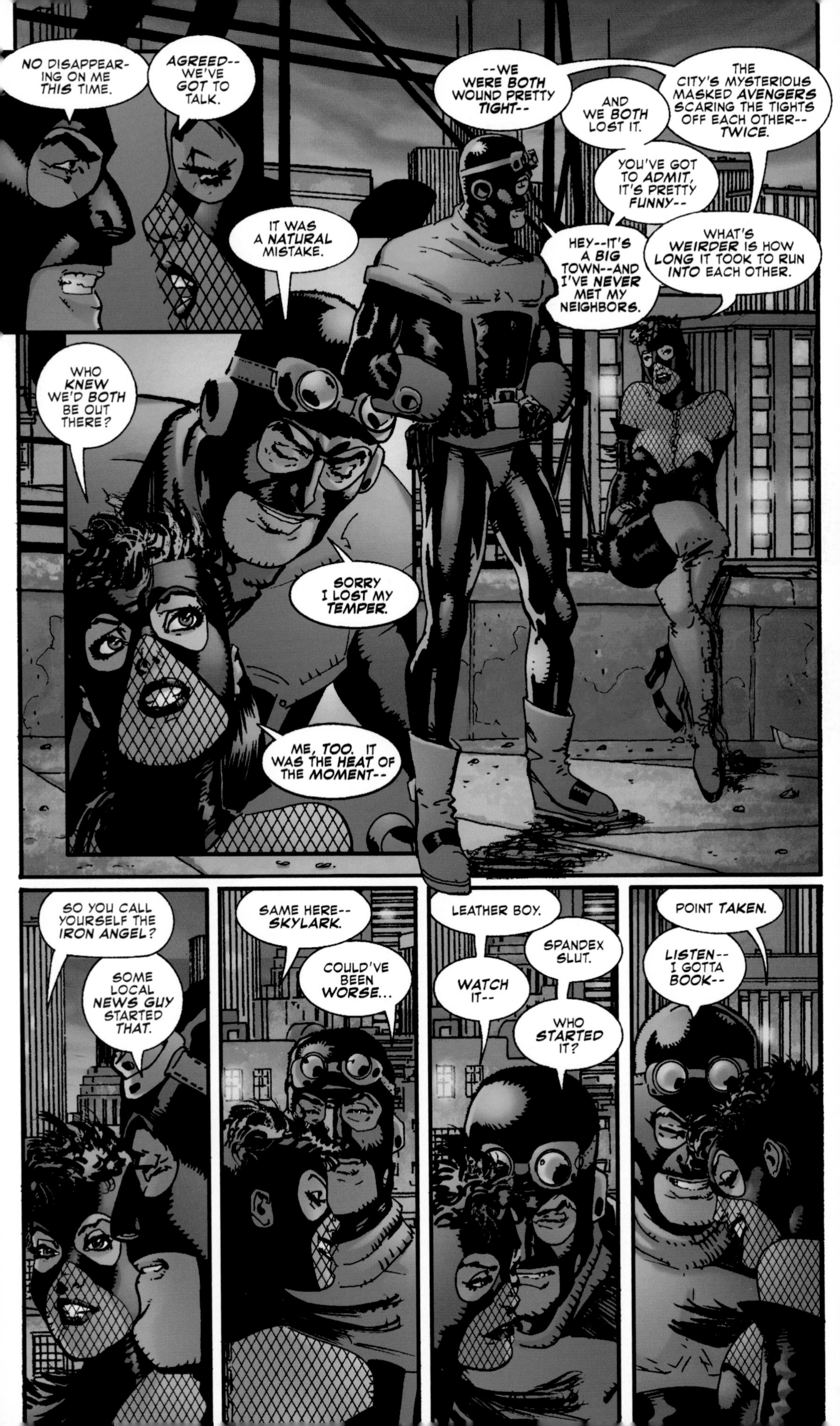
NO DISAPPEARING ON ME THIS TIME.
AGREED-- WE'VE GOT TO TALK.
IT WAS A NATURAL MISTAKE.
--WE WERE BOTH WOUND PRETTY TIGHT--
AND WE BOTH LOST IT.
THE CITY'S MYSTERIOUS MASKED AVENGERS SCARING THE TIGHTS OFF EACH OTHER-- TWICE.
YOU'VE GOT TO ADMIT, IT'S PRETTY FUNNY--
HEY--IT'S A BIG TOWN--AND I'VE NEVER MET MY NEIGHBORS.
WHAT'S WEIRDER IS HOW LONG IT TOOK TO RUN INTO EACH OTHER.
WHO KNEW WE'D BOTH BE OUT THERE?
SORRY I LOST MY TEMPER.
ME, TOO. IT WAS THE HEAT OF THE MOMENT--
SO YOU CALL YOURSELF THE IRON ANGEL?
SOME LOCAL NEWS GUY STARTED THAT.
SAME HERE-- SKYLARK.
COULD'VE BEEN WORSE...
LEATHER BOY.
SPANDEX SLUT.
WATCH IT--
WHO STARTED IT?
POINT TAKEN.
LISTEN-- I GOTTA BOOK--

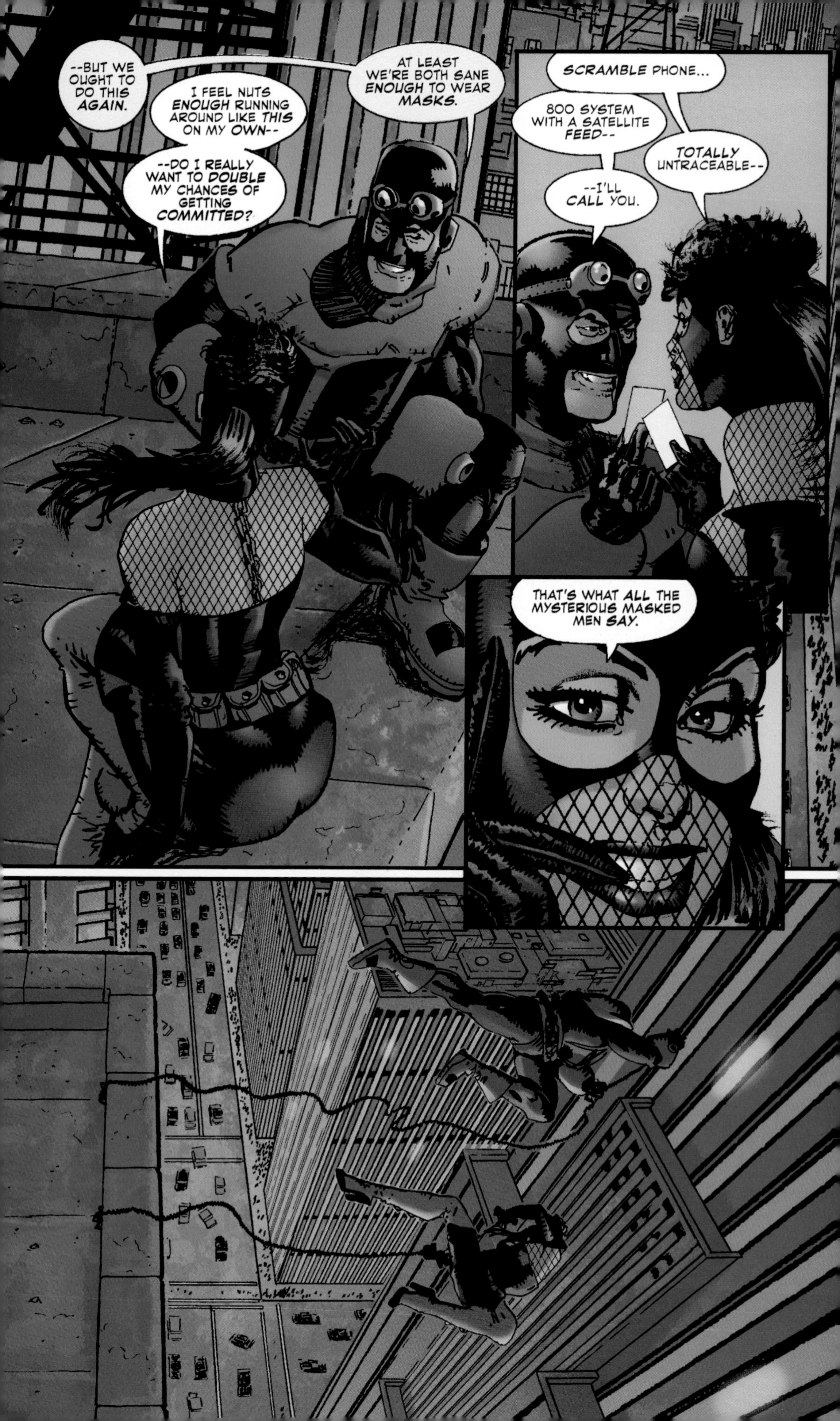
--BUT WE OUGHT TO DO THIS AGAIN.
AT LEAST WE'RE BOTH SANE ENOUGH TO WEAR MASKS.
I FEEL NUTS ENOUGH RUNNING AROUND LIKE THIS ON MY OWN--
--DO I REALLY WANT TO DOUBLE MY CHANCES OF GETTING COMMITTED?
SCRAMBLE PHONE...
800 SYSTEM WITH A SATELLITE FEED--
TOTALLY UNTRACEABLE--
--I'LL CALL YOU.
THAT'S WHAT ALL THE MYSTERIOUS MASKED MEN SAY.

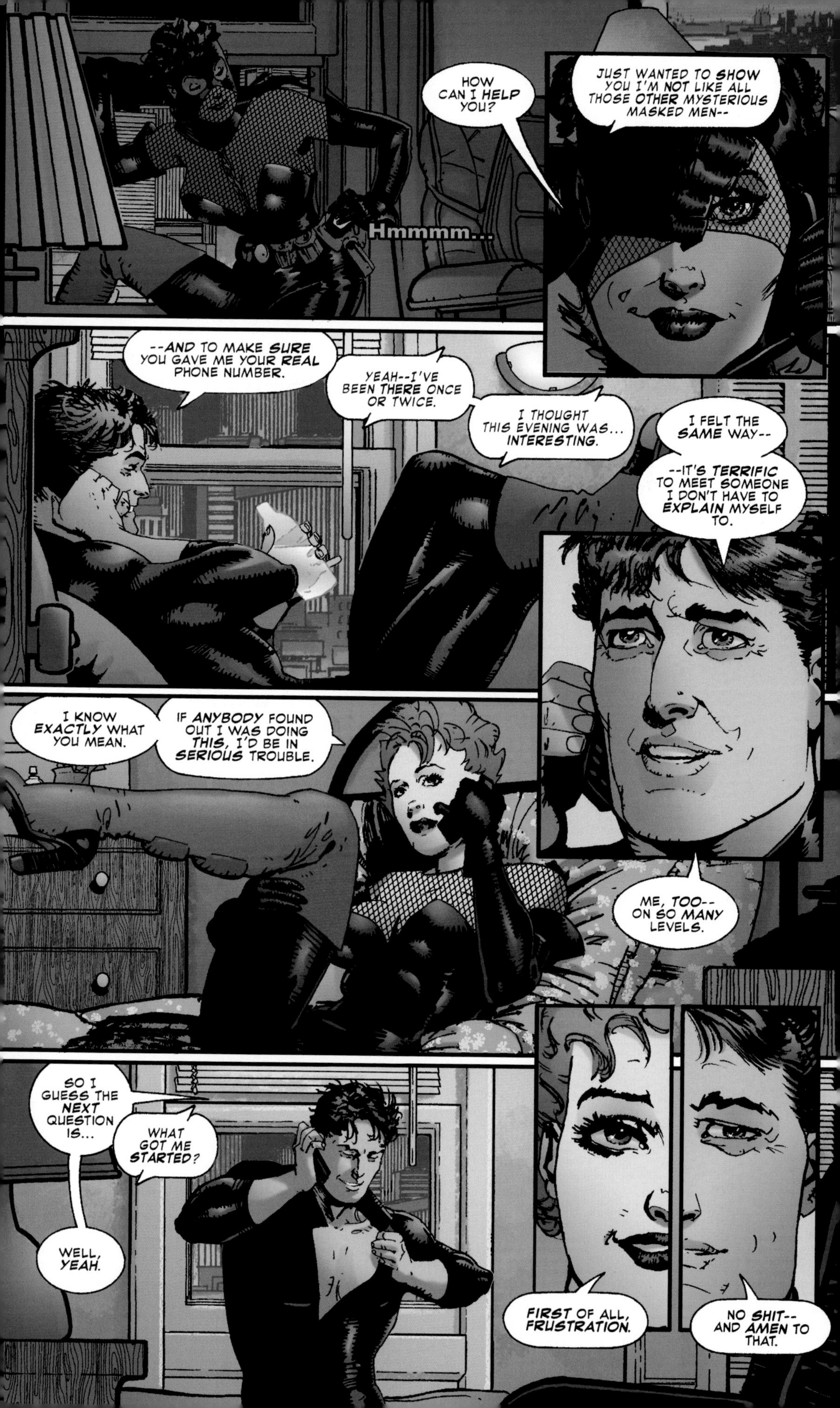

HOW CAN I HELP YOU?
Hmmmm...
JUST WANTED TO SHOW YOU I'M NOT LIKE ALL THOSE OTHER MYSTERIOUS MASKED MEN--
--AND TO MAKE SURE YOU GAVE ME YOUR REAL PHONE NUMBER.
YEAH--I'VE BEEN THERE ONCE OR TWICE.
I THOUGHT THIS EVENING WAS... INTERESTING.
I FELT THE SAME WAY--
--IT'S TERRIFIC TO MEET SOMEONE I DON'T HAVE TO EXPLAIN MYSELF TO.
I KNOW EXACTLY WHAT YOU MEAN.
IF ANYBODY FOUND OUT I WAS DOING THIS, I'D BE IN SERIOUS TROUBLE.
ME, TOO-- ON SO MANY LEVELS.
SO I GUESS THE NEXT QUESTION IS...
WHAT GOT ME STARTED?
WELL, YEAH.
FIRST OF ALL, FRUSTRATION.
NO SHIT-- AND AMEN TO THAT.

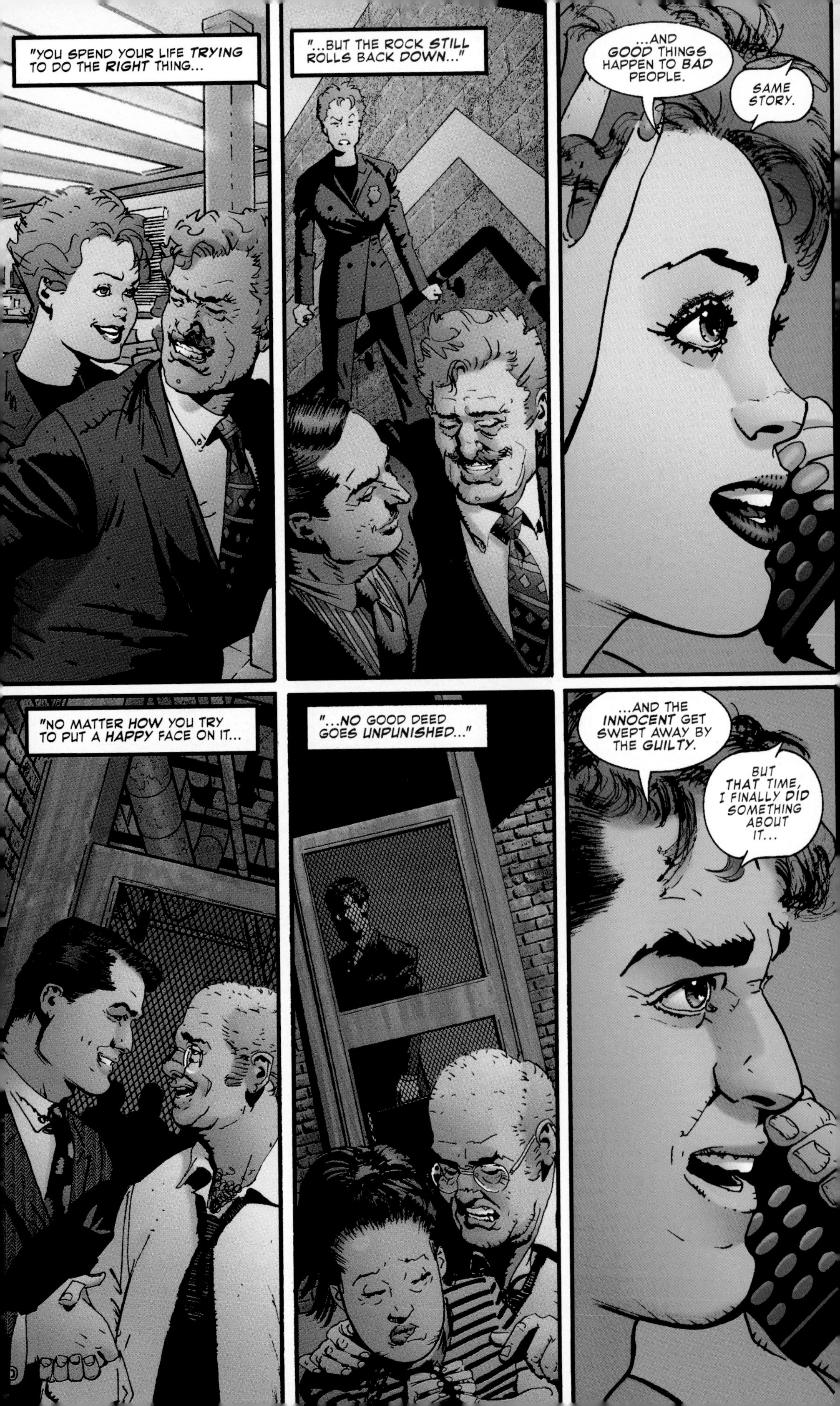
"YOU SPEND YOUR LIFE TRYING TO DO THE RIGHT THING...
"...BUT THE ROCK STILL ROLLS BACK DOWN..."
...AND GOOD THINGS HAPPEN TO BAD PEOPLE.
SAME STORY.
"NO MATTER HOW YOU TRY TO PUT A HAPPY FACE ON IT...
"...NO GOOD DEED GOES UNPUNISHED..."
...AND THE INNOCENT GET SWEPT AWAY BY THE GUILTY.
BUT THAT TIME, I FINALLY DID SOMETHING ABOUT IT...

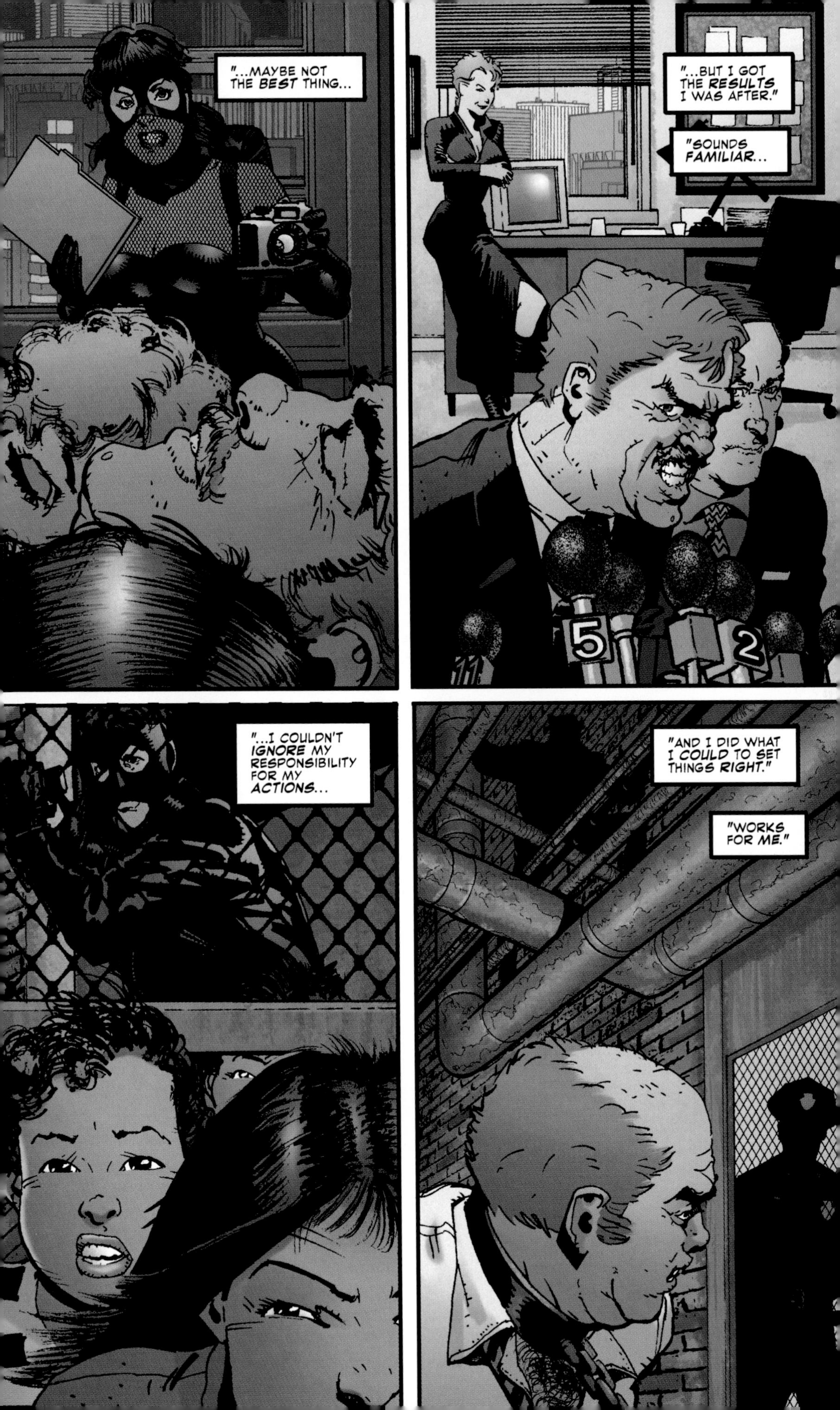
"...MAYBE NOT THE BEST THING...
"...BUT I GOT THE RESULTS I WAS AFTER."
"SOUNDS FAMILIAR...
5
2
"...I COULDN'T IGNORE MY RESPONSIBILITY FOR MY ACTIONS...
"AND I DID WHAT I COULD TO SET THINGS RIGHT."
"WORKS FOR ME."

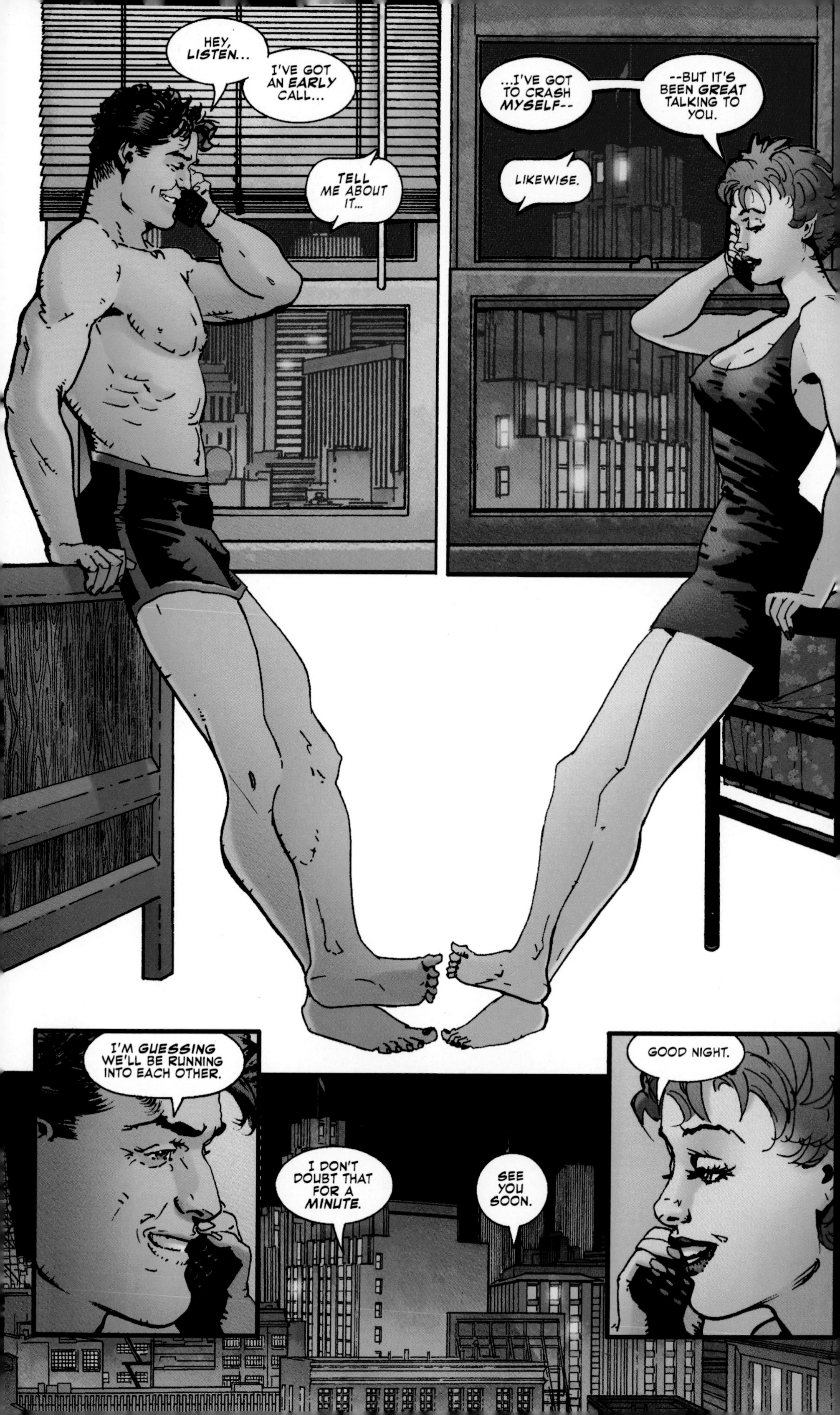
HEY, LISTEN...
I'VE GOT AN EARLY CALL...
TELL ME ABOUT IT...
...I'VE GOT TO CRASH MYSELF--
--BUT IT'S BEEN GREAT TALKING TO YOU.
LIKEWISE.
I'M GUESSING WE'LL BE RUNNING INTO EACH OTHER.
I DON'T DOUBT THAT FOR A MINUTE.
SEE YOU SOON.
GOOD NIGHT.

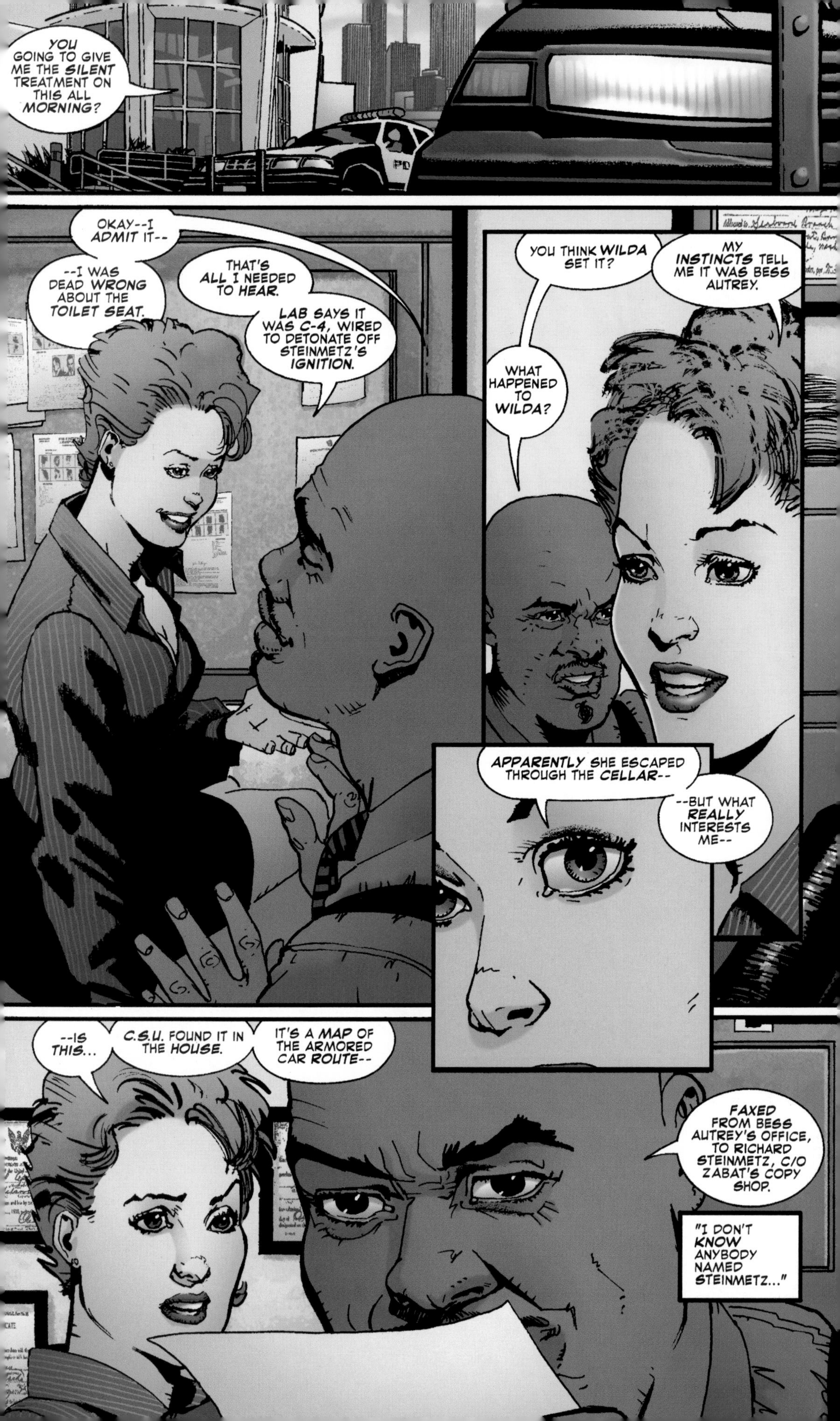
YOU GOING TO GIVE ME THE SILENT TREATMENT ON THIS ALL MORNING?
OKAY--I ADMIT IT--
--I WAS DEAD WRONG ABOUT THE TOILET SEAT.
THAT'S ALL I NEEDED TO HEAR.
LAB SAYS IT WAS C-4, WIRED TO DETONATE OFF STEINMETZ'S IGNITION.
YOU THINK WILDA SET IT?
MY INSTINCTS TELL ME IT WAS BESS AUTREY.
WHAT HAPPENED TO WILDA?
APPARENTLY SHE ESCAPED THROUGH THE CELLAR--
--BUT WHAT REALLY INTERESTS ME--
--IS THIS...
C.S.U. FOUND IT IN THE HOUSE.
IT'S A MAP OF THE ARMORED CAR ROUTE--
FAXED FROM BESS AUTREY'S OFFICE, TO RICHARD STEINMETZ, C/O ZABAT'S COPY SHOP.
"I DON'T KNOW ANYBODY NAMED STEINMETZ..."

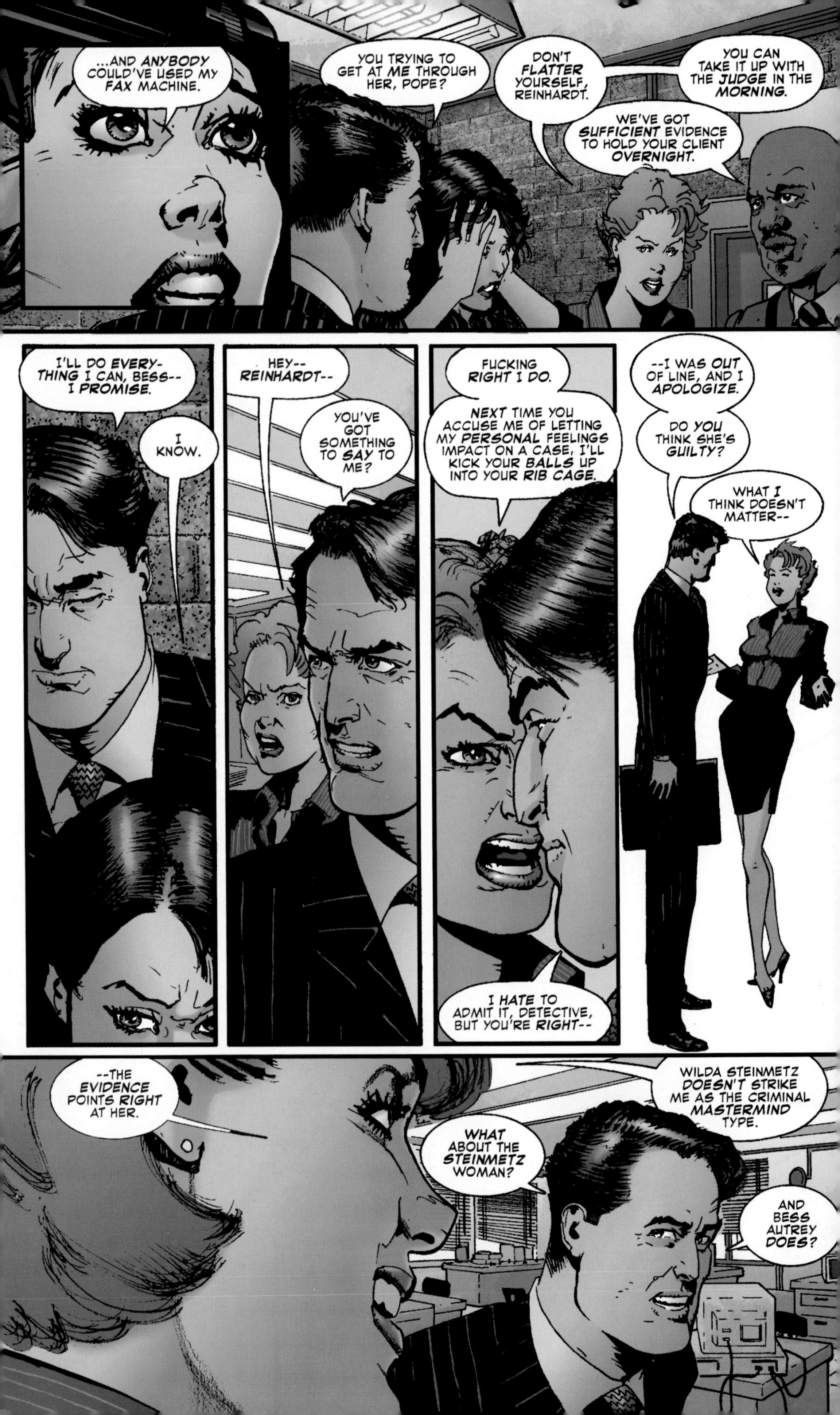
...AND ANYBODY COULD'VE USED MY FAX MACHINE.
YOU TRYING TO GET AT ME THROUGH HER, POPE?
DON'T FLATTER YOURSELF, REINHARDT.
WE'VE GOT SUFFICIENT EVIDENCE TO HOLD YOUR CLIENT OVERNIGHT.
YOU CAN TAKE IT UP WITH THE JUDGE IN THE MORNING.
I'LL DO EVERY-THING I CAN, BESS-- I PROMISE.
I KNOW.
HEY-- REINHARDT--
YOU'VE GOT SOMETHING TO SAY TO ME?
FUCKING RIGHT I DO.
NEXT TIME YOU ACCUSE ME OF LETTING MY PERSONAL FEELINGS IMPACT ON A CASE, I'LL KICK YOUR BALLS UP INTO YOUR RIB CAGE.
I HATE TO ADMIT IT, DETECTIVE, BUT YOU'RE RIGHT--
--I WAS OUT OF LINE, AND I APOLOGIZE.
DO YOU THINK SHE'S GUILTY?
WHAT I THINK DOESN'T MATTER--
--THE EVIDENCE POINTS RIGHT AT HER.
WHAT ABOUT THE STEINMETZ WOMAN?
WILDA STEINMETZ DOESN'T STRIKE ME AS THE CRIMINAL MASTERMIND TYPE.
AND BESS AUTREY DOES?

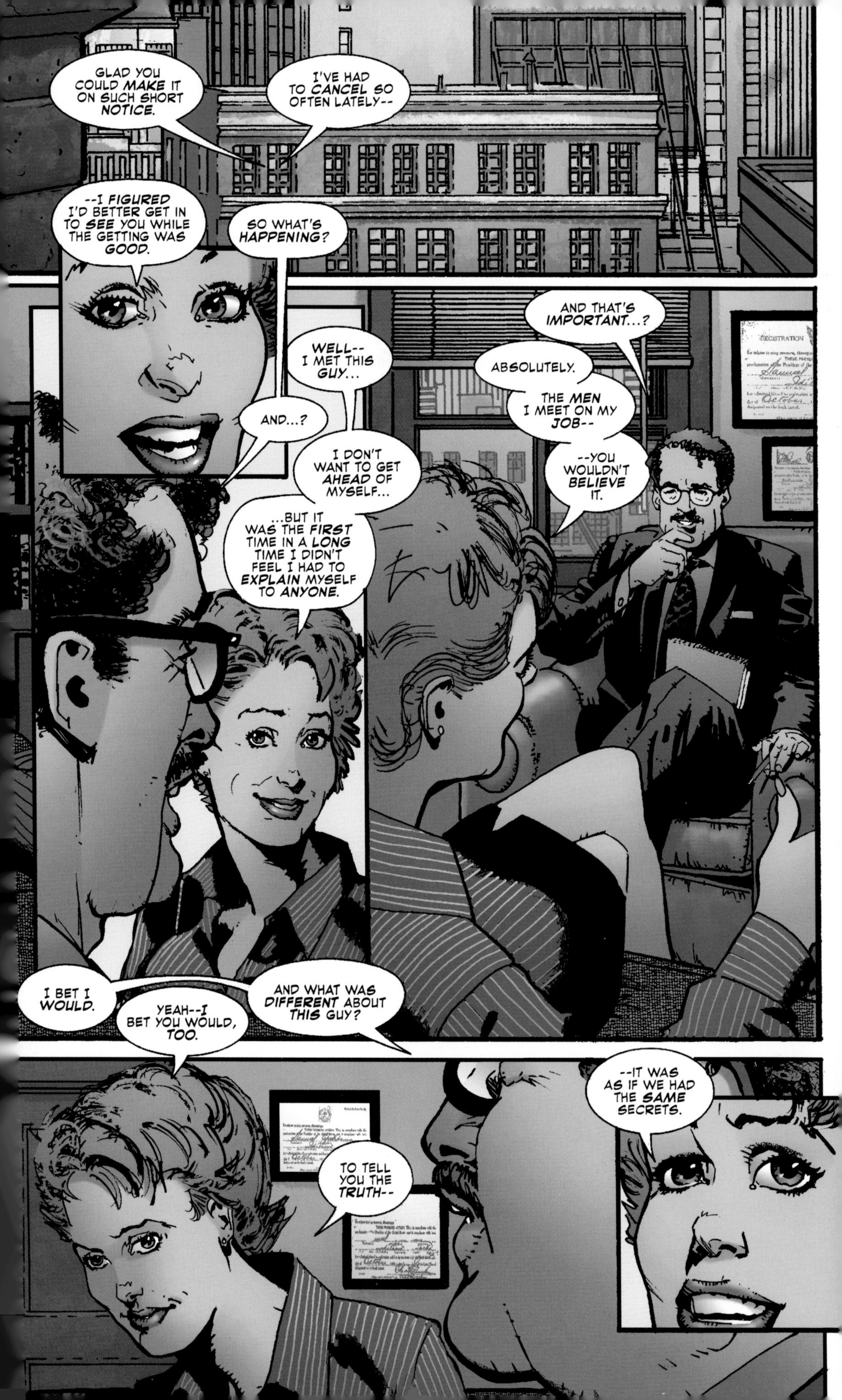

GLAD YOU COULD MAKE IT ON SUCH SHORT NOTICE.
I'VE HAD TO CANCEL SO OFTEN LATELY--
--I FIGURED I'D BETTER GET IN TO SEE YOU WHILE THE GETTING WAS GOOD.
SO WHAT'S HAPPENING?
WELL-- I MET THIS GUY...
AND...?
I DON'T WANT TO GET AHEAD OF MYSELF...
...BUT IT WAS THE FIRST TIME IN A LONG TIME I DIDN'T FEEL I HAD TO EXPLAIN MYSELF TO ANYONE.
AND THAT'S IMPORTANT...?
ABSOLUTELY.
THE MEN I MEET ON MY JOB--
--YOU WOULDN'T BELIEVE IT.
I BET I WOULD.
YEAH--I BET YOU WOULD, TOO.
AND WHAT WAS DIFFERENT ABOUT THIS GUY?
TO TELL YOU THE TRUTH--
--IT WAS AS IF WE HAD THE SAME SECRETS.

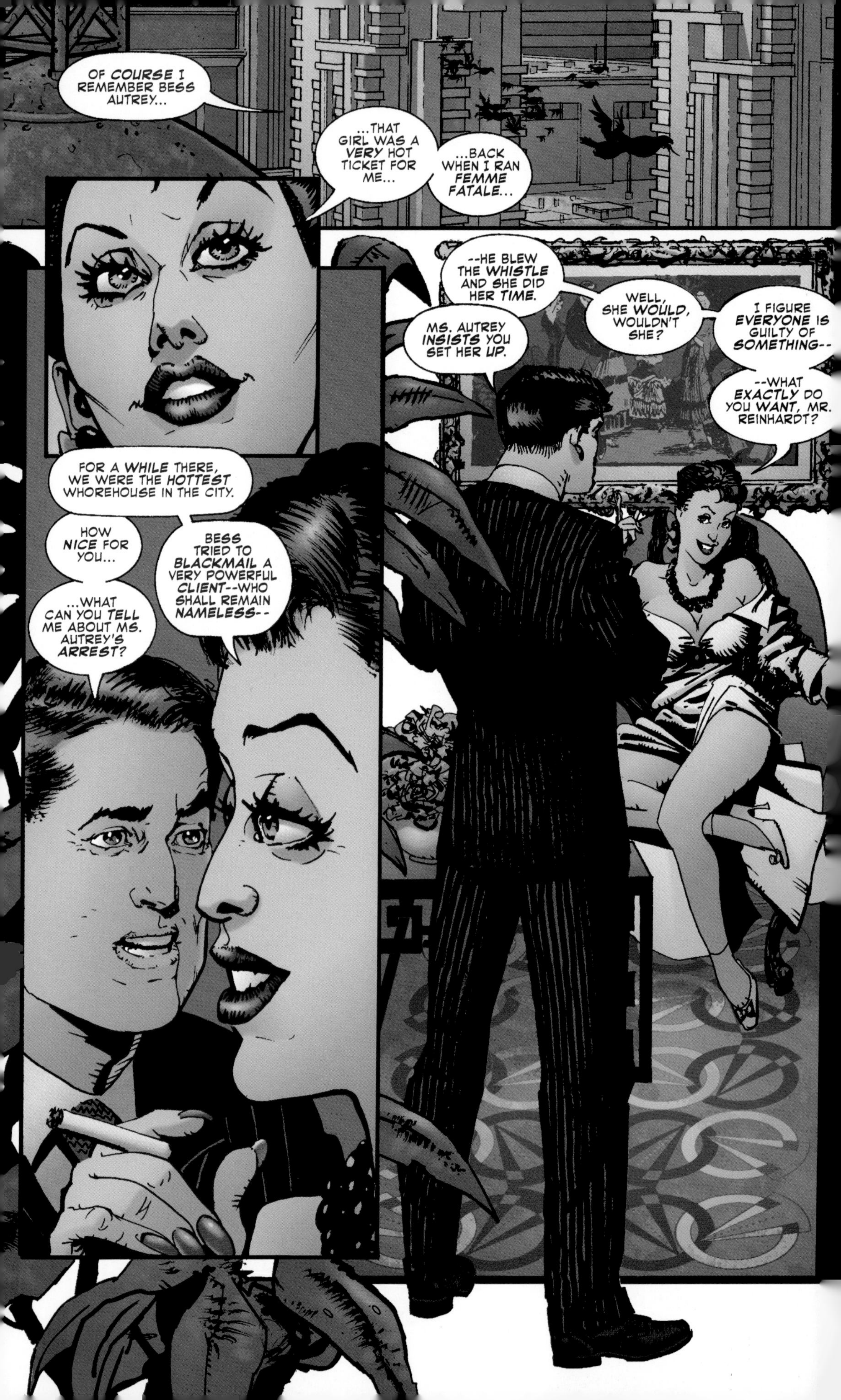
OF COURSE I REMEMBER BESS AUTREY...
...THAT GIRL WAS A VERY HOT TICKET FOR ME...
...BACK WHEN I RAN FEMME FATALE...
FOR A WHILE THERE, WE WERE THE HOTTEST WHOREHOUSE IN THE CITY.
HOW NICE FOR YOU...
...WHAT CAN YOU TELL ME ABOUT MS. AUTREY'S ARREST?
BESS TRIED TO BLACKMAIL A VERY POWERFUL CLIENT--WHO SHALL REMAIN NAMELESS--
--HE BLEW THE WHISTLE AND SHE DID HER TIME.
MS. AUTREY INSISTS YOU SET HER UP.
WELL, SHE WOULD, WOULDN'T SHE?
I FIGURE EVERYONE IS GUILTY OF SOMETHING--
--WHAT EXACTLY DO YOU WANT, MR. REINHARDT?

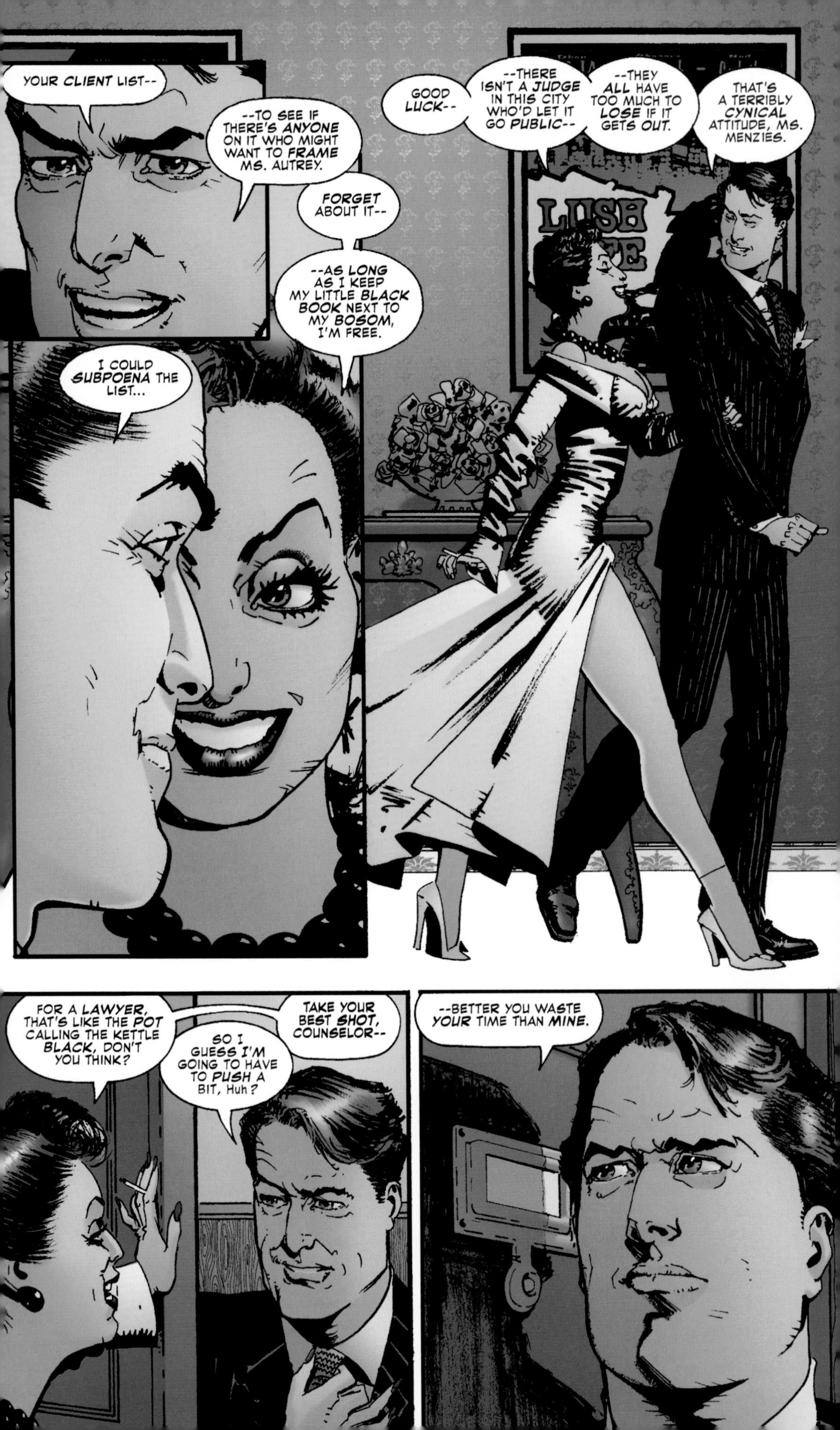
YOUR CLIENT LIST--
--TO SEE IF THERE'S ANYONE ON IT WHO MIGHT WANT TO FRAME MS. AUTREY.
FORGET ABOUT IT--
--AS LONG AS I KEEP MY LITTLE BLACK BOOK NEXT TO MY BOSOM, I'M FREE.
I COULD SUBPOENA THE LIST...
GOOD LUCK--
--THERE ISN'T A JUDGE IN THIS CITY WHO'D LET IT GO PUBLIC--
--THEY ALL HAVE TOO MUCH TO LOSE IF IT GETS OUT.
THAT'S A TERRIBLY CYNICAL ATTITUDE, MS. MENZIES.
LUSH
FOR A LAWYER, THAT'S LIKE THE POT CALLING THE KETTLE BLACK, DON'T YOU THINK?
SO I GUESS I'M GOING TO HAVE TO PUSH A BIT, Huh?
TAKE YOUR BEST SHOT, COUNSELOR--
--BETTER YOU WASTE YOUR TIME THAN MINE.

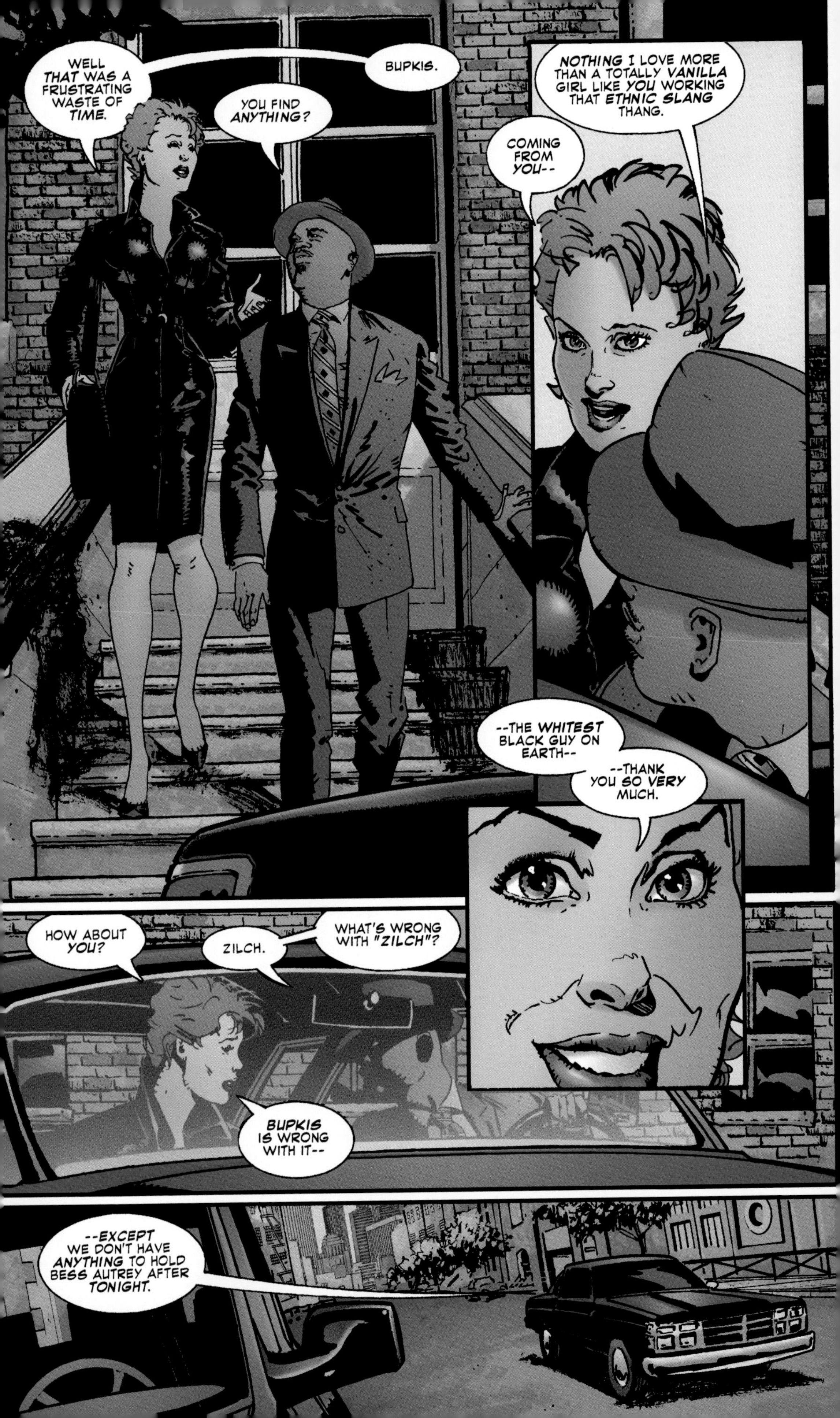
WELL THAT WAS A FRUSTRATING WASTE OF TIME.
YOU FIND ANYTHING?
BUPKIS.
NOTHING I LOVE MORE THAN A TOTALLY VANILLA GIRL LIKE YOU WORKING THAT ETHNIC SLANG THANG.
COMING FROM YOU--
--THE WHITEST BLACK GUY ON EARTH--
--THANK YOU SO VERY MUCH.
HOW ABOUT YOU?
ZILCH.
WHAT'S WRONG WITH "ZILCH"?
BUPKIS IS WRONG WITH IT--
--EXCEPT WE DON'T HAVE ANYTHING TO HOLD BESS AUTREY AFTER TONIGHT.

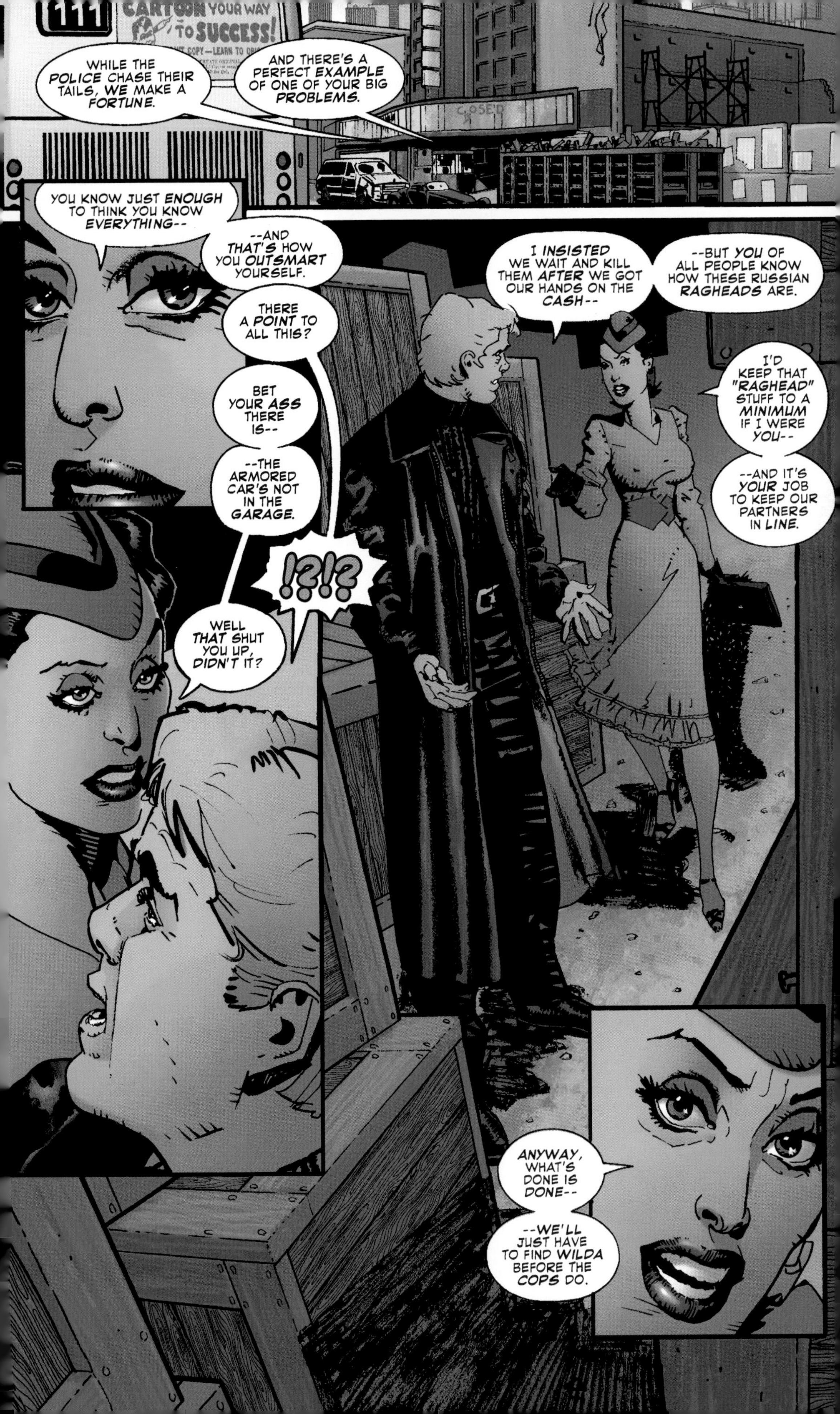
111
CARTOON YOUR WAY TO SUCCESS!
WHILE THE POLICE CHASE THEIR TAILS, WE MAKE A FORTUNE.
AND THERE'S A PERFECT EXAMPLE OF ONE OF YOUR BIG PROBLEMS.
CLOSED
YOU KNOW JUST ENOUGH TO THINK YOU KNOW EVERYTHING--
--AND THAT'S HOW YOU OUTSMART YOURSELF.
THERE A POINT TO ALL THIS?
BET YOUR ASS THERE IS--
--THE ARMORED CAR'S NOT IN THE GARAGE.
!?!?
WELL THAT SHUT YOU UP, DIDN'T IT?
I INSISTED WE WAIT AND KILL THEM AFTER WE GOT OUR HANDS ON THE CASH--
--BUT YOU OF ALL PEOPLE KNOW HOW THESE RUSSIAN RAGHEADS ARE.
I'D KEEP THAT "RAGHEAD" STUFF TO A MINIMUM IF I WERE YOU--
--AND IT'S YOUR JOB TO KEEP OUR PARTNERS IN LINE.
ANYWAY, WHAT'S DONE IS DONE--
--WE'LL JUST HAVE TO FIND WILDA BEFORE THE COPS DO.

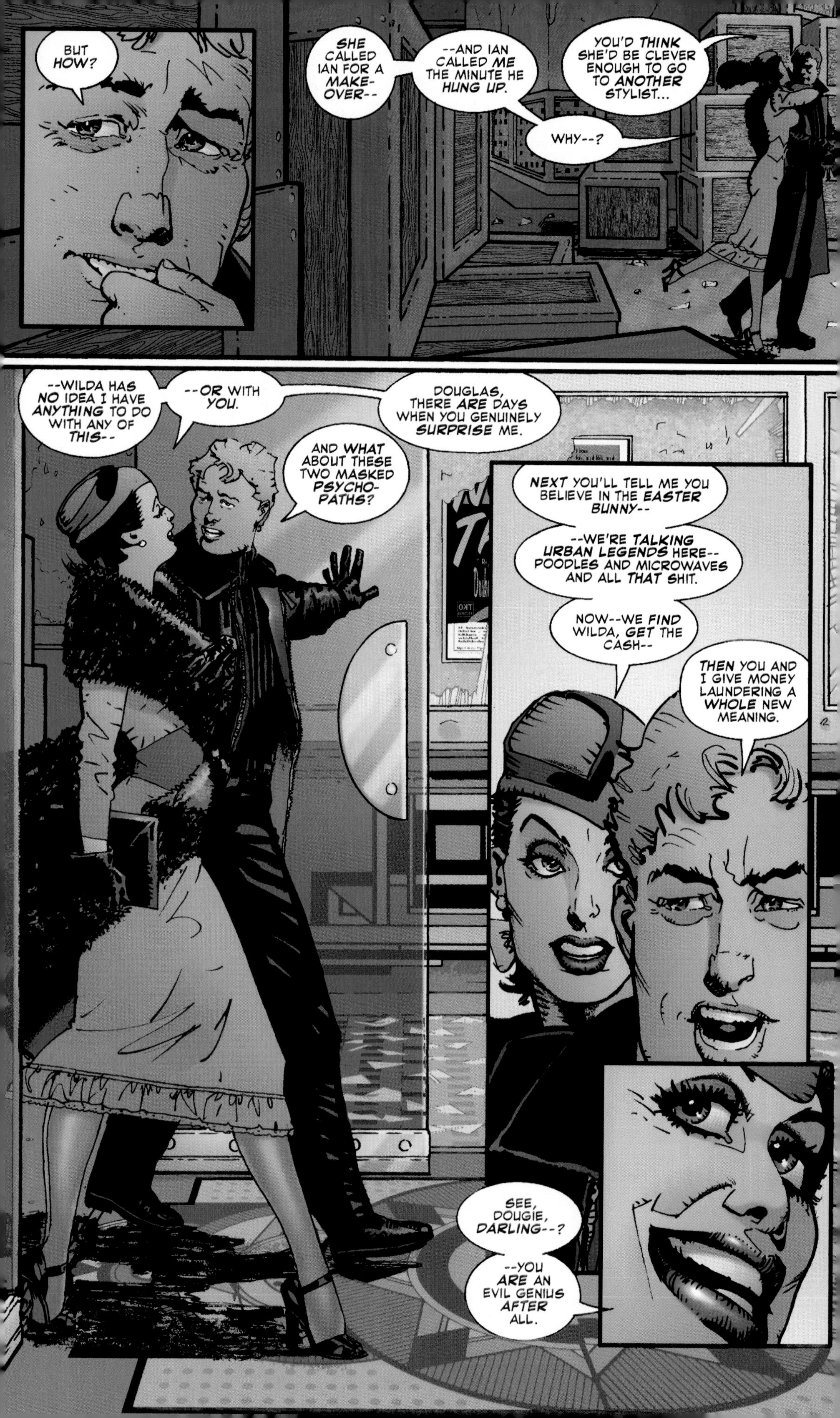
BUT HOW?
SHE CALLED IAN FOR A MAKE-OVER--
--AND IAN CALLED ME THE MINUTE HE HUNG UP.
WHY--?
YOU'D THINK SHE'D BE CLEVER ENOUGH TO GO TO ANOTHER STYLIST...
--WILDA HAS NO IDEA I HAVE ANYTHING TO DO WITH ANY OF THIS--
--OR WITH YOU.
DOUGLAS, THERE ARE DAYS WHEN YOU GENUINELY SURPRISE ME.
AND WHAT ABOUT THESE TWO MASKED PSYCHO-PATHS?
NEXT YOU'LL TELL ME YOU BELIEVE IN THE EASTER BUNNY--
--WE'RE TALKING URBAN LEGENDS HERE--POODLES AND MICROWAVES AND ALL THAT SHIT.
NOW--WE FIND WILDA, GET THE CASH--
THEN YOU AND I GIVE MONEY LAUNDERING A WHOLE NEW MEANING.
SEE, DOUGIE, DARLING--?
--YOU ARE AN EVIL GENIUS AFTER ALL.

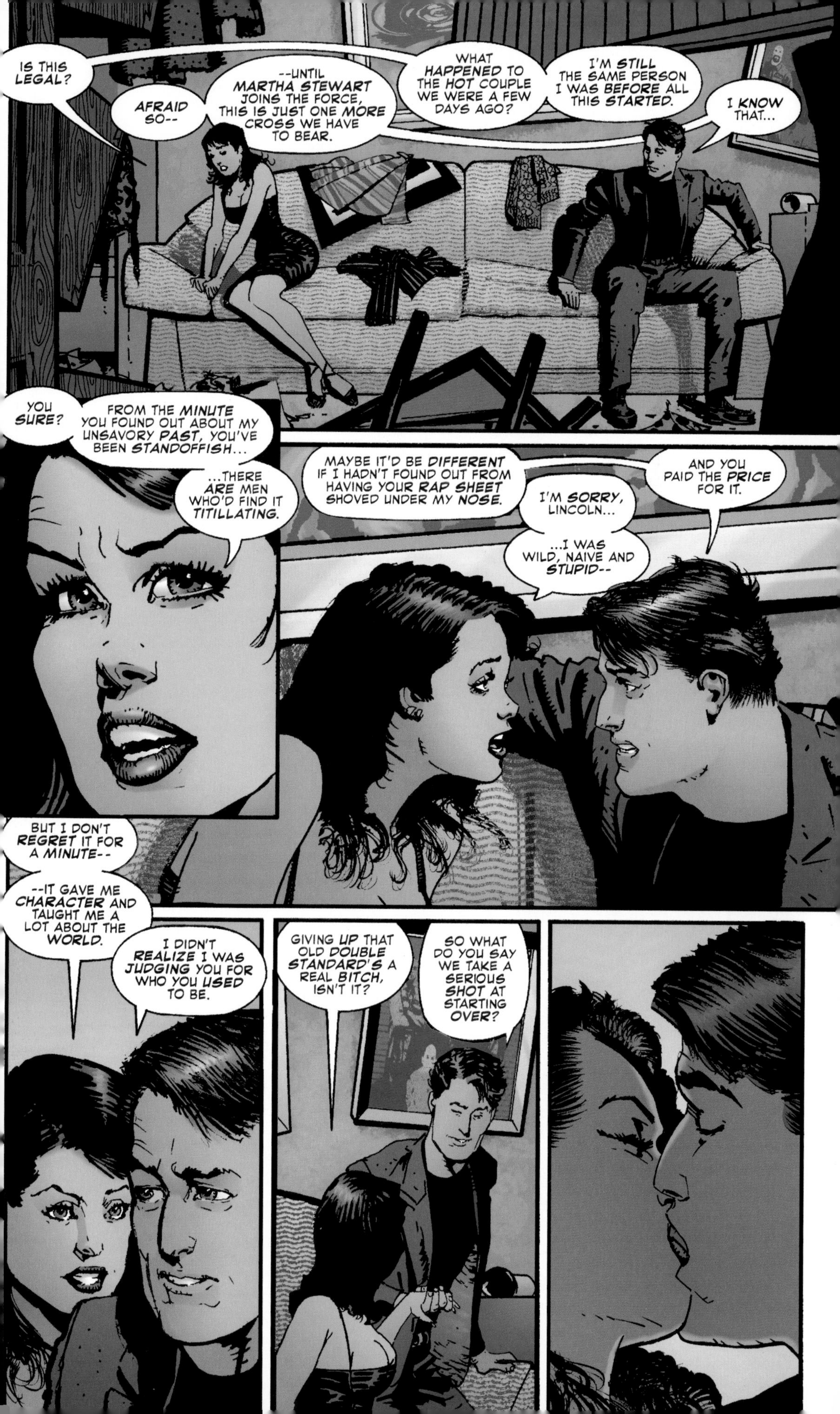
IS THIS LEGAL?
AFRAID SO--
--UNTIL MARTHA STEWART JOINS THE FORCE, THIS IS JUST ONE MORE CROSS WE HAVE TO BEAR.
WHAT HAPPENED TO THE HOT COUPLE WE WERE A FEW DAYS AGO?
I'M STILL THE SAME PERSON I WAS BEFORE ALL THIS STARTED.
I KNOW THAT...
YOU SURE?
FROM THE MINUTE YOU FOUND OUT ABOUT MY UNSAVORY PAST, YOU'VE BEEN STANDOFFISH...
...THERE ARE MEN WHO'D FIND IT TITILLATING.
MAYBE IT'D BE DIFFERENT IF I HADN'T FOUND OUT FROM HAVING YOUR RAP SHEET SHOVED UNDER MY NOSE.
I'M SORRY, LINCOLN...
...I WAS WILD, NAIVE AND STUPID--
AND YOU PAID THE PRICE FOR IT.
BUT I DON'T REGRET IT FOR A MINUTE--
--IT GAVE ME CHARACTER AND TAUGHT ME A LOT ABOUT THE WORLD.
I DIDN'T REALIZE I WAS JUDGING YOU FOR WHO YOU USED TO BE.
GIVING UP THAT OLD DOUBLE STANDARD'S A REAL BITCH, ISN'T IT?
SO WHAT DO YOU SAY WE TAKE A SERIOUS SHOT AT STARTING OVER?

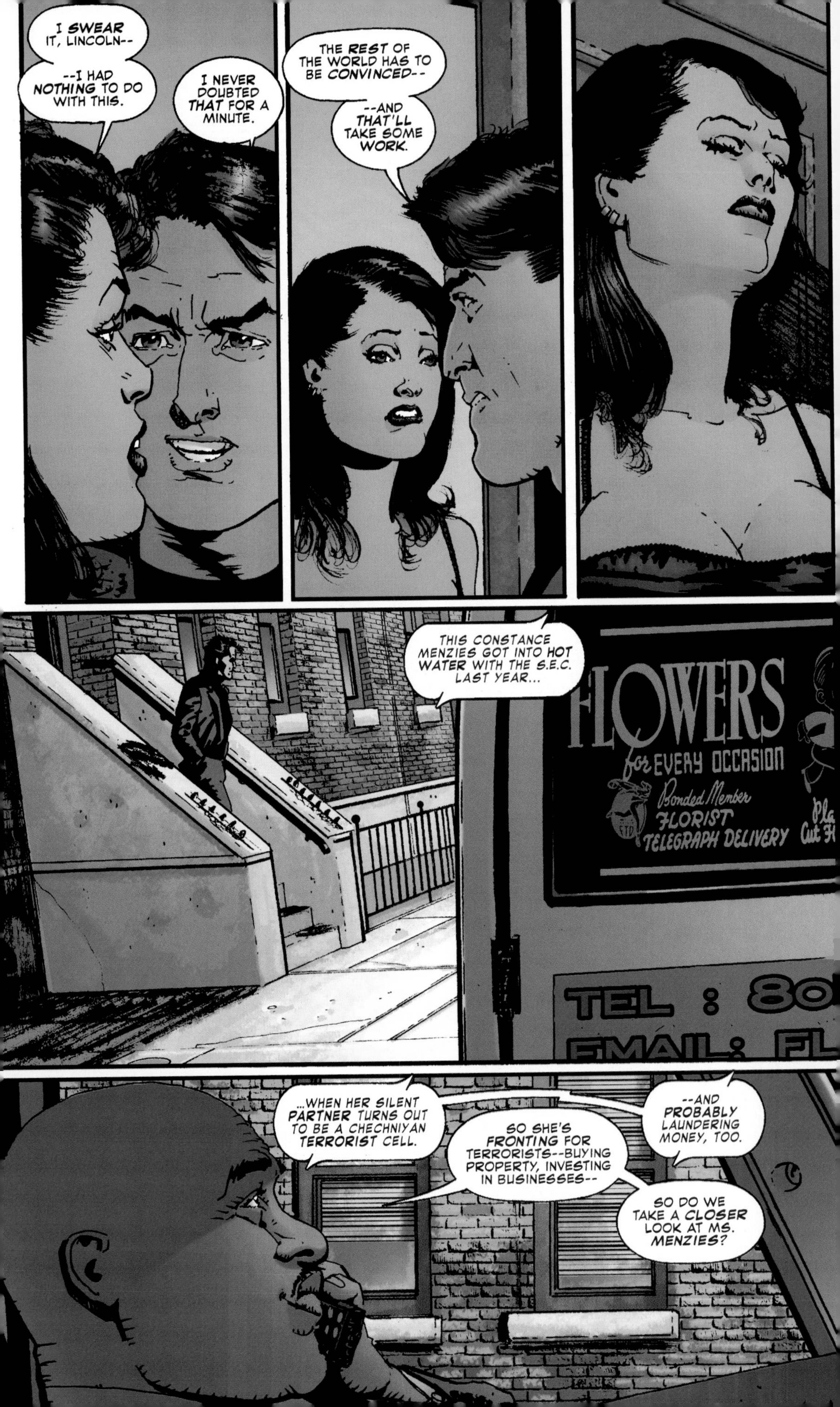
I SWEAR IT, LINCOLN--
--I HAD NOTHING TO DO WITH THIS.
I NEVER DOUBTED THAT FOR A MINUTE.
THE REST OF THE WORLD HAS TO BE CONVINCED--
--AND THAT'LL TAKE SOME WORK.
THIS CONSTANCE MENZIES GOT INTO HOT WATER WITH THE S.E.C. LAST YEAR...
FLOWERS
for EVERY OCCASION
Bonded Member
FLORIST
TELEGRAPH DELIVERY
...WHEN HER SILENT PARTNER TURNS OUT TO BE A CHECHNIYAN TERRORIST CELL.
SO SHE'S FRONTING FOR TERRORISTS--BUYING PROPERTY, INVESTING IN BUSINESSES--
--AND PROBABLY LAUNDERING MONEY, TOO.
SO DO WE TAKE A CLOSER LOOK AT MS. MENZIES?

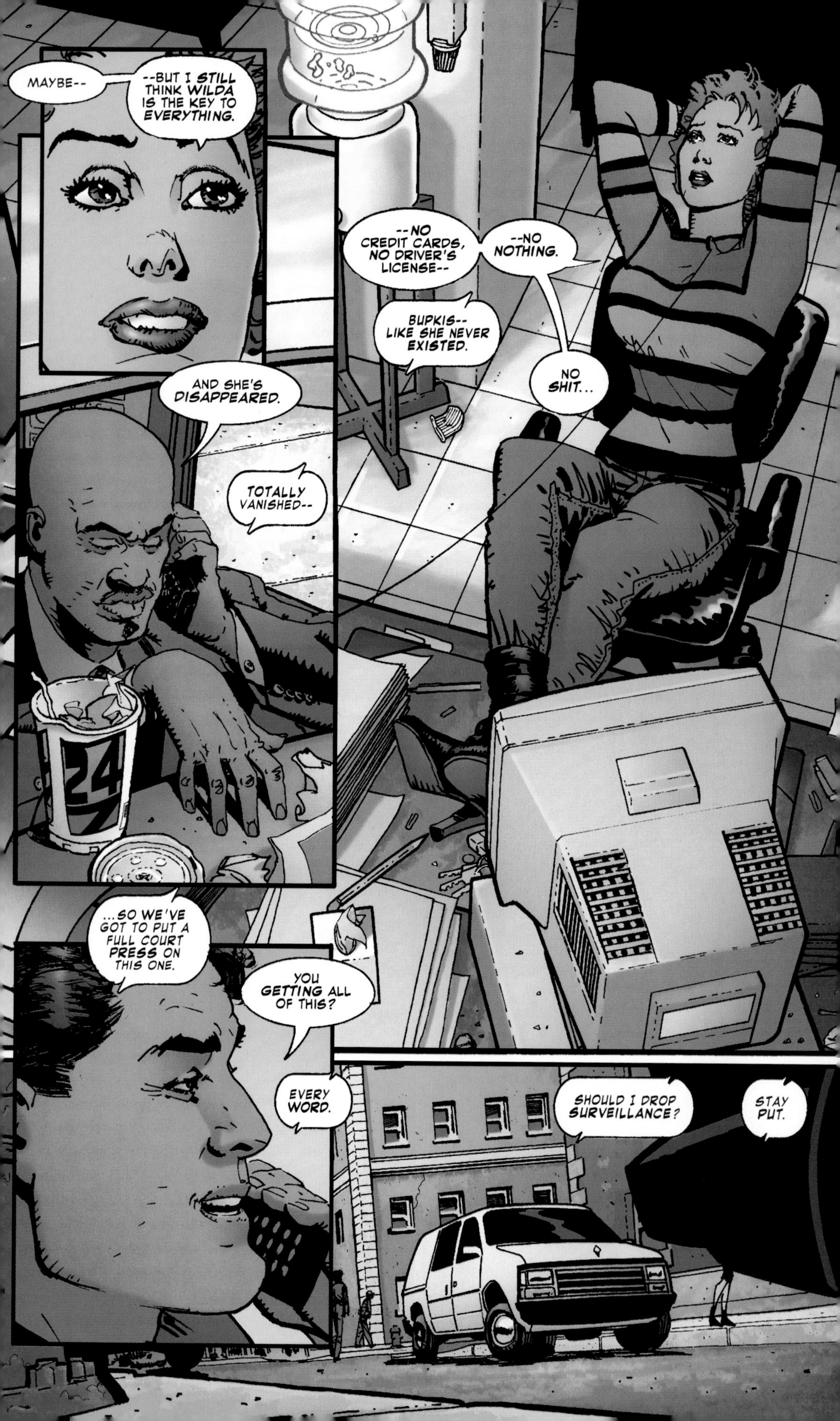
MAYBE--
--BUT I STILL THINK WILDA IS THE KEY TO EVERYTHING.
AND SHE'S DISAPPEARED.
TOTALLY VANISHED--
--NO CREDIT CARDS, NO DRIVER'S LICENSE--
--NO NOTHING.
BUPKIS-- LIKE SHE NEVER EXISTED.
NO SHIT...
...SO WE'VE GOT TO PUT A FULL COURT PRESS ON THIS ONE.
YOU GETTING ALL OF THIS?
EVERY WORD.
SHOULD I DROP SURVEILLANCE?
STAY PUT.

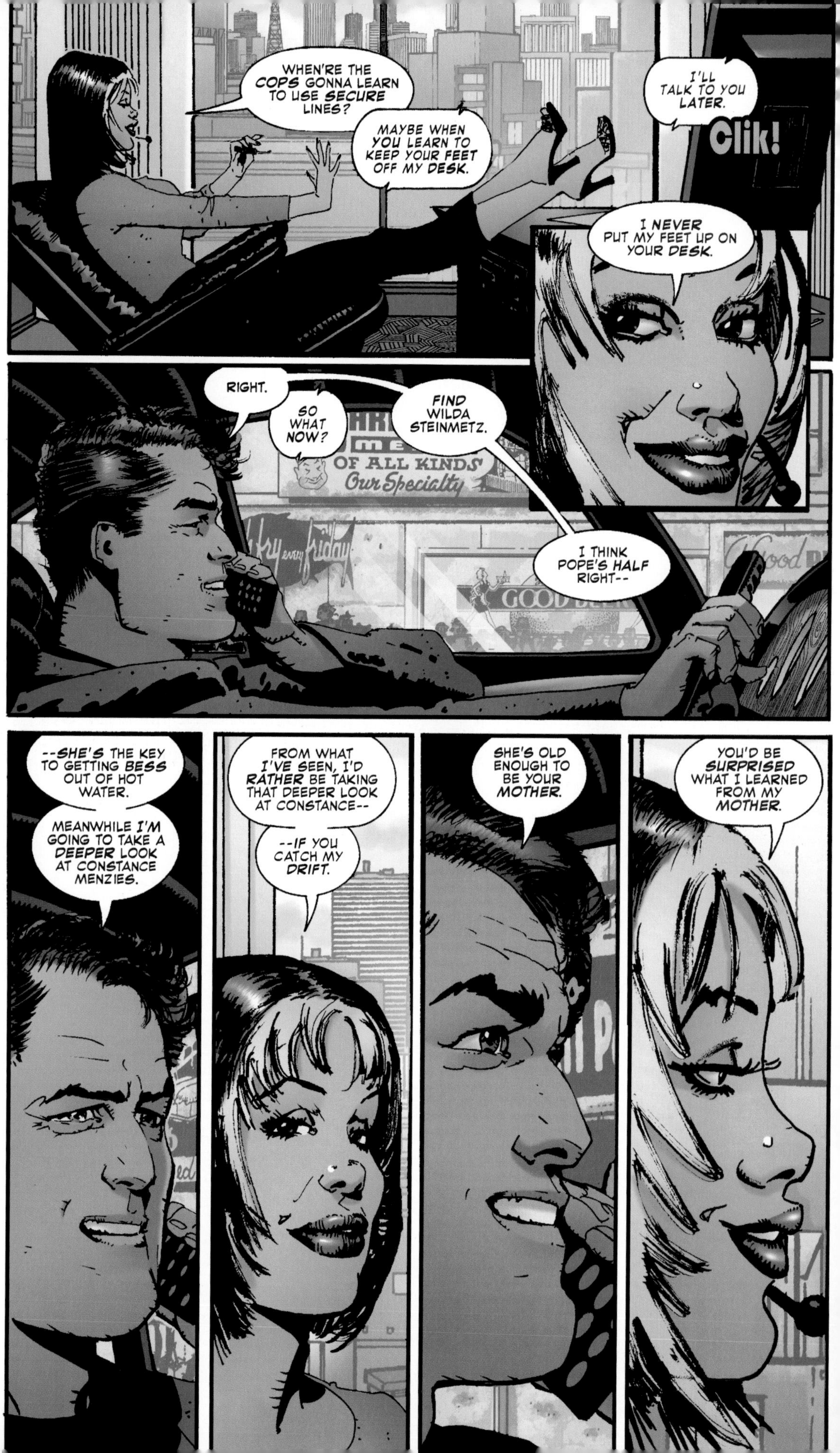
WHEN'RE THE COPS GONNA LEARN TO USE SECURE LINES?
MAYBE WHEN YOU LEARN TO KEEP YOUR FEET OFF MY DESK.
I'LL TALK TO YOU LATER.
Clik!
I NEVER PUT MY FEET UP ON YOUR DESK.
RIGHT.
SO WHAT NOW?
FIND WILDA STEINMETZ.
OF ALL KINDS
Our Specialty
GOOD
I THINK POPE'S HALF RIGHT--
--SHE'S THE KEY TO GETTING BESS OUT OF HOT WATER.
MEANWHILE I'M GOING TO TAKE A DEEPER LOOK AT CONSTANCE MENZIES.
FROM WHAT I'VE SEEN, I'D RATHER BE TAKING THAT DEEPER LOOK AT CONSTANCE--
--IF YOU CATCH MY DRIFT.
SHE'S OLD ENOUGH TO BE YOUR MOTHER.
YOU'D BE SURPRISED WHAT I LEARNED FROM MY MOTHER.

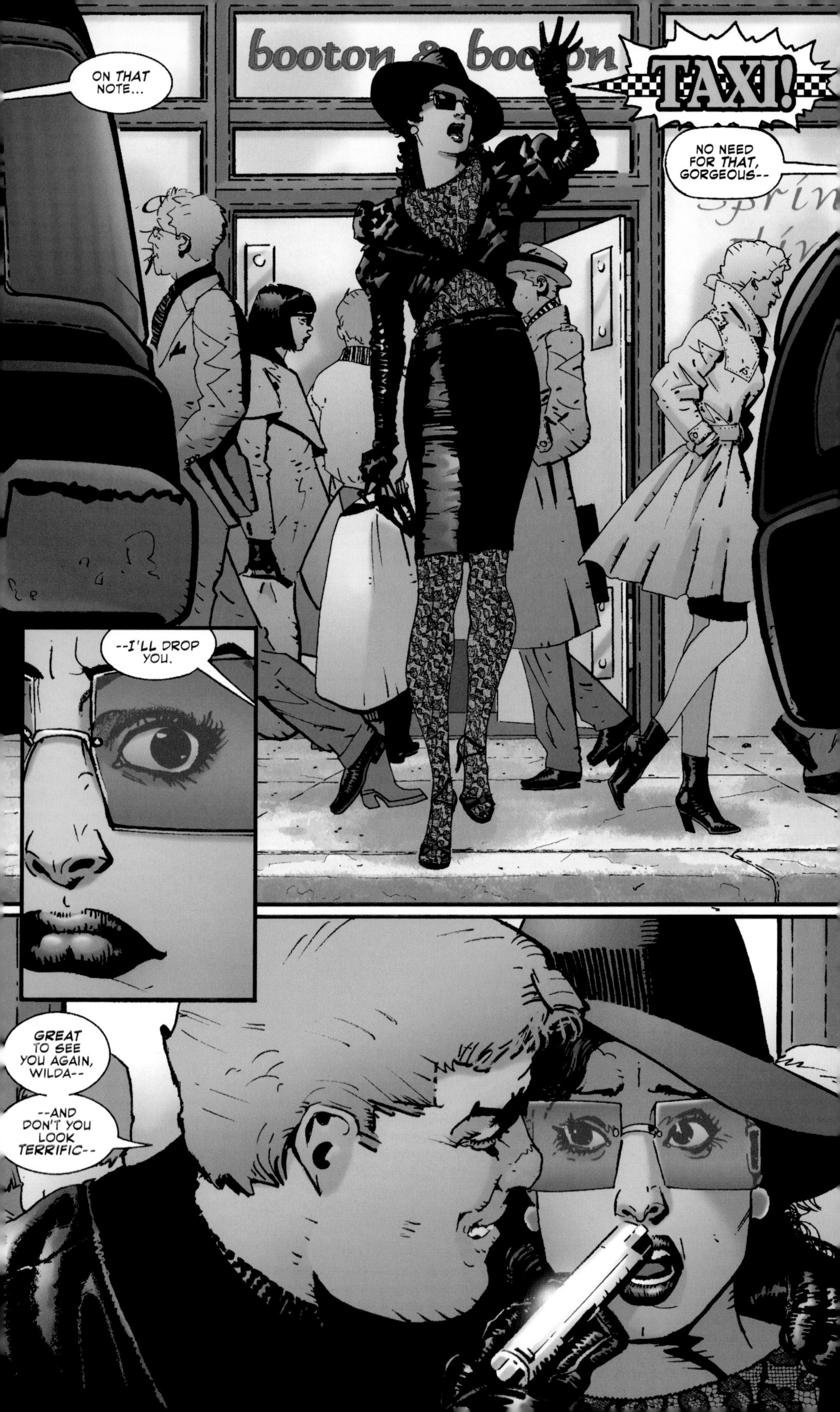
booton & booton
ON THAT NOTE...
TAXI!
NO NEED FOR THAT, GORGEOUS--
--I'LL DROP YOU.
GREAT TO SEE YOU AGAIN, WILDA--
--AND DON'T YOU LOOK TERRIFIC--

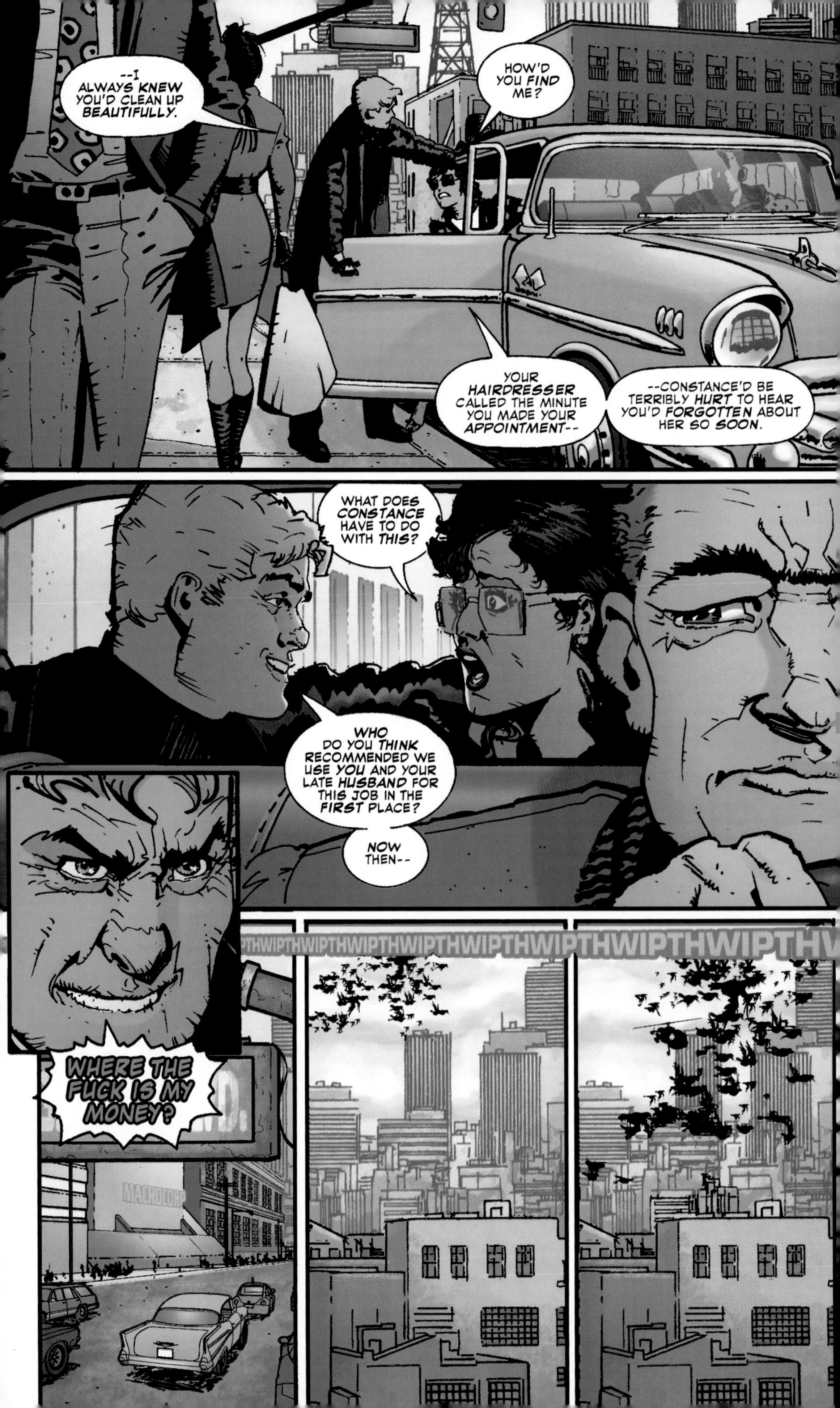
--I ALWAYS KNEW YOU'D CLEAN UP BEAUTIFULLY.
HOW'D YOU FIND ME?
YOUR HAIRDRESSER CALLED THE MINUTE YOU MADE YOUR APPOINTMENT--
--CONSTANCE'D BE TERRIBLY HURT TO HEAR YOU'D FORGOTTEN ABOUT HER SO SOON.
WHAT DOES CONSTANCE HAVE TO DO WITH THIS?
WHO DO YOU THINK RECOMMENDED WE USE YOU AND YOUR LATE HUSBAND FOR THIS JOB IN THE FIRST PLACE?
NOW THEN--
WHERE THE FUCK IS MY MONEY?
PTHWIPTHWIPTHWIPTHWIPTHWIPTHWIPTHWIPTHV
MACROCORP

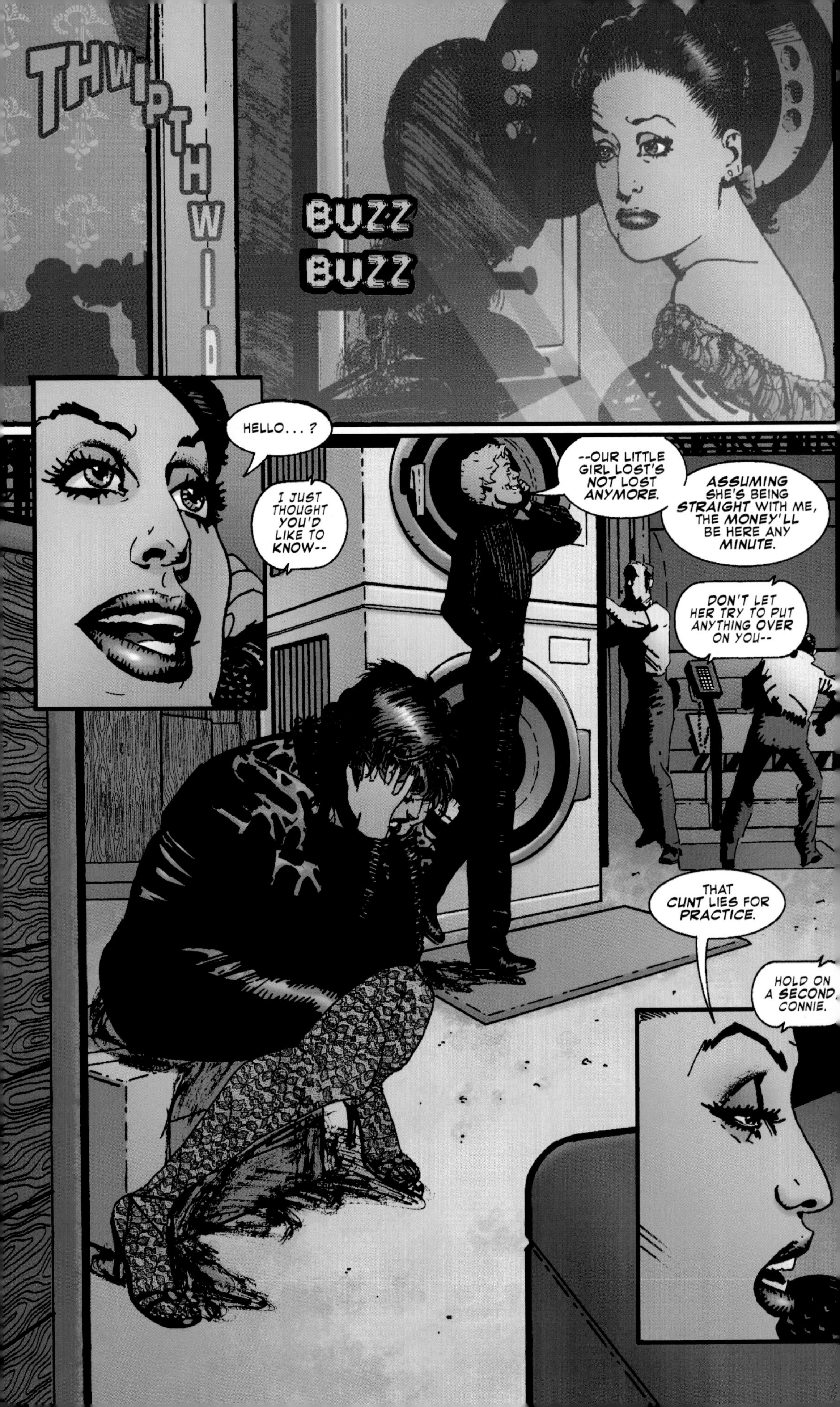
THWIPTHWIP
BUZZ BUZZ
HELLO. . . ?
I JUST THOUGHT YOU'D LIKE TO KNOW--
--OUR LITTLE GIRL LOST'S NOT LOST ANYMORE.
ASSUMING SHE'S BEING STRAIGHT WITH ME, THE MONEY'LL BE HERE ANY MINUTE.
DON'T LET HER TRY TO PUT ANYTHING OVER ON YOU--
THAT CUNT LIES FOR PRACTICE.
HOLD ON A SECOND, CONNIE.

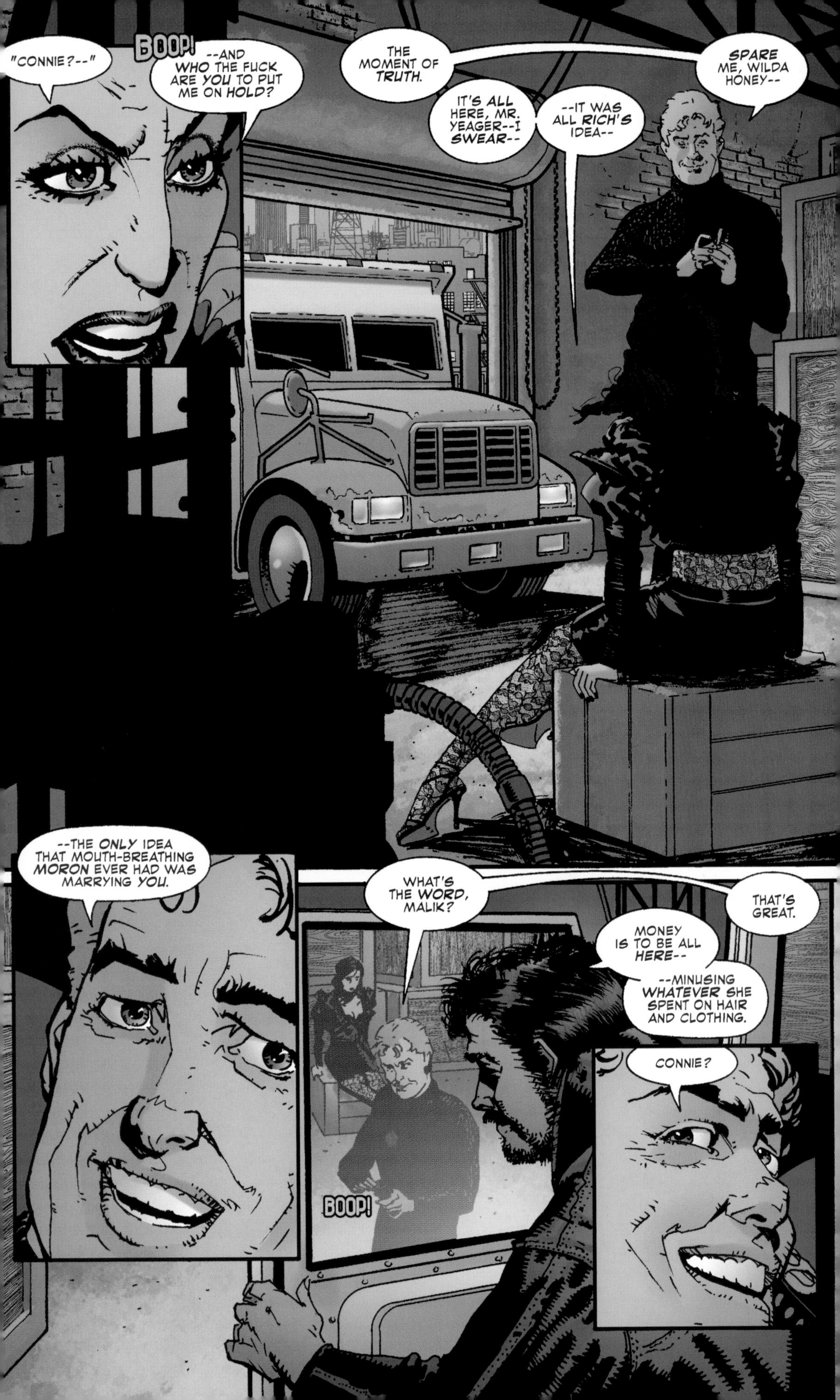
"CONNIE?--"
BOOP!
--AND WHO THE FUCK ARE YOU TO PUT ME ON HOLD?
THE MOMENT OF TRUTH.
SPARE ME, WILDA HONEY--
IT'S ALL HERE, MR. YEAGER--I SWEAR--
--IT WAS ALL RICH'S IDEA--
--THE ONLY IDEA THAT MOUTH-BREATHING MORON EVER HAD WAS MARRYING YOU.
WHAT'S THE WORD, MALIK?
THAT'S GREAT.
MONEY IS TO BE ALL HERE--
--MINUSING WHATEVER SHE SPENT ON HAIR AND CLOTHING.
CONNIE?
BOOP!

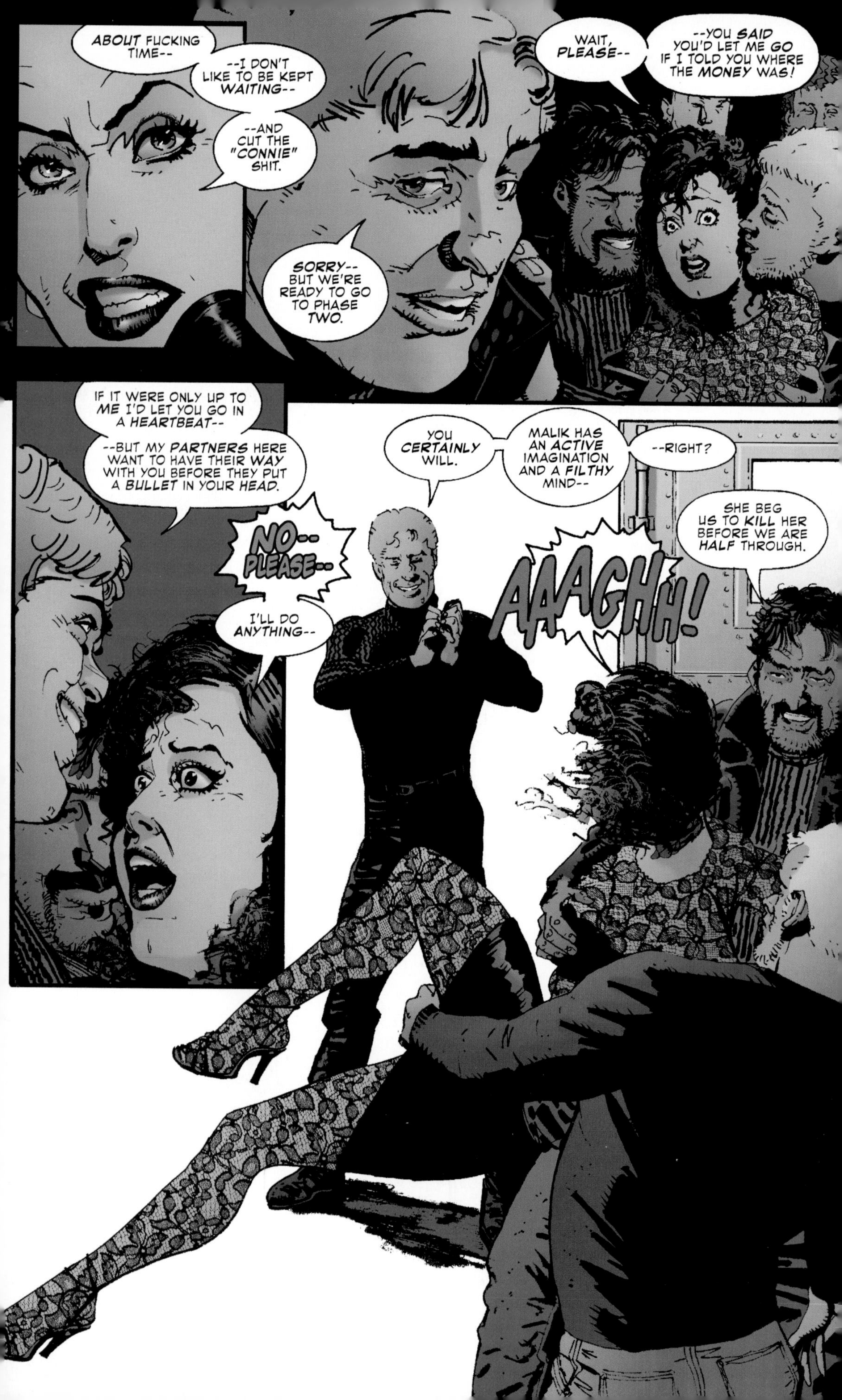
ABOUT FUCKING TIME--
--I DON'T LIKE TO BE KEPT WAITING--
--AND CUT THE "CONNIE" SHIT.
SORRY-- BUT WE'RE READY TO GO TO PHASE TWO.
WAIT, PLEASE--
--YOU SAID YOU'D LET ME GO IF I TOLD YOU WHERE THE MONEY WAS!
IF IT WERE ONLY UP TO ME I'D LET YOU GO IN A HEARTBEAT--
--BUT MY PARTNERS HERE WANT TO HAVE THEIR WAY WITH YOU BEFORE THEY PUT A BULLET IN YOUR HEAD.
NO-- PLEASE--
I'LL DO ANYTHING--
YOU CERTAINLY WILL.
MALIK HAS AN ACTIVE IMAGINATION AND A FILTHY MIND--
--RIGHT?
SHE BEG US TO KILL HER BEFORE WE ARE HALF THROUGH.
AAAGHH!

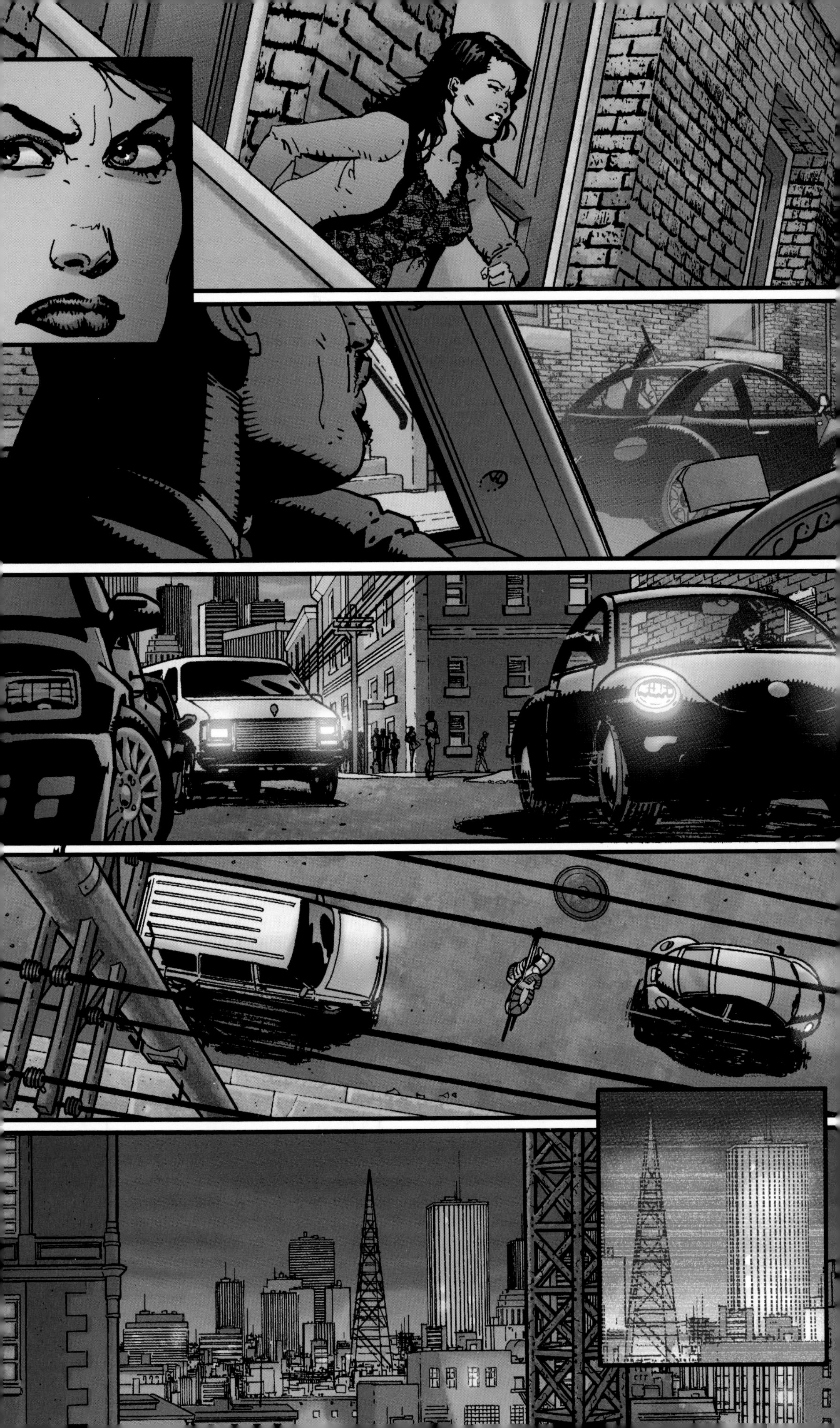

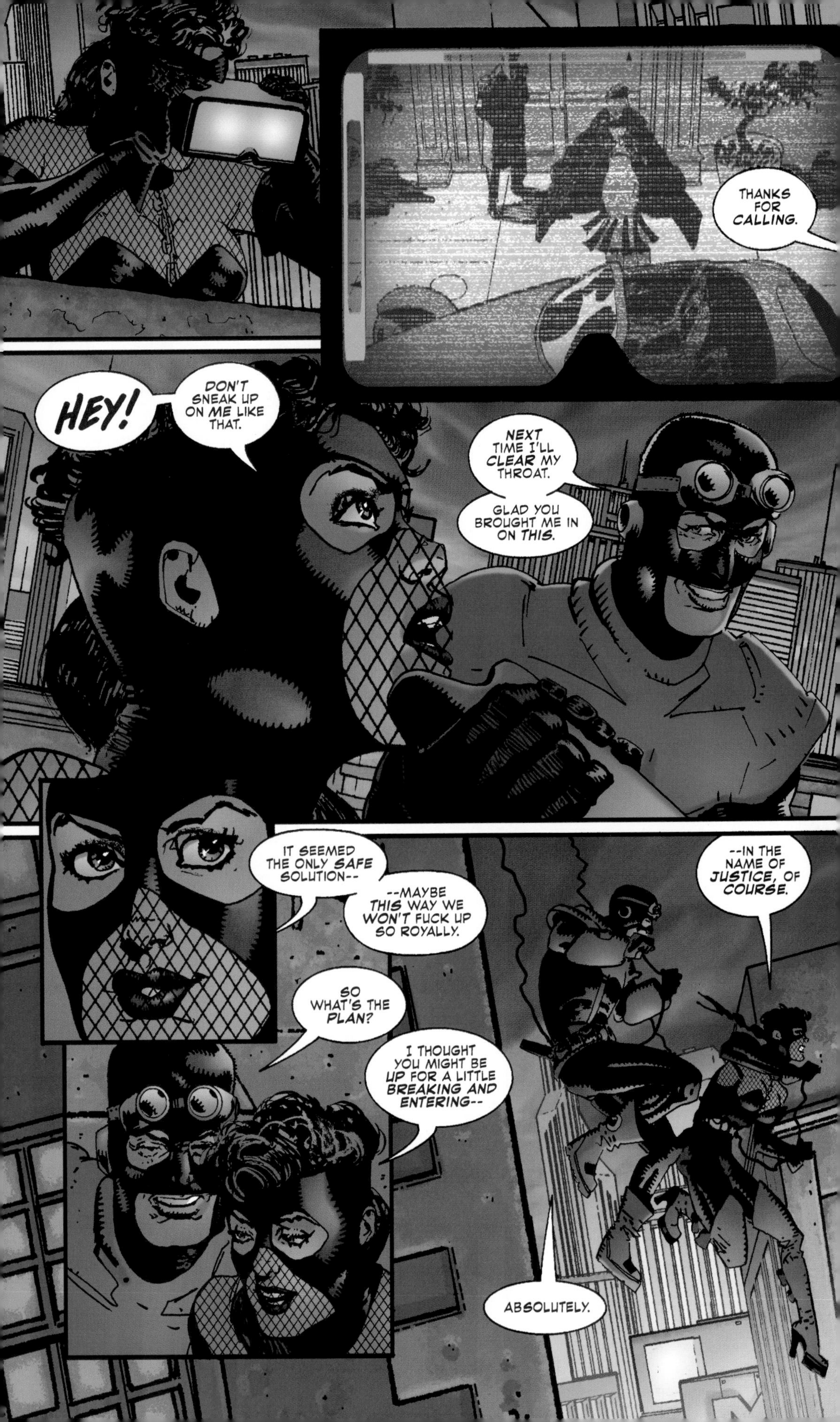
THANKS FOR CALLING.
HEY!
DON'T SNEAK UP ON ME LIKE THAT.
NEXT TIME I'LL CLEAR MY THROAT.
GLAD YOU BROUGHT ME IN ON THIS.
IT SEEMED THE ONLY SAFE SOLUTION--
--MAYBE THIS WAY WE WON'T FUCK UP SO ROYALLY.
SO WHAT'S THE PLAN?
I THOUGHT YOU MIGHT BE UP FOR A LITTLE BREAKING AND ENTERING--
--IN THE NAME OF JUSTICE, OF COURSE.
ABSOLUTELY.

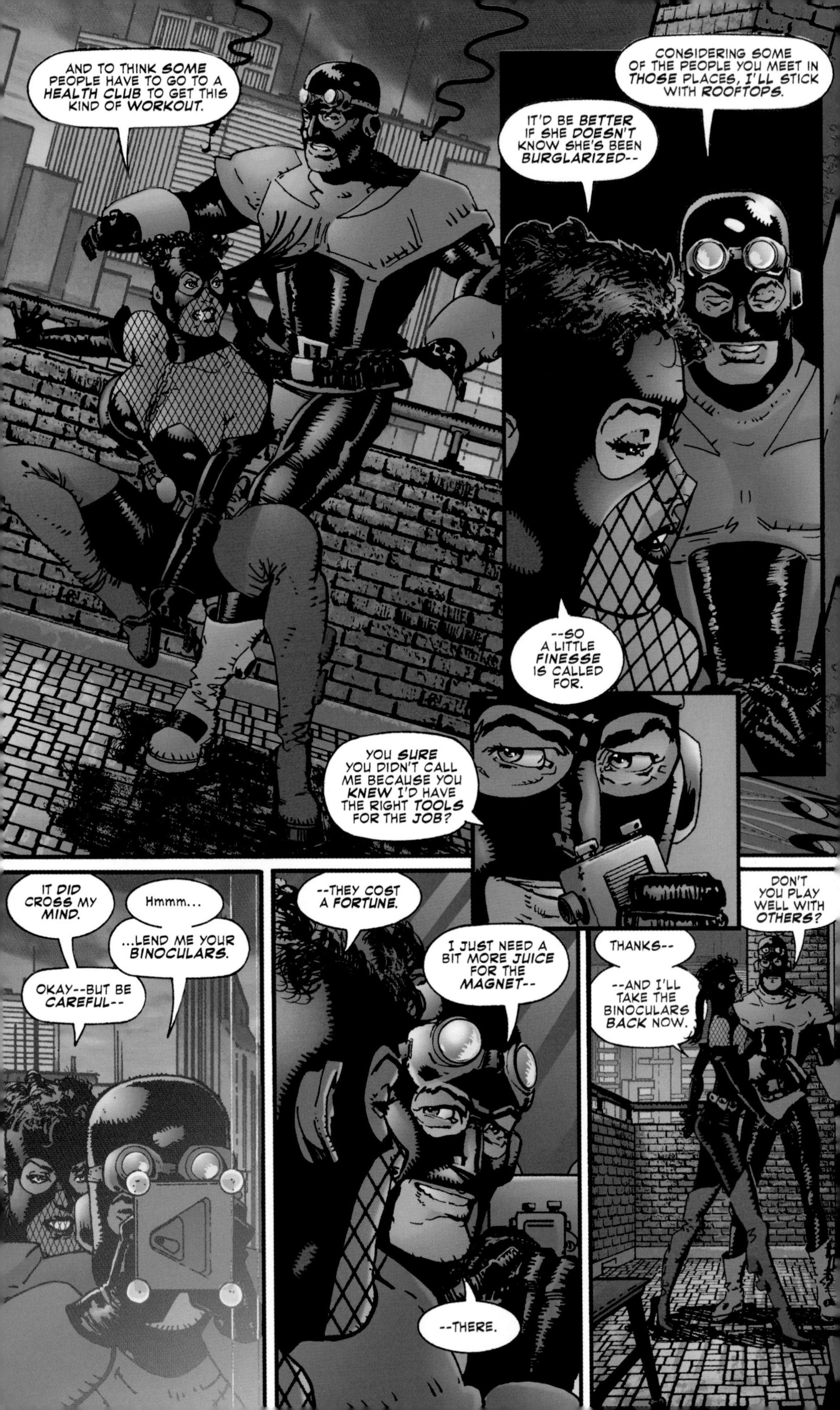

AND TO THINK SOME PEOPLE HAVE TO GO TO A HEALTH CLUB TO GET THIS KIND OF WORKOUT.
CONSIDERING SOME OF THE PEOPLE YOU MEET IN THOSE PLACES, I'LL STICK WITH ROOFTOPS.
IT'D BE BETTER IF SHE DOESN'T KNOW SHE'S BEEN BURGLARIZED--
--SO A LITTLE FINESSE IS CALLED FOR.
YOU SURE YOU DIDN'T CALL ME BECAUSE YOU KNEW I'D HAVE THE RIGHT TOOLS FOR THE JOB?
IT DID CROSS MY MIND.
Hmmm...
...LEND ME YOUR BINOCULARS.
OKAY--BUT BE CAREFUL--
--THEY COST A FORTUNE.
I JUST NEED A BIT MORE JUICE FOR THE MAGNET--
--THERE.
THANKS--
--AND I'LL TAKE THE BINOCULARS BACK NOW.
DON'T YOU PLAY WELL WITH OTHERS?

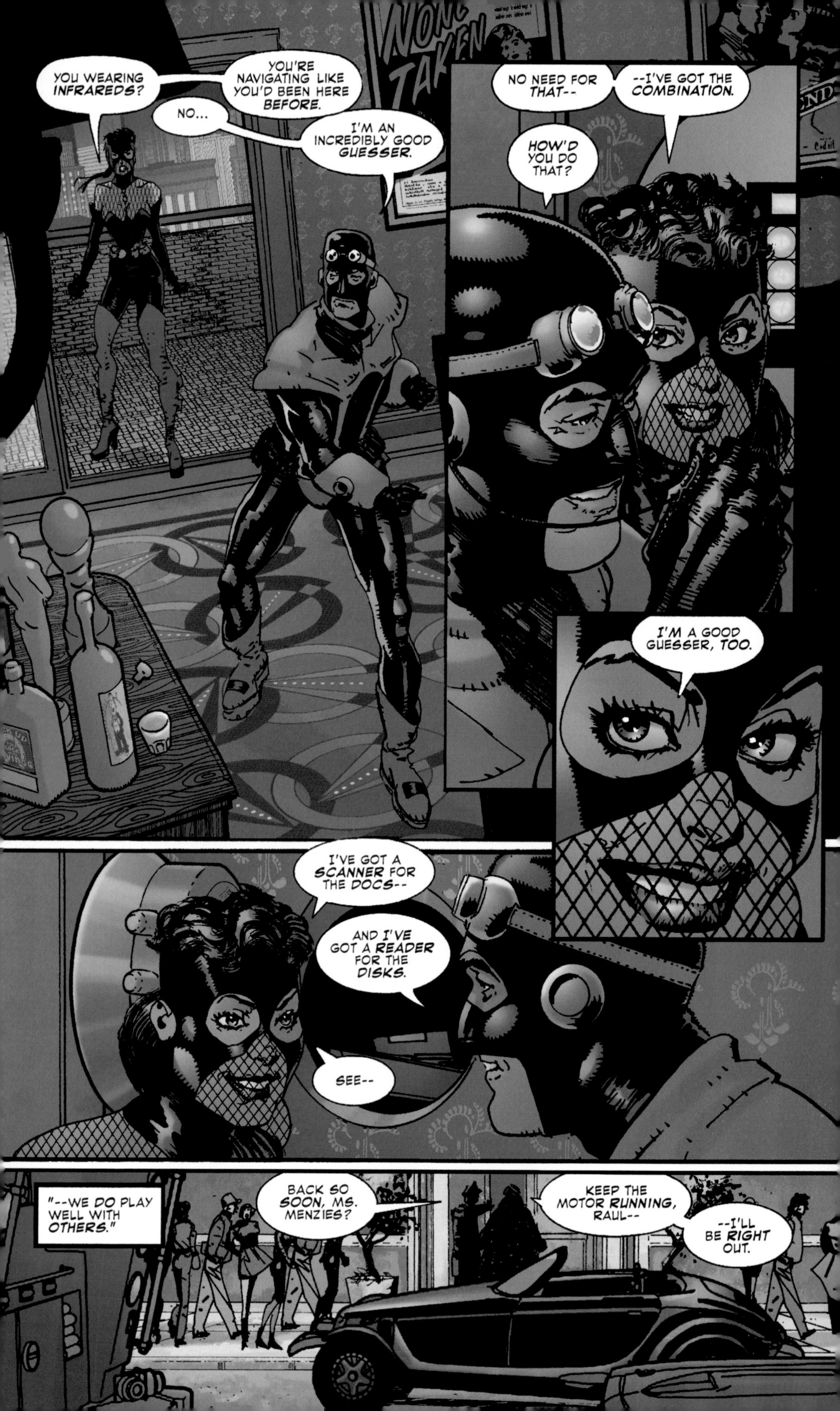
YOU WEARING INFRAREDS?
YOU'RE NAVIGATING LIKE YOU'D BEEN HERE BEFORE.
NO...
I'M AN INCREDIBLY GOOD GUESSER.
NO NEED FOR THAT--
--I'VE GOT THE COMBINATION.
HOW'D YOU DO THAT?
I'M A GOOD GUESSER, TOO.
I'VE GOT A SCANNER FOR THE DOCS--
AND I'VE GOT A READER FOR THE DISKS.
SEE--
"--WE DO PLAY WELL WITH OTHERS."
BACK SO SOON, MS. MENZIES?
KEEP THE MOTOR RUNNING, RAUL--
--I'LL BE RIGHT OUT.

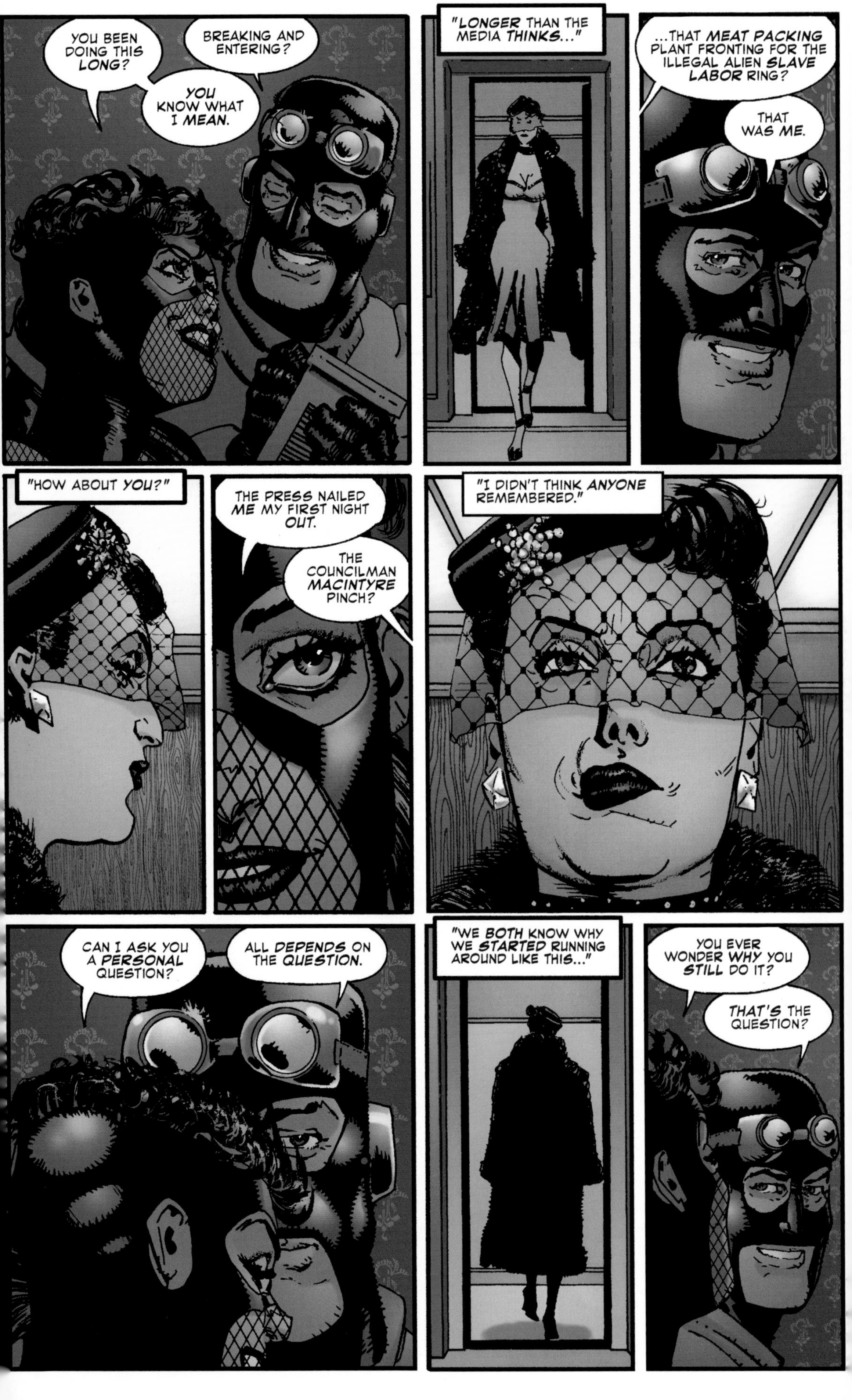
YOU BEEN DOING THIS LONG?
BREAKING AND ENTERING?
YOU KNOW WHAT I MEAN.
"LONGER THAN THE MEDIA THINKS..."
...THAT MEAT PACKING PLANT FRONTING FOR THE ILLEGAL ALIEN SLAVE LABOR RING?
THAT WAS ME.
"HOW ABOUT YOU?"
THE PRESS NAILED ME MY FIRST NIGHT OUT.
THE COUNCILMAN MACINTYRE PINCH?
"I DIDN'T THINK ANYONE REMEMBERED."
CAN I ASK YOU A PERSONAL QUESTION?
ALL DEPENDS ON THE QUESTION.
"WE BOTH KNOW WHY WE STARTED RUNNING AROUND LIKE THIS..."
YOU EVER WONDER WHY YOU STILL DO IT?
THAT'S THE QUESTION?

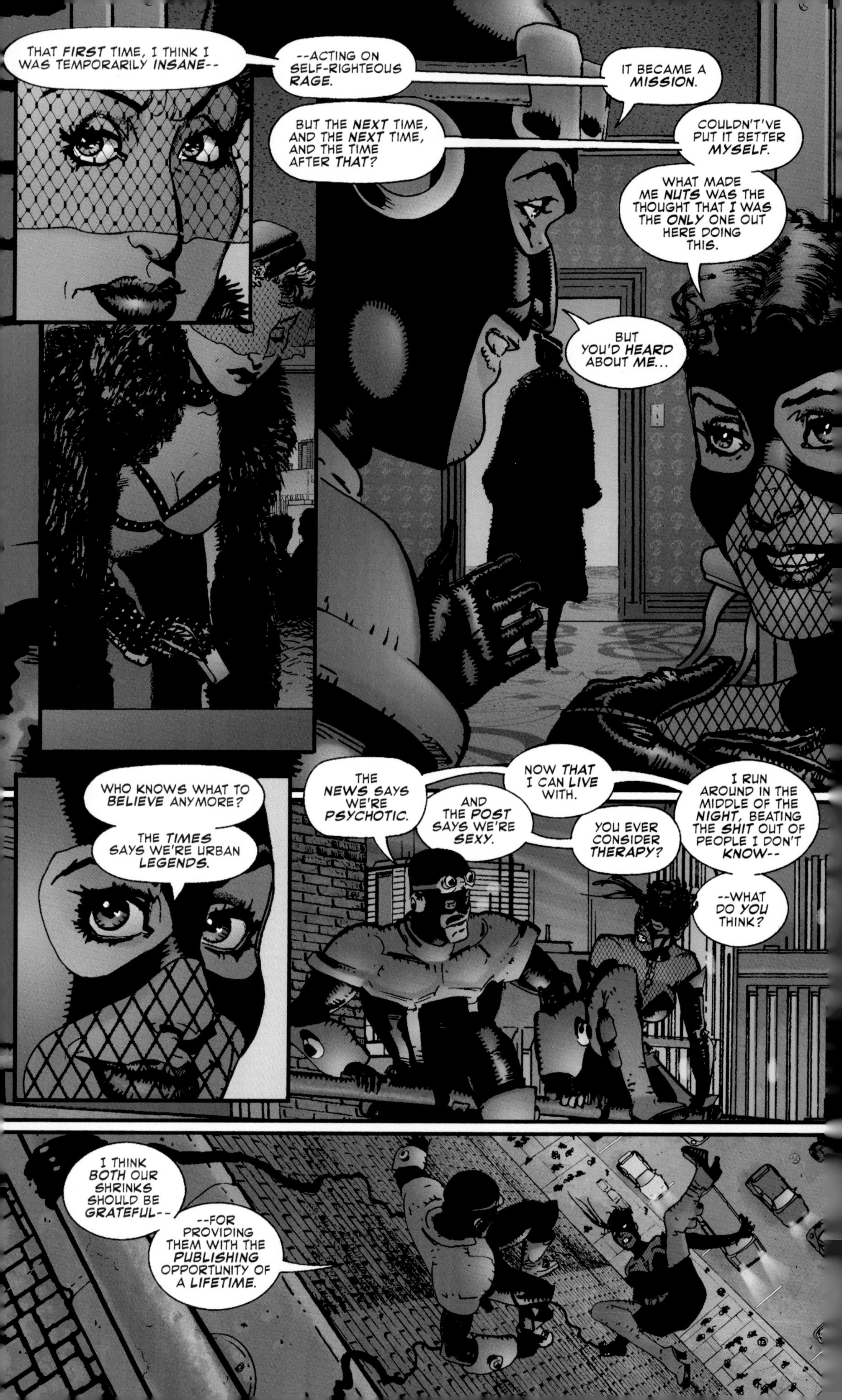
THAT FIRST TIME, I THINK I WAS TEMPORARILY INSANE--
--ACTING ON SELF-RIGHTEOUS RAGE.
IT BECAME A MISSION.
BUT THE NEXT TIME, AND THE NEXT TIME, AND THE TIME AFTER THAT?
COULDN'T'VE PUT IT BETTER MYSELF.
WHAT MADE ME NUTS WAS THE THOUGHT THAT I WAS THE ONLY ONE OUT HERE DOING THIS.
BUT YOU'D HEARD ABOUT ME...
WHO KNOWS WHAT TO BELIEVE ANYMORE?
THE TIMES SAYS WE'RE URBAN LEGENDS.
THE NEWS SAYS WE'RE PSYCHOTIC.
AND THE POST SAYS WE'RE SEXY.
NOW THAT I CAN LIVE WITH.
YOU EVER CONSIDER THERAPY?
I RUN AROUND IN THE MIDDLE OF THE NIGHT, BEATING THE SHIT OUT OF PEOPLE I DON'T KNOW--
--WHAT DO YOU THINK?
I THINK BOTH OUR SHRINKS SHOULD BE GRATEFUL--
--FOR PROVIDING THEM WITH THE PUBLISHING OPPORTUNITY OF A LIFETIME.

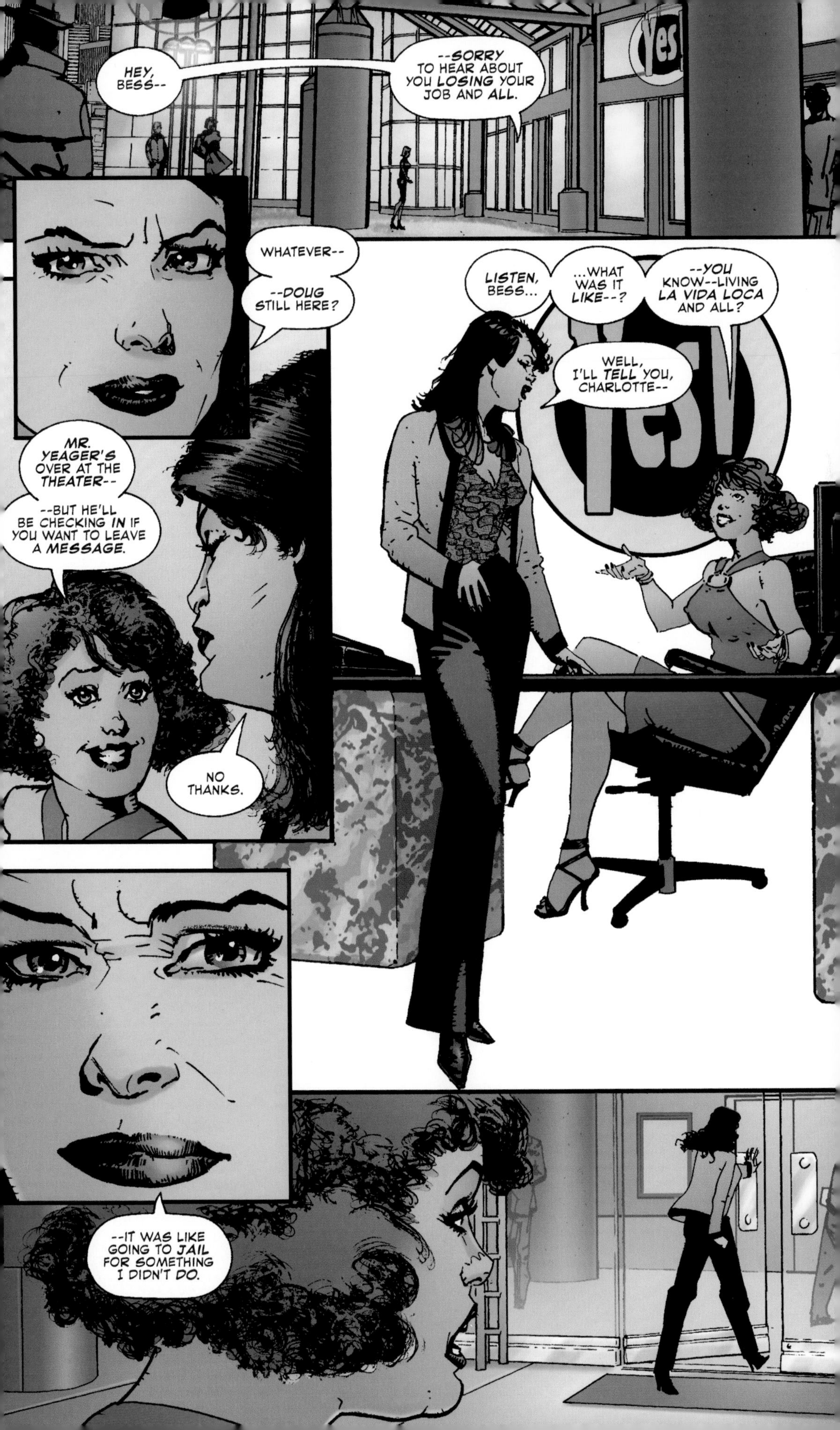
HEY, BESS--
--SORRY TO HEAR ABOUT YOU LOSING YOUR JOB AND ALL.
WHATEVER--
--DOUG STILL HERE?
MR. YEAGER'S OVER AT THE THEATER--
--BUT HE'LL BE CHECKING IN IF YOU WANT TO LEAVE A MESSAGE.
NO THANKS.
LISTEN, BESS...
...WHAT WAS IT LIKE--?
--YOU KNOW--LIVING LA VIDA LOCA AND ALL?
WELL, I'LL TELL YOU, CHARLOTTE--
--IT WAS LIKE GOING TO JAIL FOR SOMETHING I DIDN'T DO.

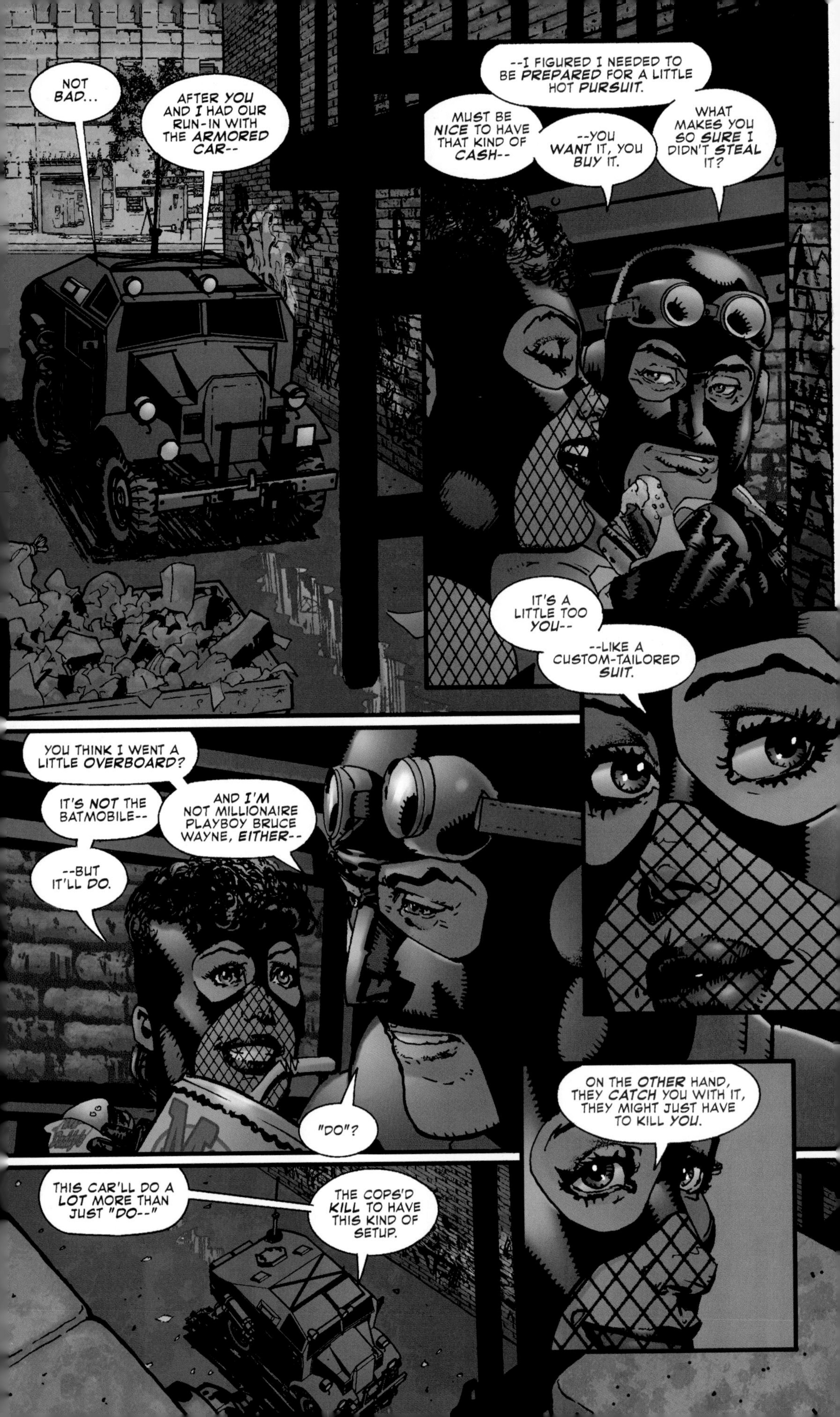
NOT BAD...
AFTER YOU AND I HAD OUR RUN-IN WITH THE ARMORED CAR--
--I FIGURED I NEEDED TO BE PREPARED FOR A LITTLE HOT PURSUIT.
MUST BE NICE TO HAVE THAT KIND OF CASH--
--YOU WANT IT, YOU BUY IT.
WHAT MAKES YOU SO SURE I DIDN'T STEAL IT?
IT'S A LITTLE TOO YOU--
--LIKE A CUSTOM-TAILORED SUIT.
YOU THINK I WENT A LITTLE OVERBOARD?
IT'S NOT THE BATMOBILE--
--BUT IT'LL DO.
AND I'M NOT MILLIONAIRE PLAYBOY BRUCE WAYNE, EITHER--
"DO"?
ON THE OTHER HAND, THEY CATCH YOU WITH IT, THEY MIGHT JUST HAVE TO KILL YOU.
THIS CAR'LL DO A LOT MORE THAN JUST "DO--"
THE COPS'D KILL TO HAVE THIS KIND OF SETUP.

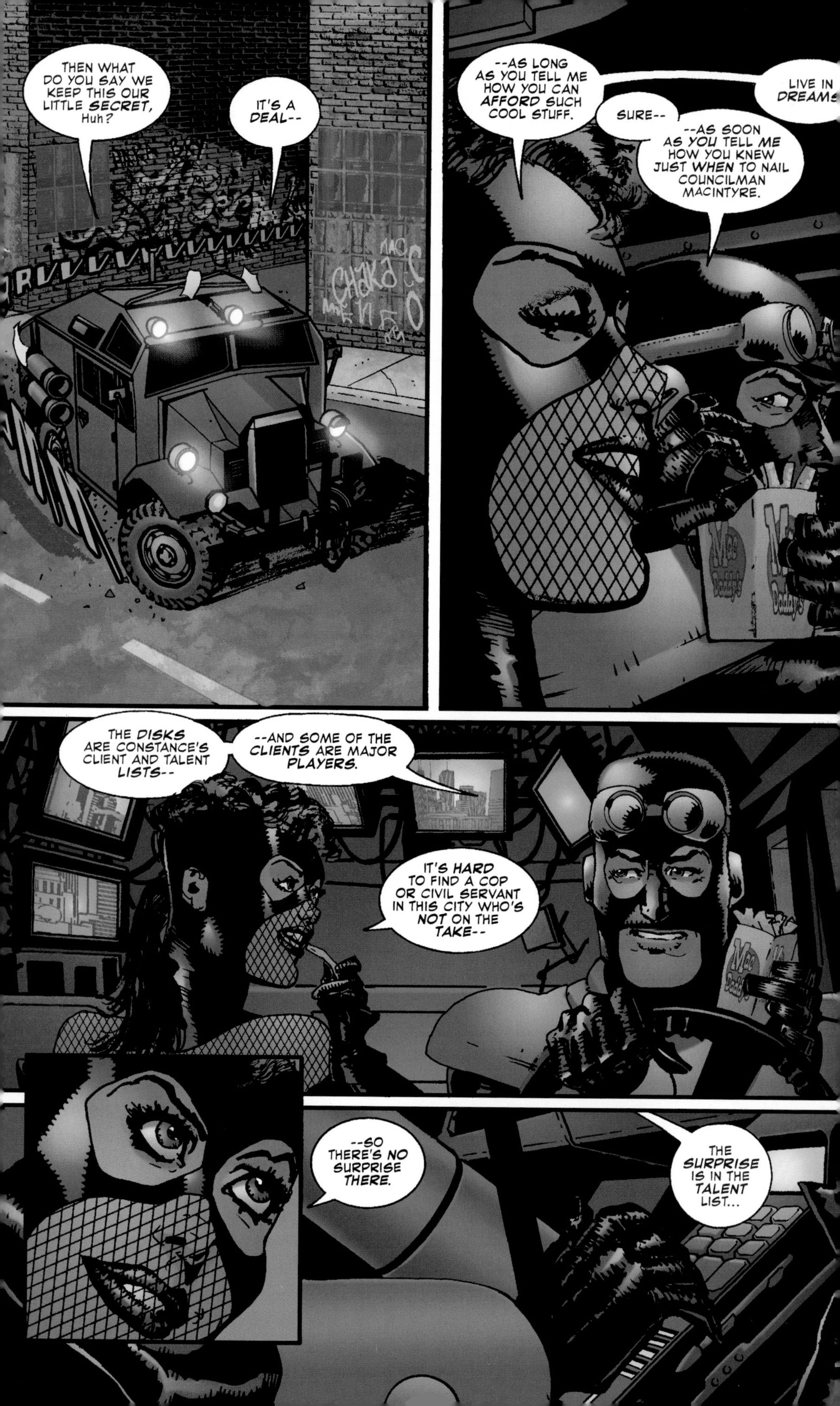

THEN WHAT DO YOU SAY WE KEEP THIS OUR LITTLE SECRET, Huh?
IT'S A DEAL--
--AS LONG AS YOU TELL ME HOW YOU CAN AFFORD SUCH COOL STUFF.
LIVE IN DREAMS
SURE--
--AS SOON AS YOU TELL ME HOW YOU KNEW JUST WHEN TO NAIL COUNCILMAN MACINTYRE.
THE DISKS ARE CONSTANCE'S CLIENT AND TALENT LISTS--
--AND SOME OF THE CLIENTS ARE MAJOR PLAYERS.
IT'S HARD TO FIND A COP OR CIVIL SERVANT IN THIS CITY WHO'S NOT ON THE TAKE--
--SO THERE'S NO SURPRISE THERE.
THE SURPRISE IS IN THE TALENT LIST...

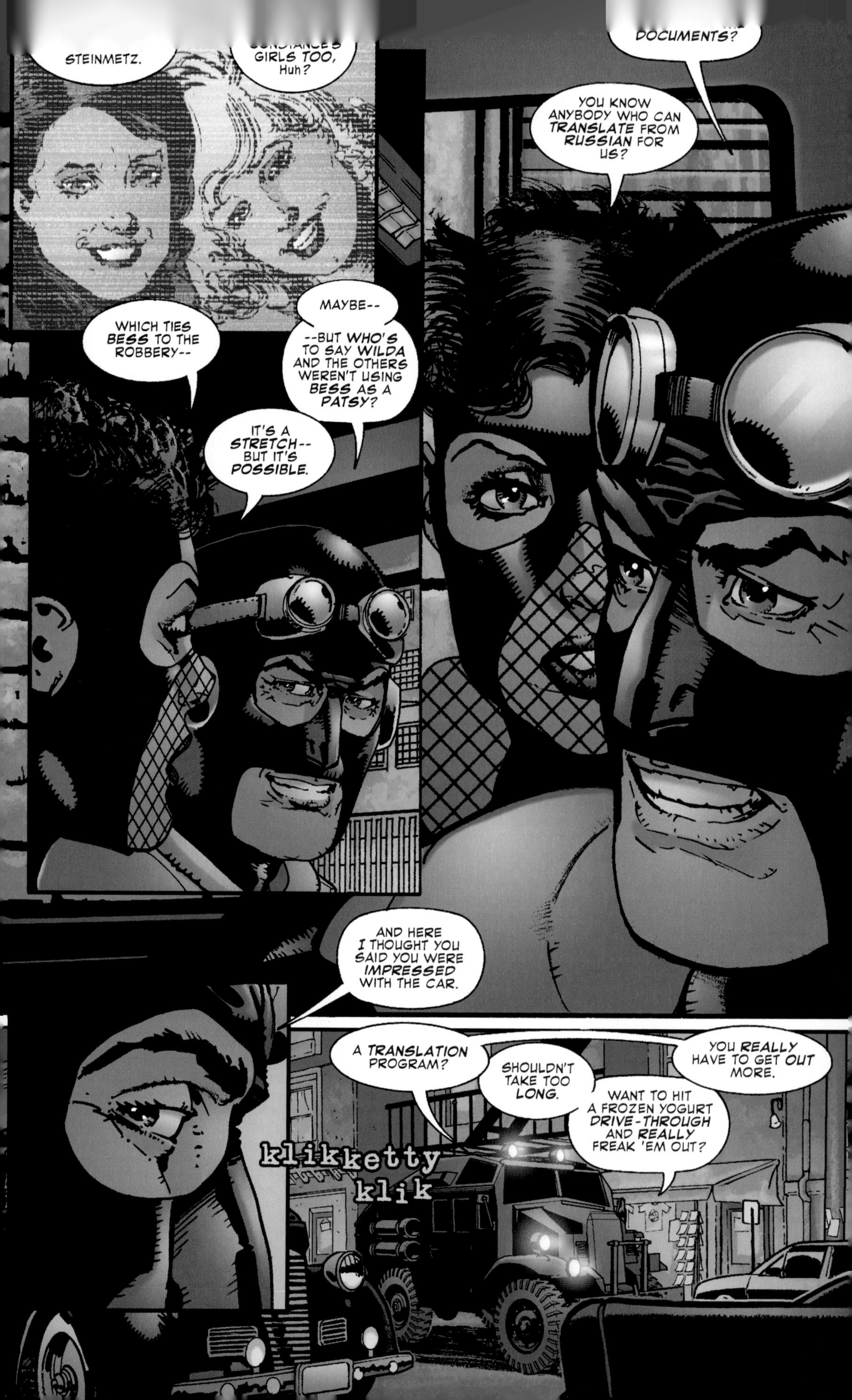

STEINMETZ.
GIRLS TOO, Huh?
DOCUMENTS?
YOU KNOW ANYBODY WHO CAN TRANSLATE FROM RUSSIAN FOR US?
WHICH TIES BESS TO THE ROBBERY--
MAYBE--
--BUT WHO'S TO SAY WILDA AND THE OTHERS WEREN'T USING BESS AS A PATSY?
IT'S A STRETCH--BUT IT'S POSSIBLE.
AND HERE I THOUGHT YOU SAID YOU WERE IMPRESSED WITH THE CAR.
A TRANSLATION PROGRAM?
SHOULDN'T TAKE TOO LONG.
YOU REALLY HAVE TO GET OUT MORE.
WANT TO HIT A FROZEN YOGURT DRIVE-THROUGH AND REALLY FREAK 'EM OUT?
klikketty klik

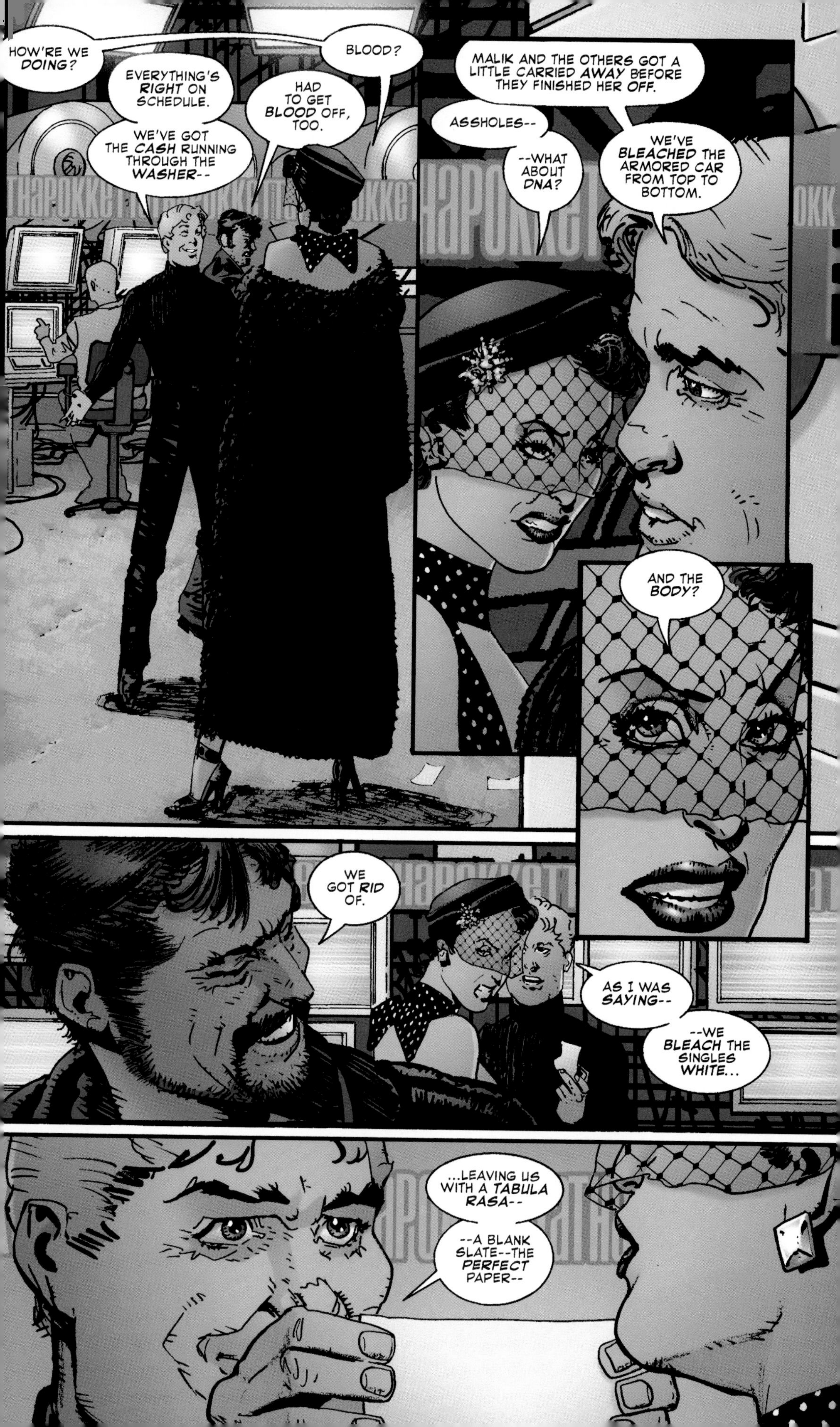

HOW'RE WE DOING?
EVERYTHING'S RIGHT ON SCHEDULE.
WE'VE GOT THE CASH RUNNING THROUGH THE WASHER--
BLOOD?
HAD TO GET BLOOD OFF, TOO.
MALIK AND THE OTHERS GOT A LITTLE CARRIED AWAY BEFORE THEY FINISHED HER OFF.
ASSHOLES--
--WHAT ABOUT DNA?
WE'VE BLEACHED THE ARMORED CAR FROM TOP TO BOTTOM.
AND THE BODY?
WE GOT RID OF.
AS I WAS SAYING--
--WE BLEACH THE SINGLES WHITE...
...LEAVING US WITH A TABULA RASA--
--A BLANK SLATE--THE PERFECT PAPER--

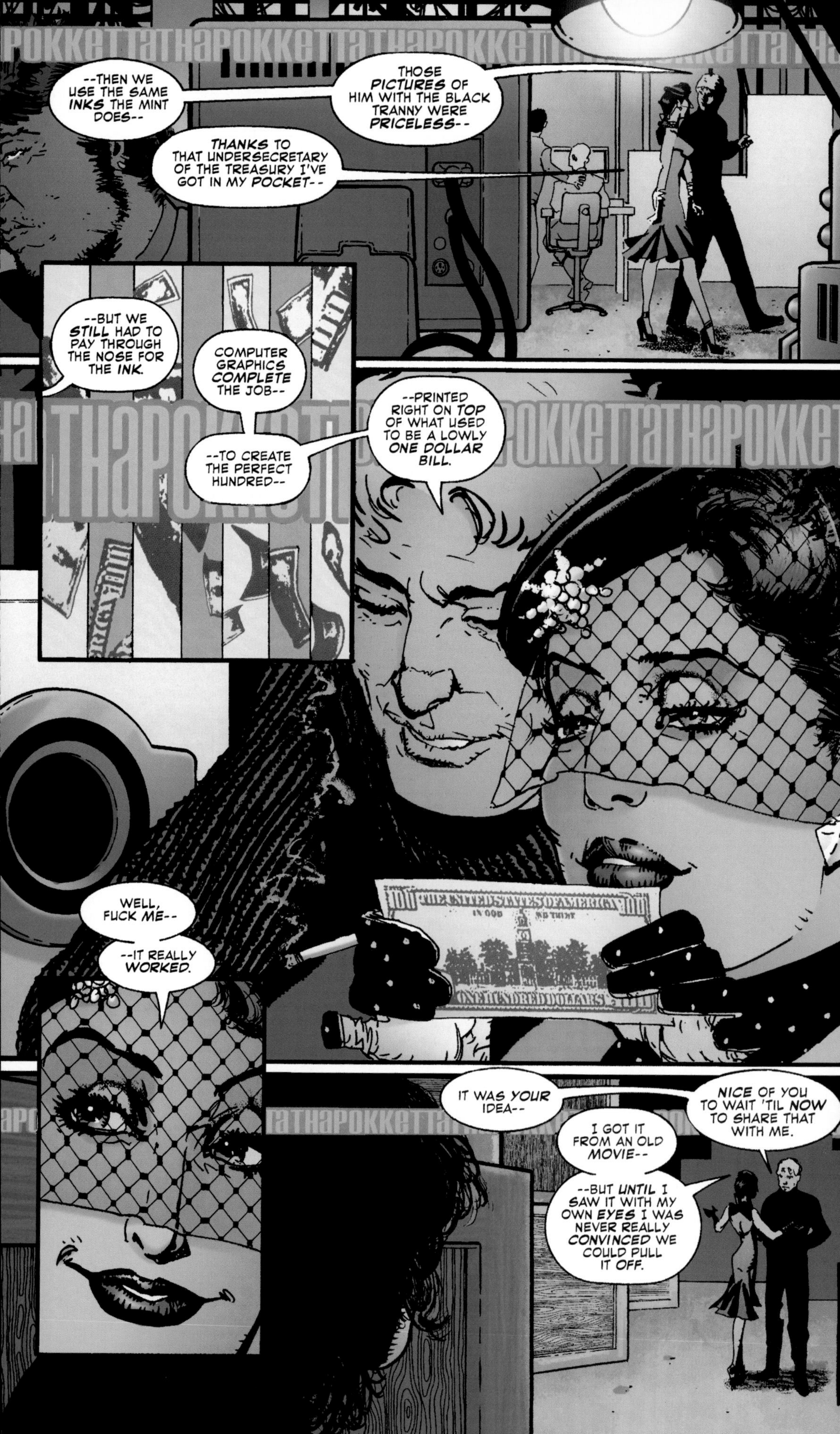
--THEN WE USE THE SAME INKS THE MINT DOES--
THOSE PICTURES OF HIM WITH THE BLACK TRANNY WERE PRICELESS--
THANKS TO THAT UNDERSECRETARY OF THE TREASURY I'VE GOT IN MY POCKET--
--BUT WE STILL HAD TO PAY THROUGH THE NOSE FOR THE INK.
COMPUTER GRAPHICS COMPLETE THE JOB--
--TO CREATE THE PERFECT HUNDRED--
--PRINTED RIGHT ON TOP OF WHAT USED TO BE A LOWLY ONE DOLLAR BILL.
WELL, FUCK ME--
--IT REALLY WORKED.
IT WAS YOUR IDEA--
NICE OF YOU TO WAIT 'TIL NOW TO SHARE THAT WITH ME.
I GOT IT FROM AN OLD MOVIE--
--BUT UNTIL I SAW IT WITH MY OWN EYES I WAS NEVER REALLY CONVINCED WE COULD PULL IT OFF.

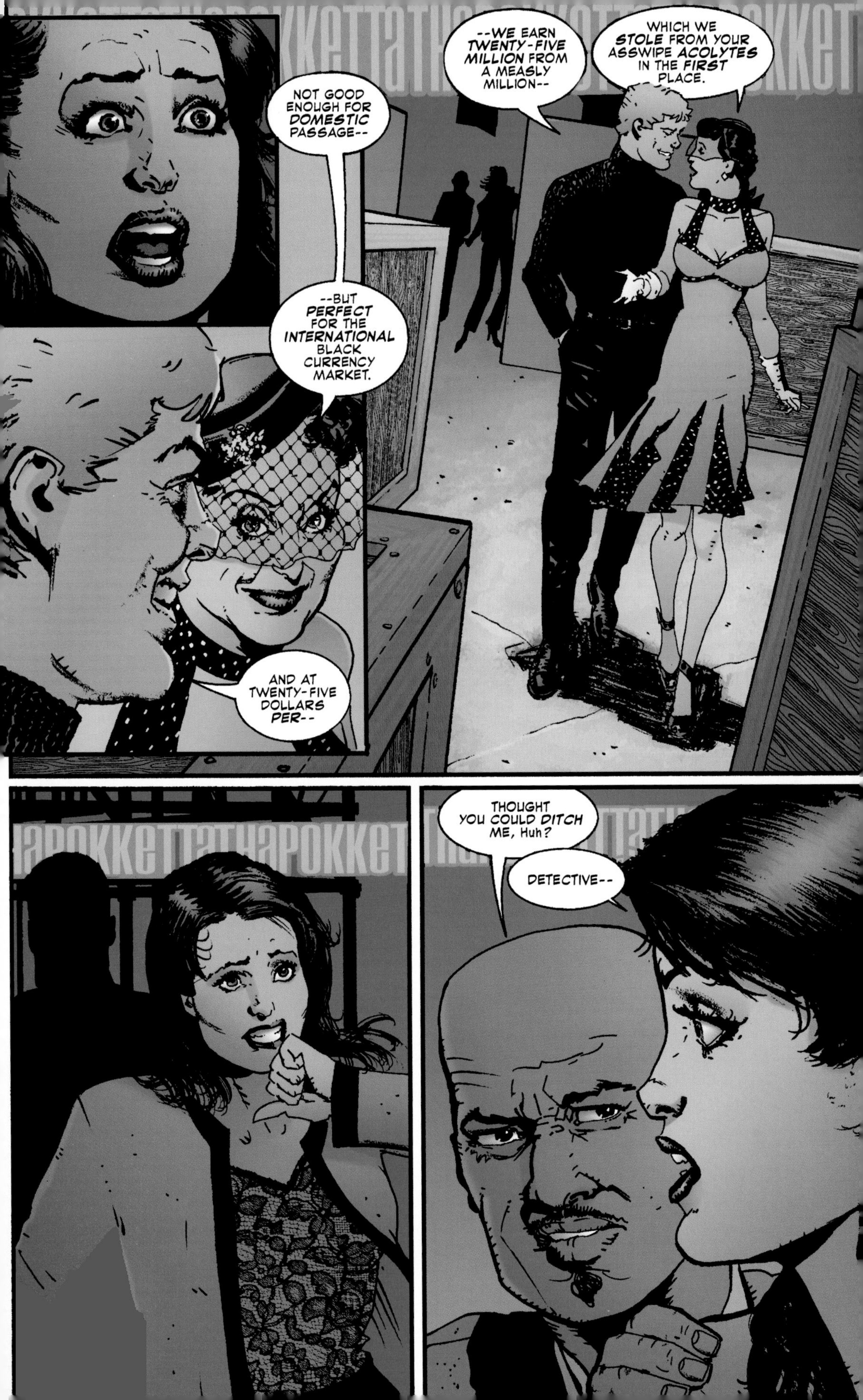
NOT GOOD ENOUGH FOR DOMESTIC PASSAGE--
--BUT PERFECT FOR THE INTERNATIONAL BLACK CURRENCY MARKET.
AND AT TWENTY-FIVE DOLLARS PER--
--WE EARN TWENTY-FIVE MILLION FROM A MEASLY MILLION--
WHICH WE STOLE FROM YOUR ASSWIPE ACOLYTES IN THE FIRST PLACE.
THOUGHT YOU COULD DITCH ME, Huh?
DETECTIVE--

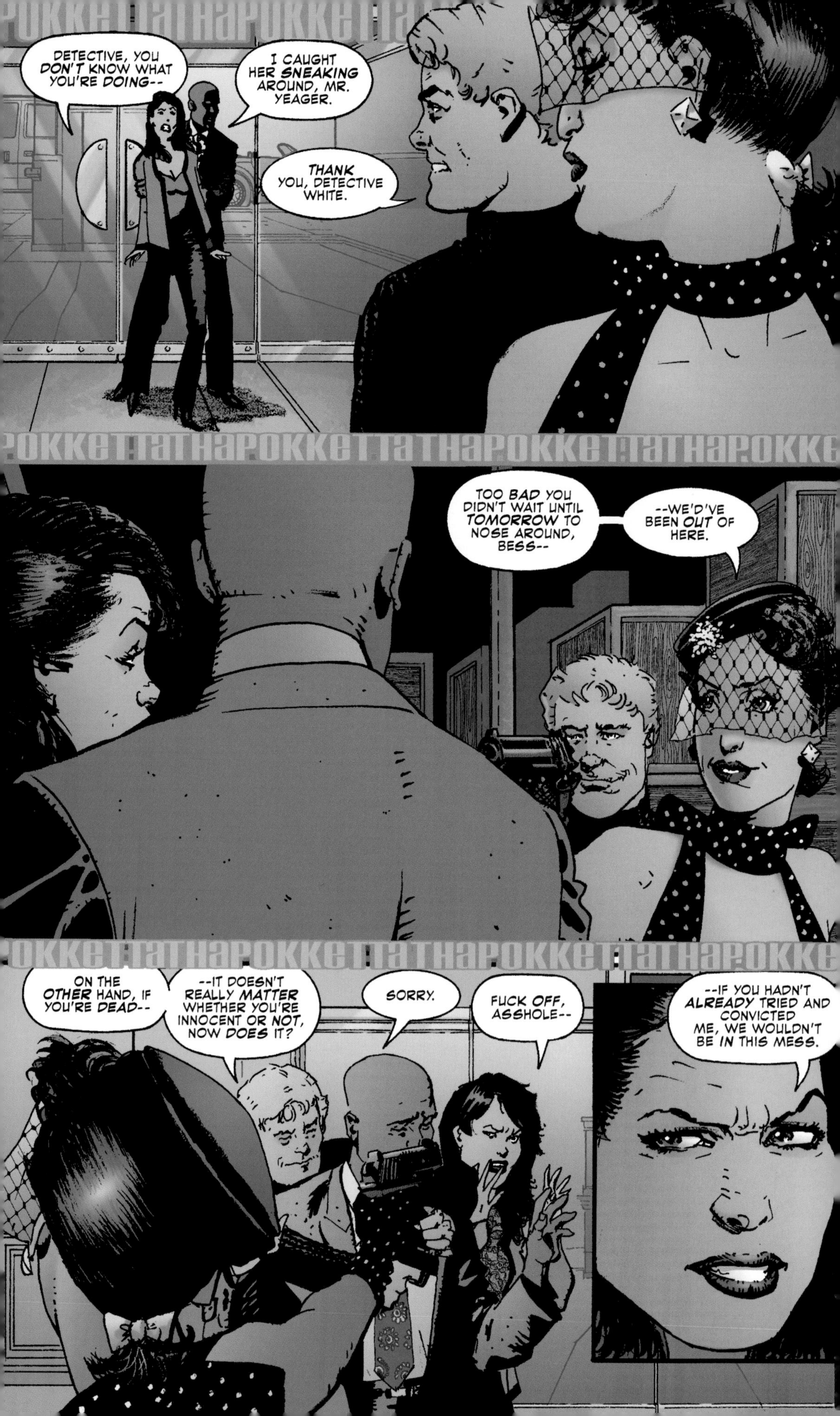
DETECTIVE, YOU DON'T KNOW WHAT YOU'RE DOING--
I CAUGHT HER SNEAKING AROUND, MR. YEAGER.
THANK YOU, DETECTIVE WHITE.
TOO BAD YOU DIDN'T WAIT UNTIL TOMORROW TO NOSE AROUND, BESS--
--WE'D'VE BEEN OUT OF HERE.
ON THE OTHER HAND, IF YOU'RE DEAD--
--IT DOESN'T REALLY MATTER WHETHER YOU'RE INNOCENT OR NOT, NOW DOES IT?
SORRY.
FUCK OFF, ASSHOLE--
--IF YOU HADN'T ALREADY TRIED AND CONVICTED ME, WE WOULDN'T BE IN THIS MESS.

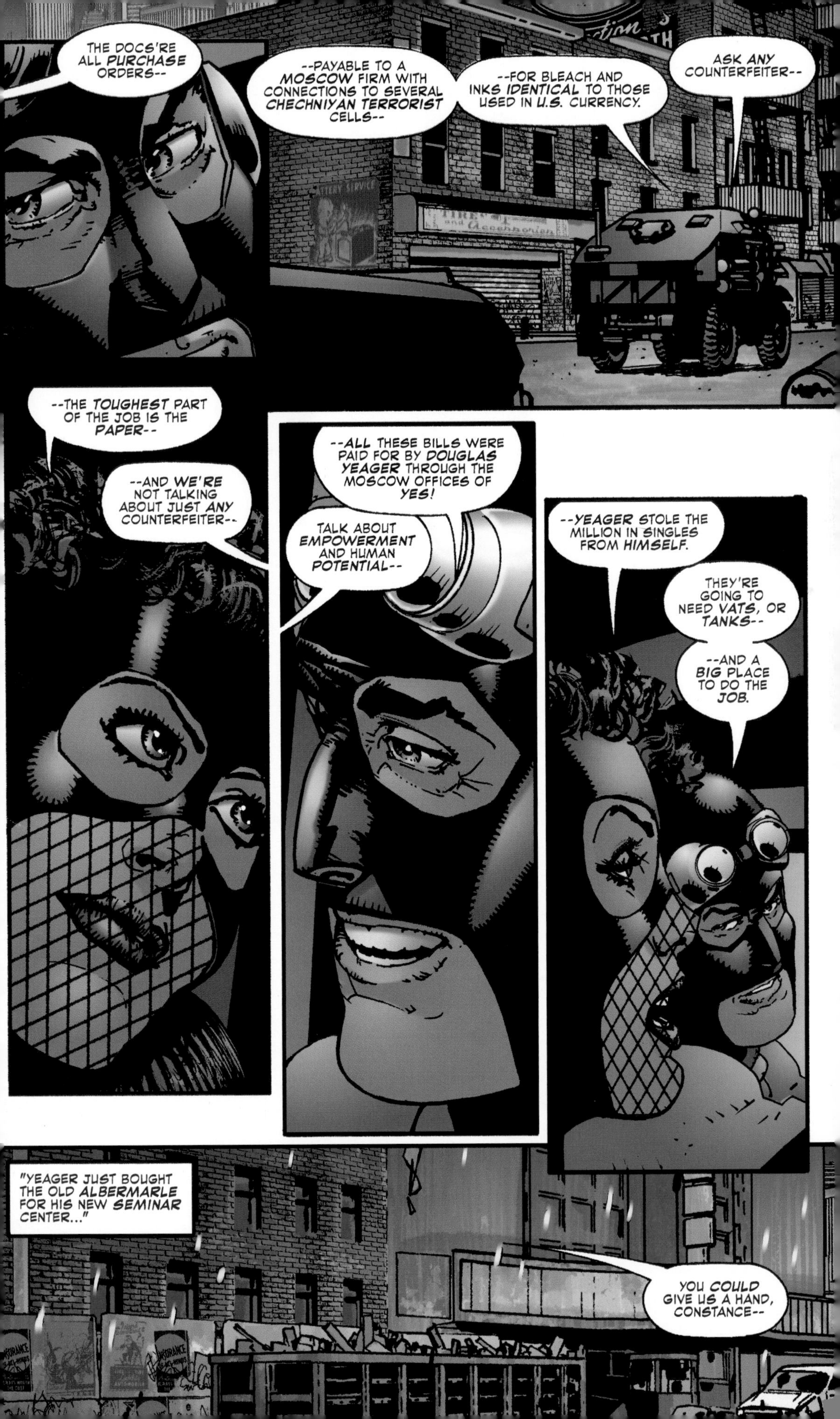
THE DOCS'RE ALL PURCHASE ORDERS--
--PAYABLE TO A MOSCOW FIRM WITH CONNECTIONS TO SEVERAL CHECHNIYAN TERRORIST CELLS--
--FOR BLEACH AND INKS IDENTICAL TO THOSE USED IN U.S. CURRENCY.
ASK ANY COUNTERFEITER--
--THE TOUGHEST PART OF THE JOB IS THE PAPER--
--AND WE'RE NOT TALKING ABOUT JUST ANY COUNTERFEITER--
--ALL THESE BILLS WERE PAID FOR BY DOUGLAS YEAGER THROUGH THE MOSCOW OFFICES OF YES!
TALK ABOUT EMPOWERMENT AND HUMAN POTENTIAL--
--YEAGER STOLE THE MILLION IN SINGLES FROM HIMSELF.
THEY'RE GOING TO NEED VATS, OR TANKS--
--AND A BIG PLACE TO DO THE JOB.
"YEAGER JUST BOUGHT THE OLD ALBERMARLE FOR HIS NEW SEMINAR CENTER..."
YOU COULD GIVE US A HAND, CONSTANCE--

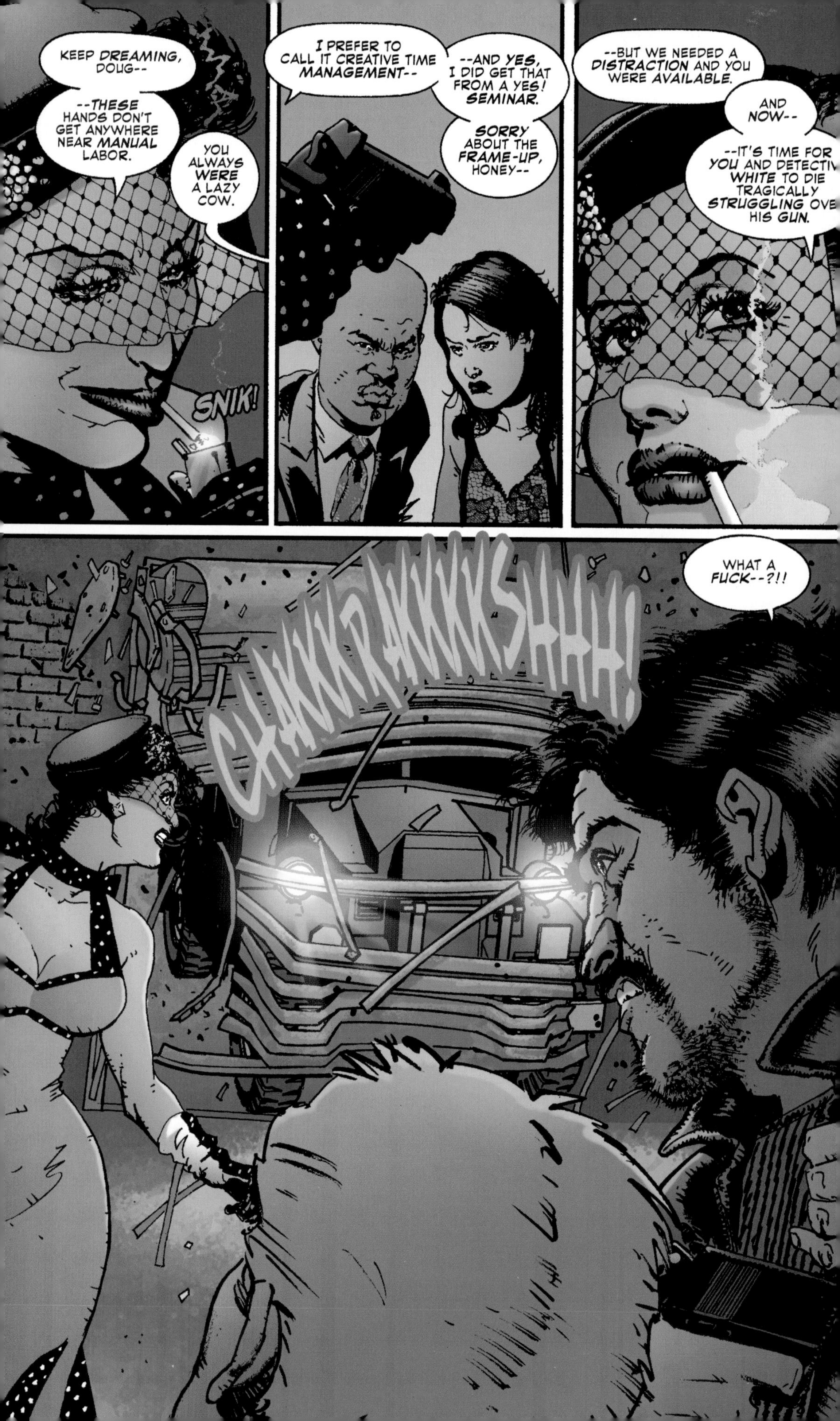
KEEP DREAMING, DOUG--
--THESE HANDS DON'T GET ANYWHERE NEAR MANUAL LABOR.
YOU ALWAYS WERE A LAZY COW.
SNIK!
I PREFER TO CALL IT CREATIVE TIME MANAGEMENT--
--AND YES, I DID GET THAT FROM A YES! SEMINAR.
SORRY ABOUT THE FRAME-UP, HONEY--
--BUT WE NEEDED A DISTRACTION AND YOU WERE AVAILABLE.
AND NOW--
--IT'S TIME FOR YOU AND DETECTIV WHITE TO DIE TRAGICALLY STRUGGLING OVE HIS GUN.
CHAKKRAKKKSHHH!
WHAT A FUCK--?!!

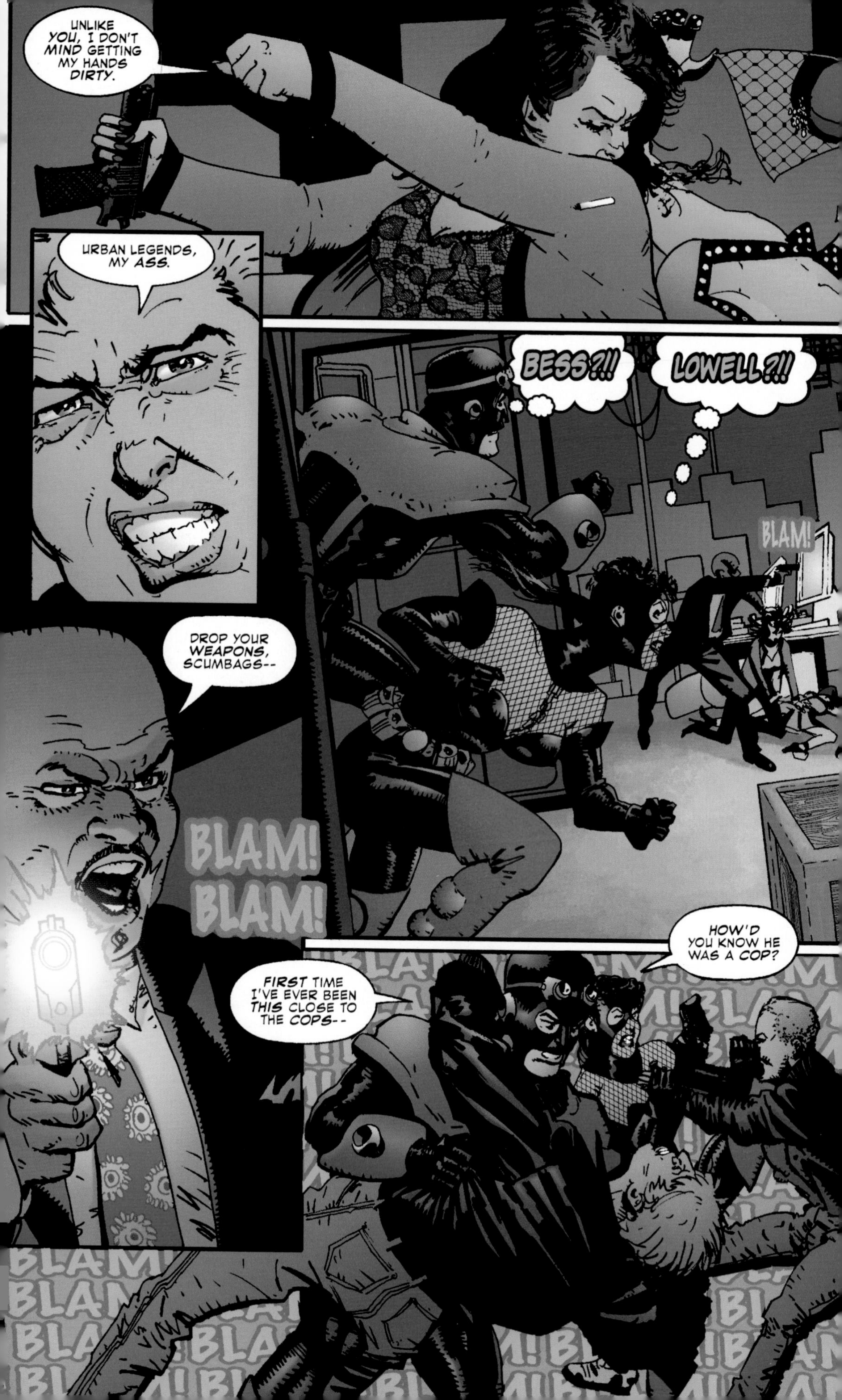
UNLIKE YOU, I DON'T MIND GETTING MY HANDS DIRTY.
URBAN LEGENDS, MY ASS.
BESS?!!
LOWELL?!!
BLAM!
DROP YOUR WEAPONS, SCUMBAGS--
BLAM! BLAM!
HOW'D YOU KNOW HE WAS A COP?
FIRST TIME I'VE EVER BEEN THIS CLOSE TO THE COPS--

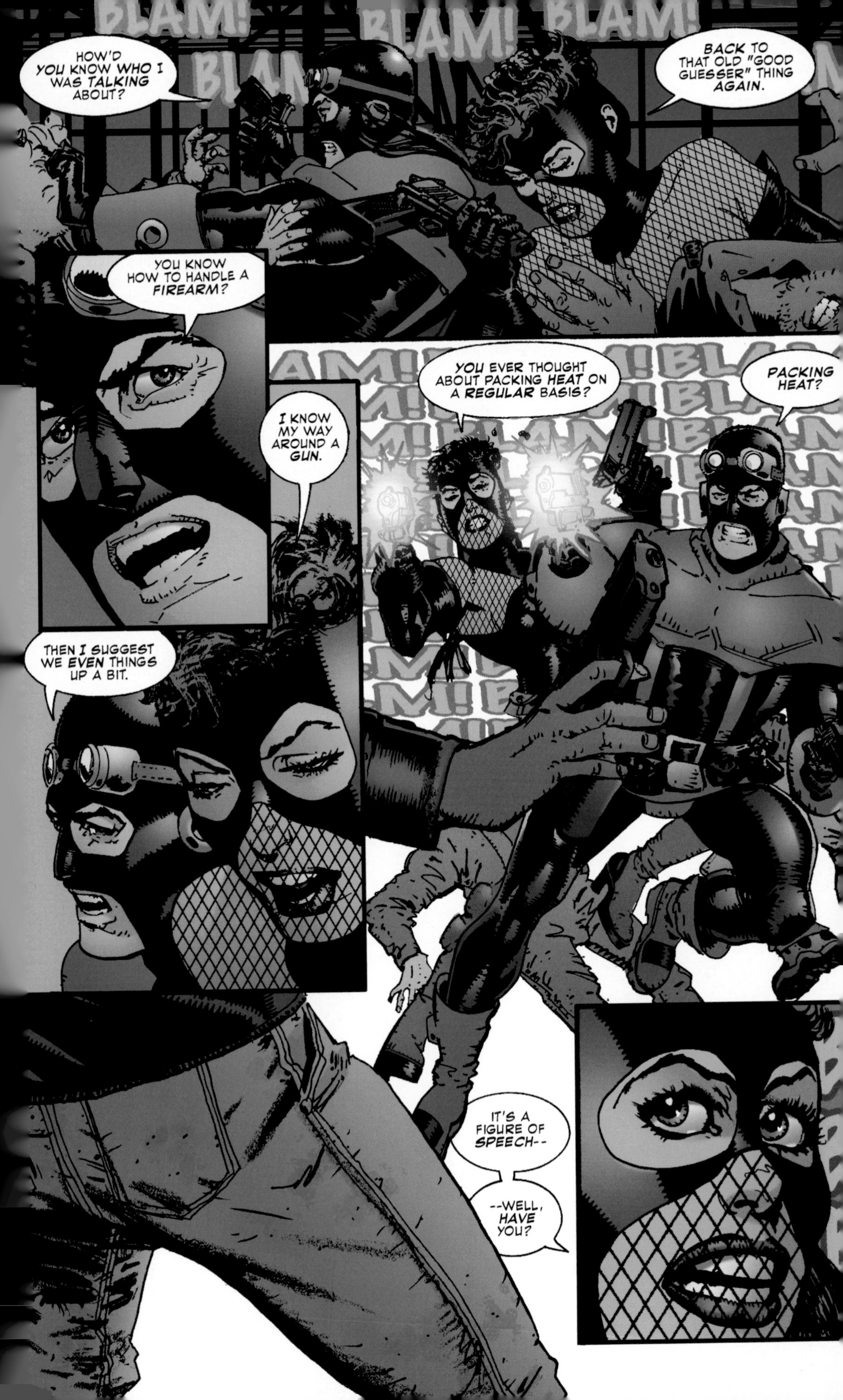
BLAM! BLAM! BLAM! BLAM!
HOW'D YOU KNOW WHO I WAS TALKING ABOUT?
BACK TO THAT OLD "GOOD GUESSER" THING AGAIN.
YOU KNOW HOW TO HANDLE A FIREARM?
I KNOW MY WAY AROUND A GUN.
YOU EVER THOUGHT ABOUT PACKING HEAT ON A REGULAR BASIS?
PACKING HEAT?
THEN I SUGGEST WE EVEN THINGS UP A BIT.
IT'S A FIGURE OF SPEECH--
--WELL, HAVE YOU?

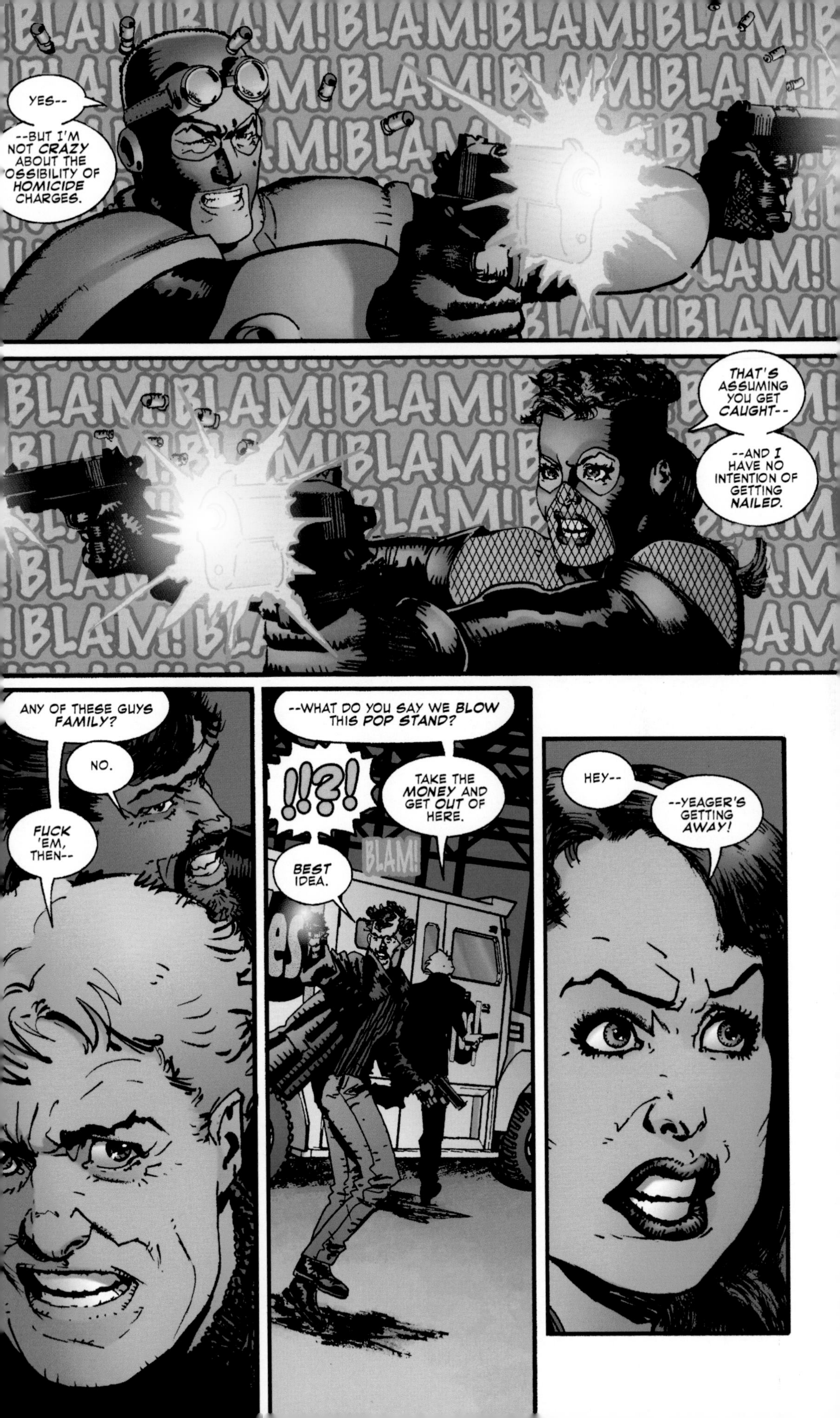
BLAM! BLAM! BLAM! BLAM!
YES--
--BUT I'M NOT CRAZY ABOUT THE POSSIBILITY OF HOMICIDE CHARGES.
BLAM! BLAM! BLAM!
THAT'S ASSUMING YOU GET CAUGHT--
--AND I HAVE NO INTENTION OF GETTING NAILED.
ANY OF THESE GUYS FAMILY?
NO.
FUCK 'EM, THEN--
--WHAT DO YOU SAY WE BLOW THIS POP STAND?
!!?!
TAKE THE MONEY AND GET OUT OF HERE.
BLAM!
BEST IDEA.
HEY--
--YEAGER'S GETTING AWAY!

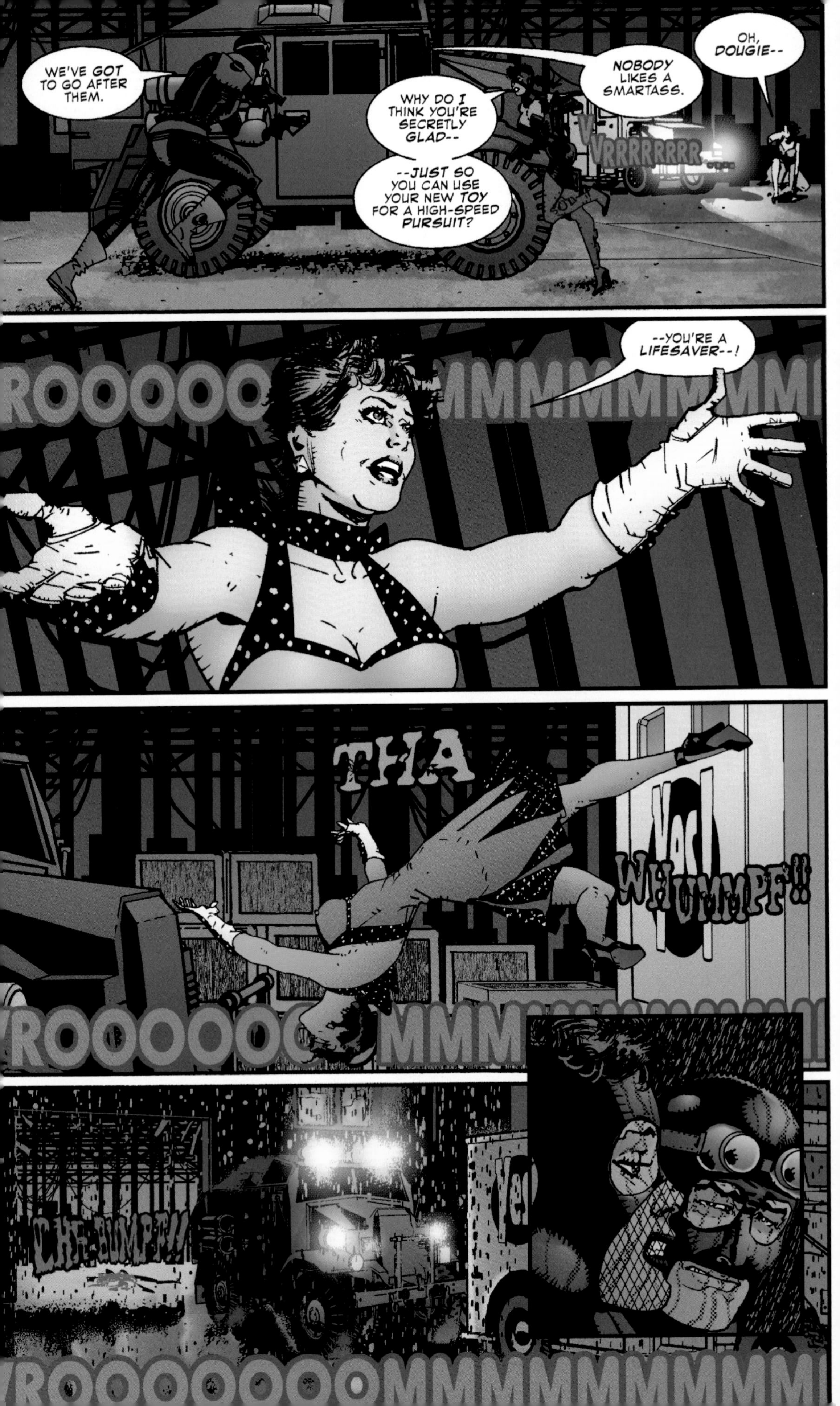

WE'VE GOT TO GO AFTER THEM.
WHY DO I THINK YOU'RE SECRETLY GLAD--
--JUST SO YOU CAN USE YOUR NEW TOY FOR A HIGH-SPEED PURSUIT?
NOBODY LIKES A SMARTASS.
OH, DOUGIE--
VVRRRRRRRR
ROOOOOOMMMMMMMMMM
--YOU'RE A LIFESAVER--!
THA
WHUMMPF!!
ROOOOOOMMMMMMMMMM
ROOOOOOOOMMMMMMMMMMM

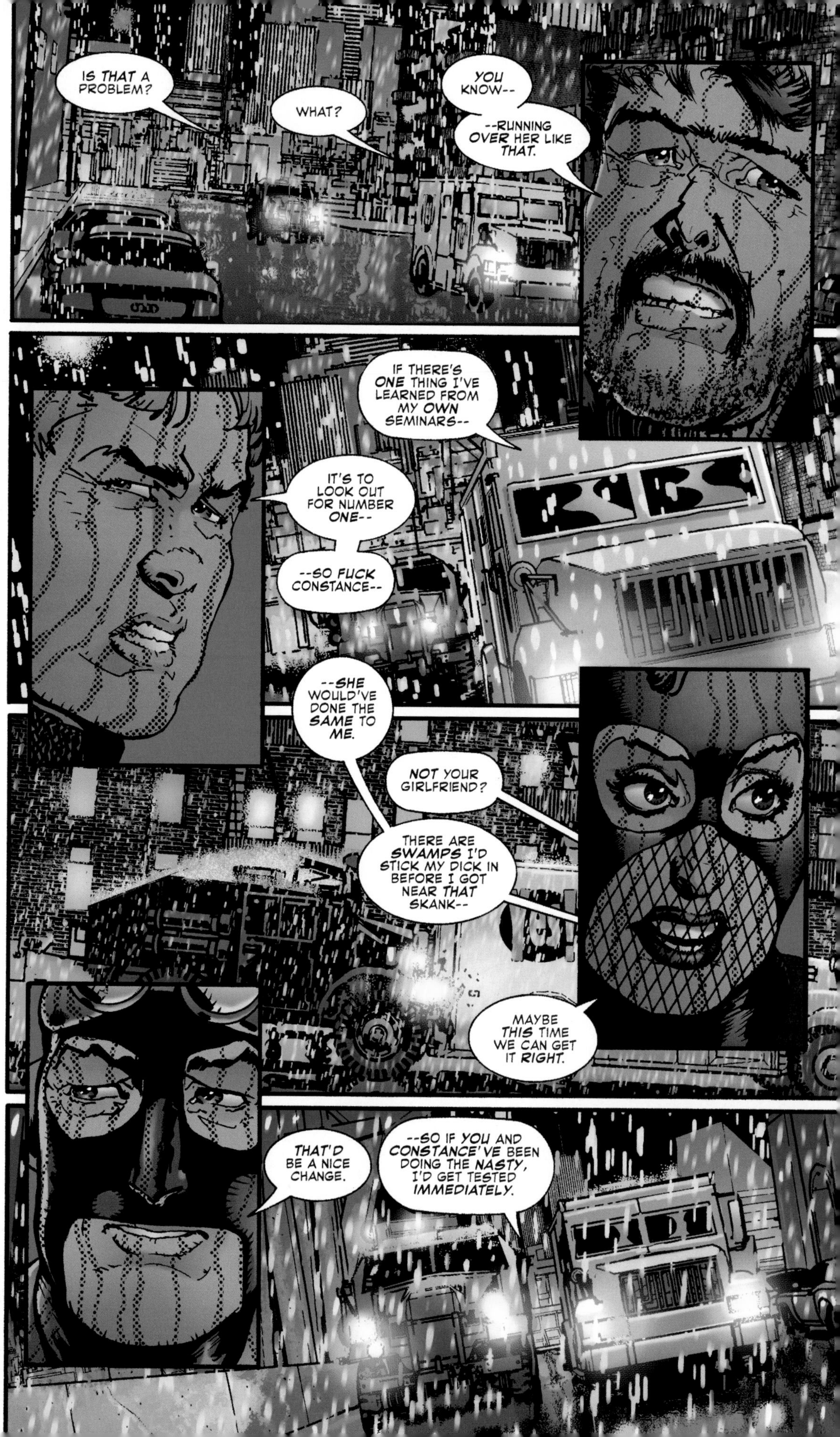

IS THAT A PROBLEM?
WHAT?
YOU KNOW--
--RUNNING OVER HER LIKE THAT.
IF THERE'S ONE THING I'VE LEARNED FROM MY OWN SEMINARS--
IT'S TO LOOK OUT FOR NUMBER ONE--
--SO FUCK CONSTANCE--
--SHE WOULD'VE DONE THE SAME TO ME.
NOT YOUR GIRLFRIEND?
THERE ARE SWAMPS I'D STICK MY DICK IN BEFORE I GOT NEAR THAT SKANK--
MAYBE THIS TIME WE CAN GET IT RIGHT.
THAT'D BE A NICE CHANGE.
--SO IF YOU AND CONSTANCE'VE BEEN DOING THE NASTY, I'D GET TESTED IMMEDIATELY.

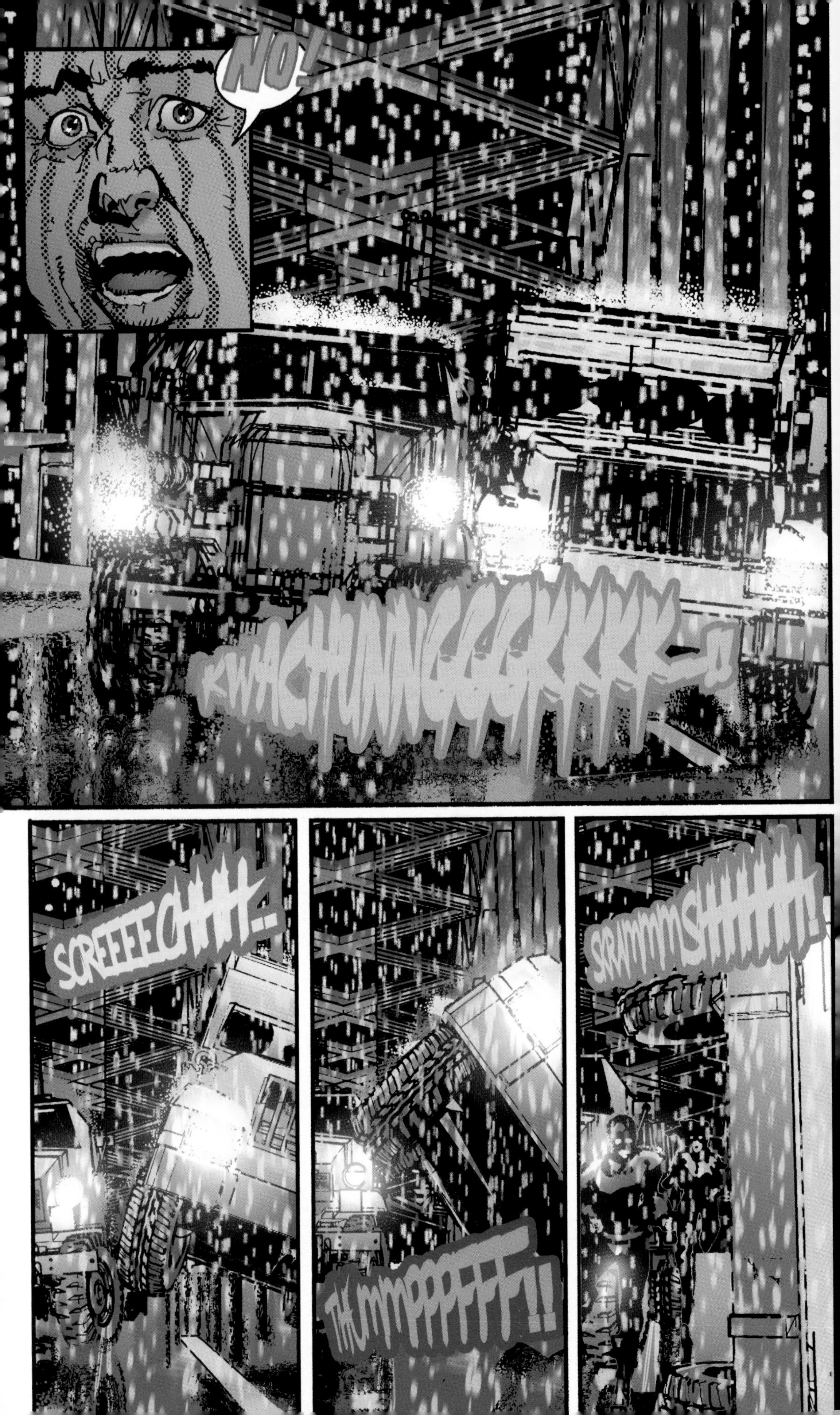
NO!
KWACHUNNGGGKKKK--!
SCREEEECHHH..
THUMMPPPFFF!!
SKRAMMMSHHHHHH!

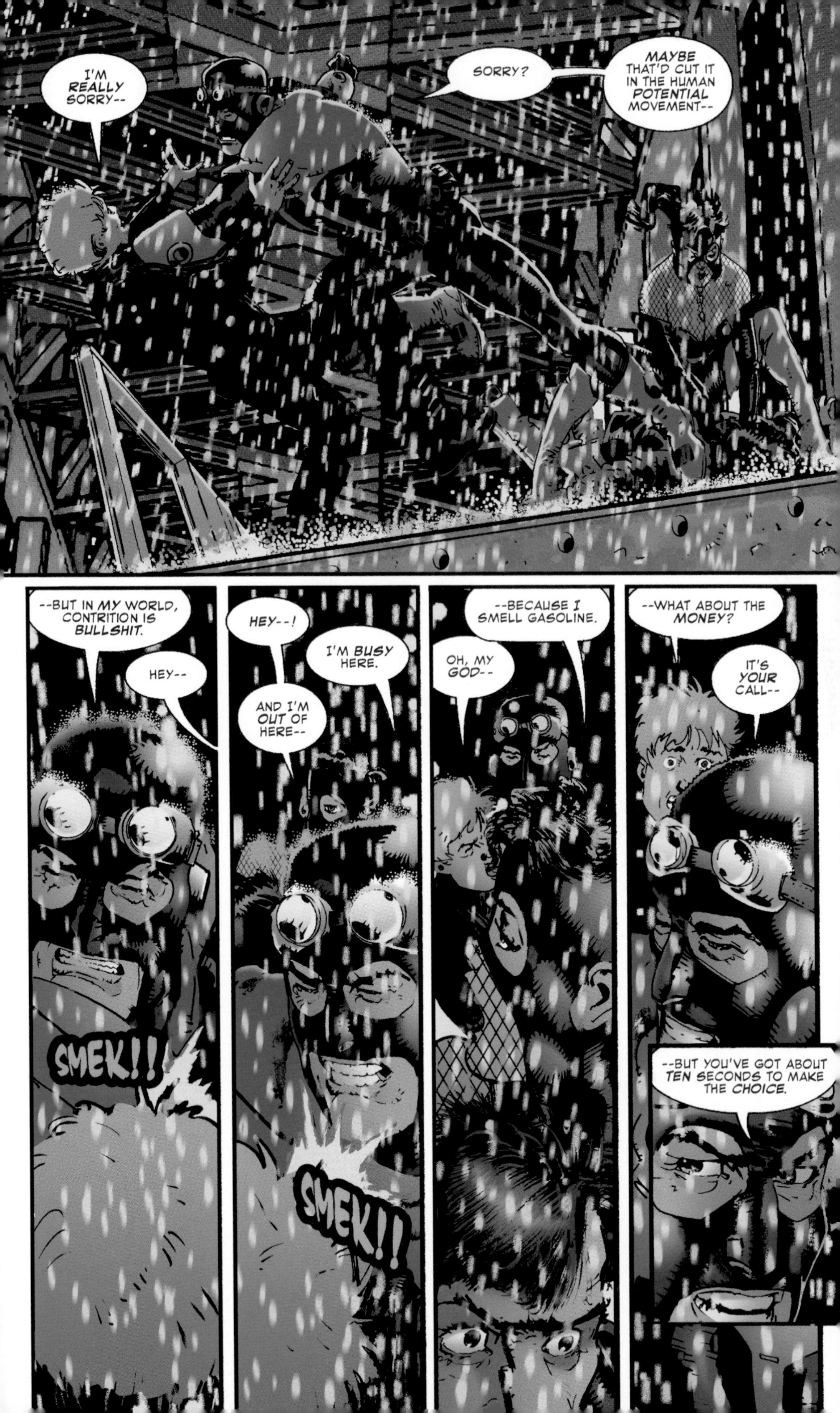

I'M REALLY SORRY--
SORRY?
MAYBE THAT'D CUT IT IN THE HUMAN POTENTIAL MOVEMENT--
--BUT IN MY WORLD, CONTRITION IS BULLSHIT.
HEY--
SMEK!!
HEY--!
I'M BUSY HERE.
AND I'M OUT OF HERE--
SMEK!!
--BECAUSE I SMELL GASOLINE.
OH, MY GOD--
--WHAT ABOUT THE MONEY?
IT'S YOUR CALL--
--BUT YOU'VE GOT ABOUT TEN SECONDS TO MAKE THE CHOICE.

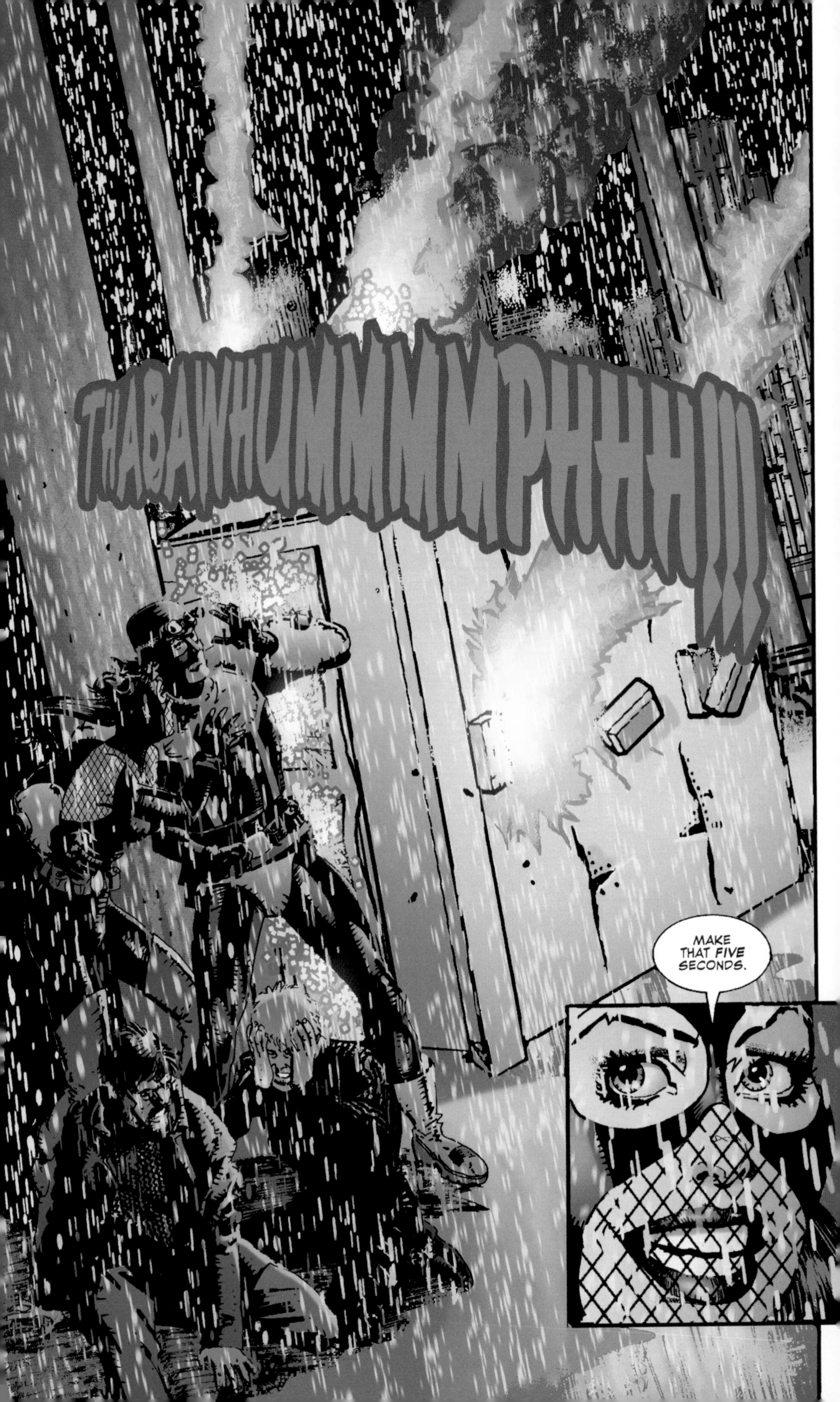
THABAWHUMMMMMPHHH!!!
MAKE THAT FIVE SECONDS.

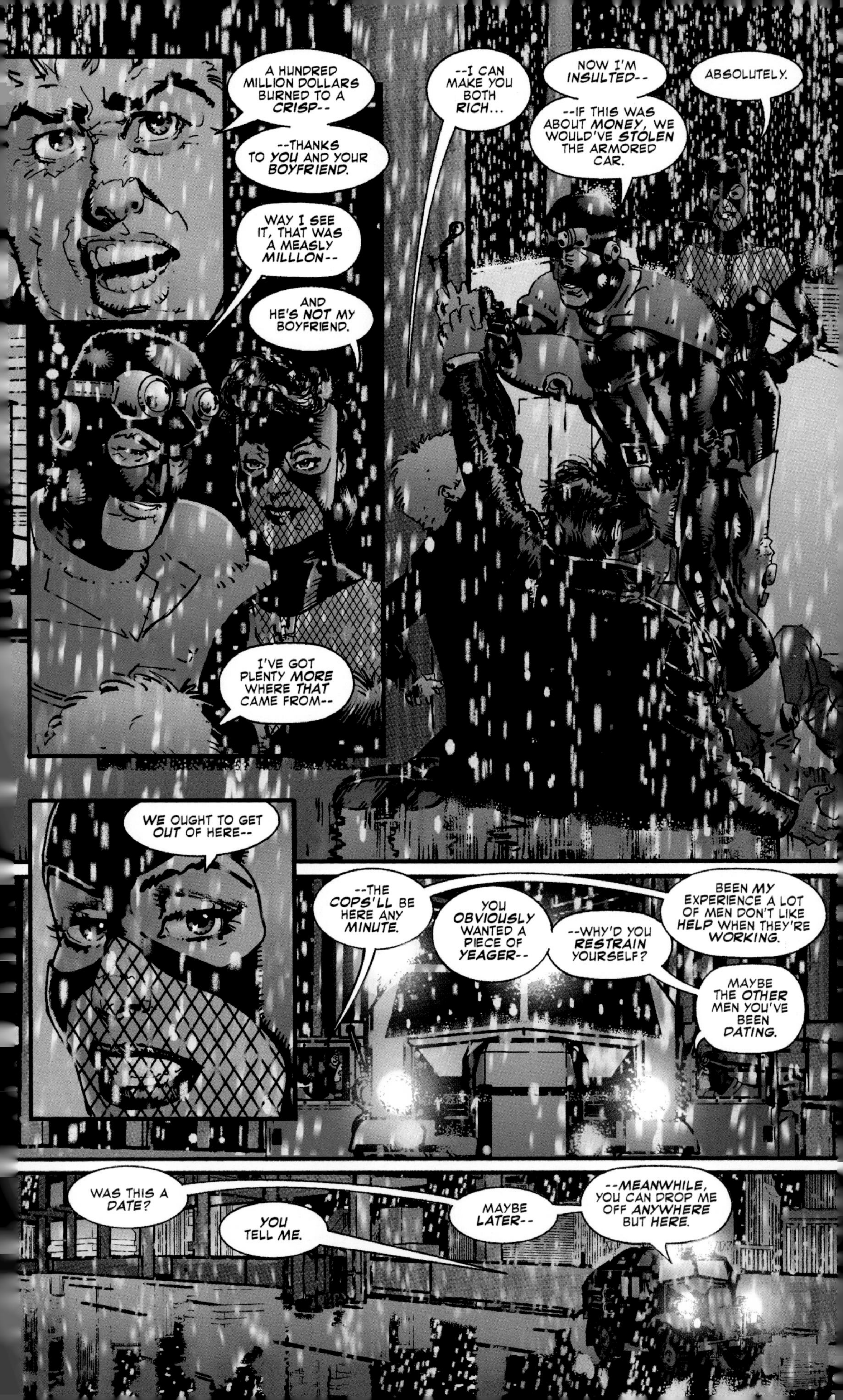
A HUNDRED MILLION DOLLARS BURNED TO A CRISP--
--THANKS TO YOU AND YOUR BOYFRIEND.
WAY I SEE IT, THAT WAS A MEASLY MILLLON--
AND HE'S NOT MY BOYFRIEND.
I'VE GOT PLENTY MORE WHERE THAT CAME FROM--
--I CAN MAKE YOU BOTH RICH...
NOW I'M INSULTED--
--IF THIS WAS ABOUT MONEY, WE WOULD'VE STOLEN THE ARMORED CAR.
ABSOLUTELY.
WE OUGHT TO GET OUT OF HERE--
--THE COPS'LL BE HERE ANY MINUTE.
YOU OBVIOUSLY WANTED A PIECE OF YEAGER--
--WHY'D YOU RESTRAIN YOURSELF?
BEEN MY EXPERIENCE A LOT OF MEN DON'T LIKE HELP WHEN THEY'RE WORKING.
MAYBE THE OTHER MEN YOU'VE BEEN DATING.
WAS THIS A DATE?
YOU TELL ME.
MAYBE LATER--
--MEANWHILE, YOU CAN DROP ME OFF ANYWHERE BUT HERE.

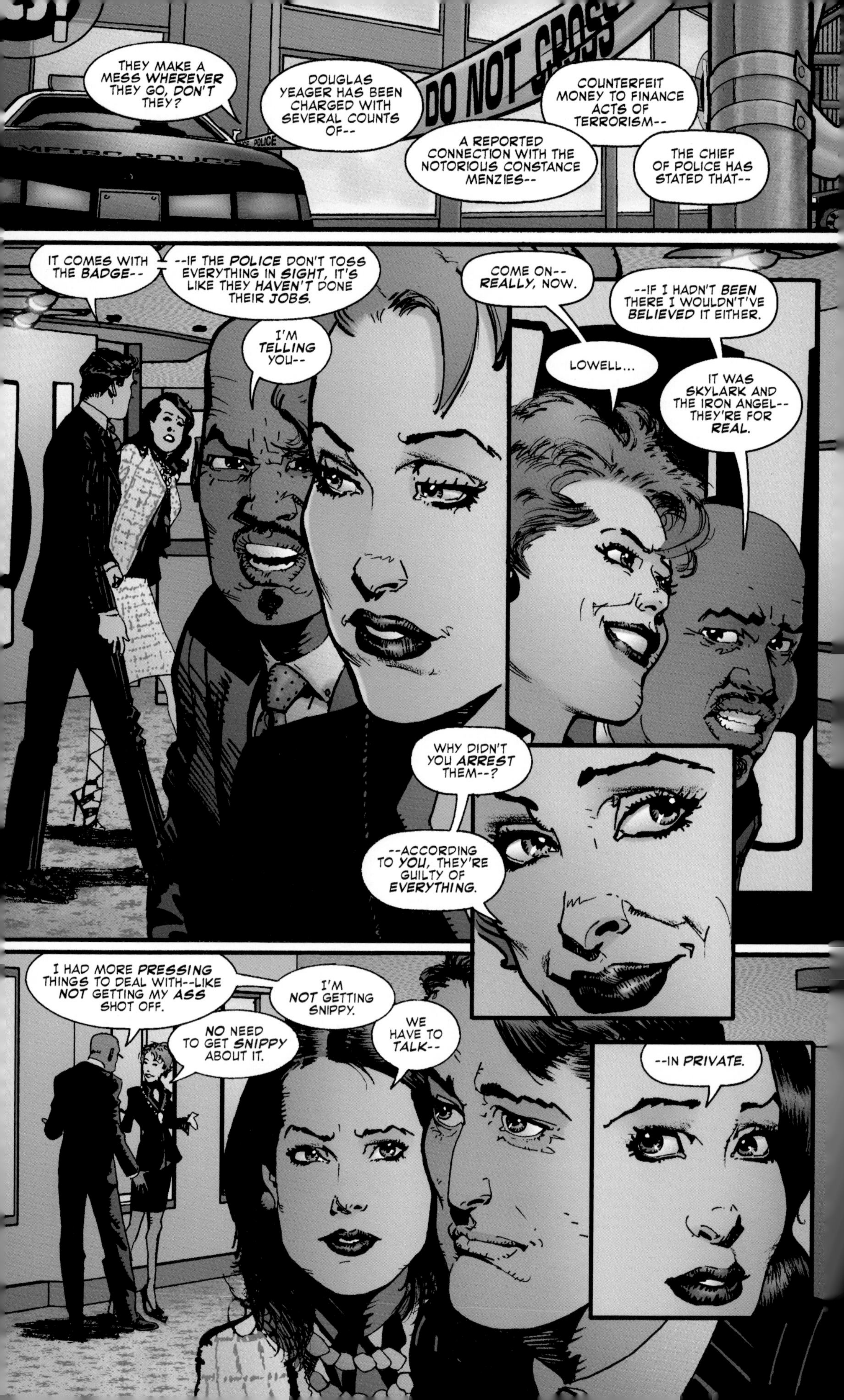
THEY MAKE A MESS WHEREVER THEY GO, DON'T THEY?
DOUGLAS YEAGER HAS BEEN CHARGED WITH SEVERAL COUNTS OF--
DO NOT CROSS
COUNTERFEIT MONEY TO FINANCE ACTS OF TERRORISM--
A REPORTED CONNECTION WITH THE NOTORIOUS CONSTANCE MENZIES--
THE CHIEF OF POLICE HAS STATED THAT--
IT COMES WITH THE BADGE--
--IF THE POLICE DON'T TOSS EVERYTHING IN SIGHT, IT'S LIKE THEY HAVEN'T DONE THEIR JOBS.
I'M TELLING YOU--
COME ON-- REALLY, NOW.
LOWELL...
--IF I HADN'T BEEN THERE I WOULDN'T'VE BELIEVED IT EITHER.
IT WAS SKYLARK AND THE IRON ANGEL-- THEY'RE FOR REAL.
WHY DIDN'T YOU ARREST THEM--?
--ACCORDING TO YOU, THEY'RE GUILTY OF EVERYTHING.
I HAD MORE PRESSING THINGS TO DEAL WITH--LIKE NOT GETTING MY ASS SHOT OFF.
NO NEED TO GET SNIPPY ABOUT IT.
I'M NOT GETTING SNIPPY.
WE HAVE TO TALK--
--IN PRIVATE.

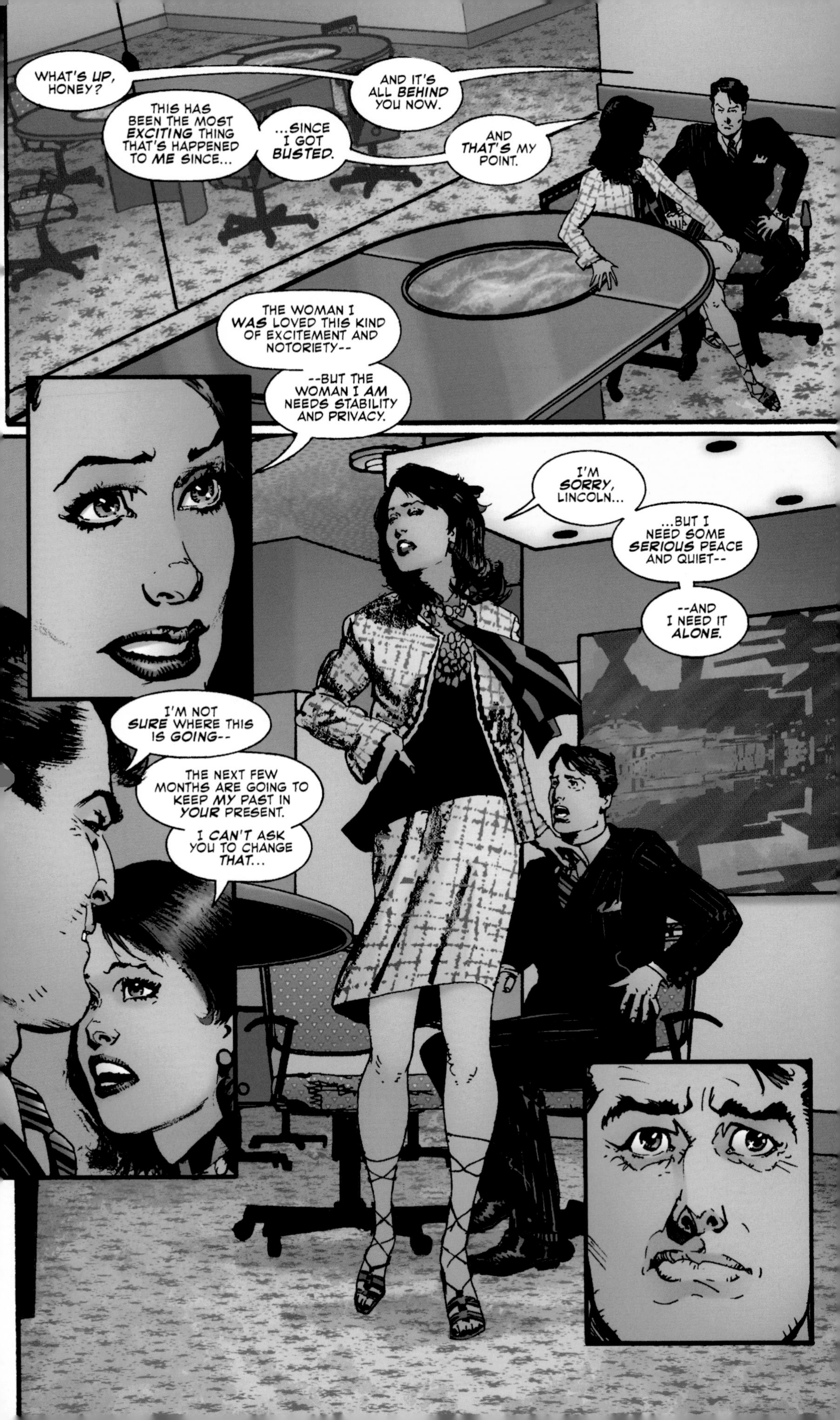
WHAT'S UP, HONEY?
THIS HAS BEEN THE MOST EXCITING THING THAT'S HAPPENED TO ME SINCE...
...SINCE I GOT BUSTED.
AND IT'S ALL BEHIND YOU NOW.
AND THAT'S MY POINT.
THE WOMAN I WAS LOVED THIS KIND OF EXCITEMENT AND NOTORIETY--
--BUT THE WOMAN I AM NEEDS STABILITY AND PRIVACY.
I'M SORRY, LINCOLN...
...BUT I NEED SOME SERIOUS PEACE AND QUIET--
--AND I NEED IT ALONE.
I'M NOT SURE WHERE THIS IS GOING--
THE NEXT FEW MONTHS ARE GOING TO KEEP MY PAST IN YOUR PRESENT.
I CAN'T ASK YOU TO CHANGE THAT...

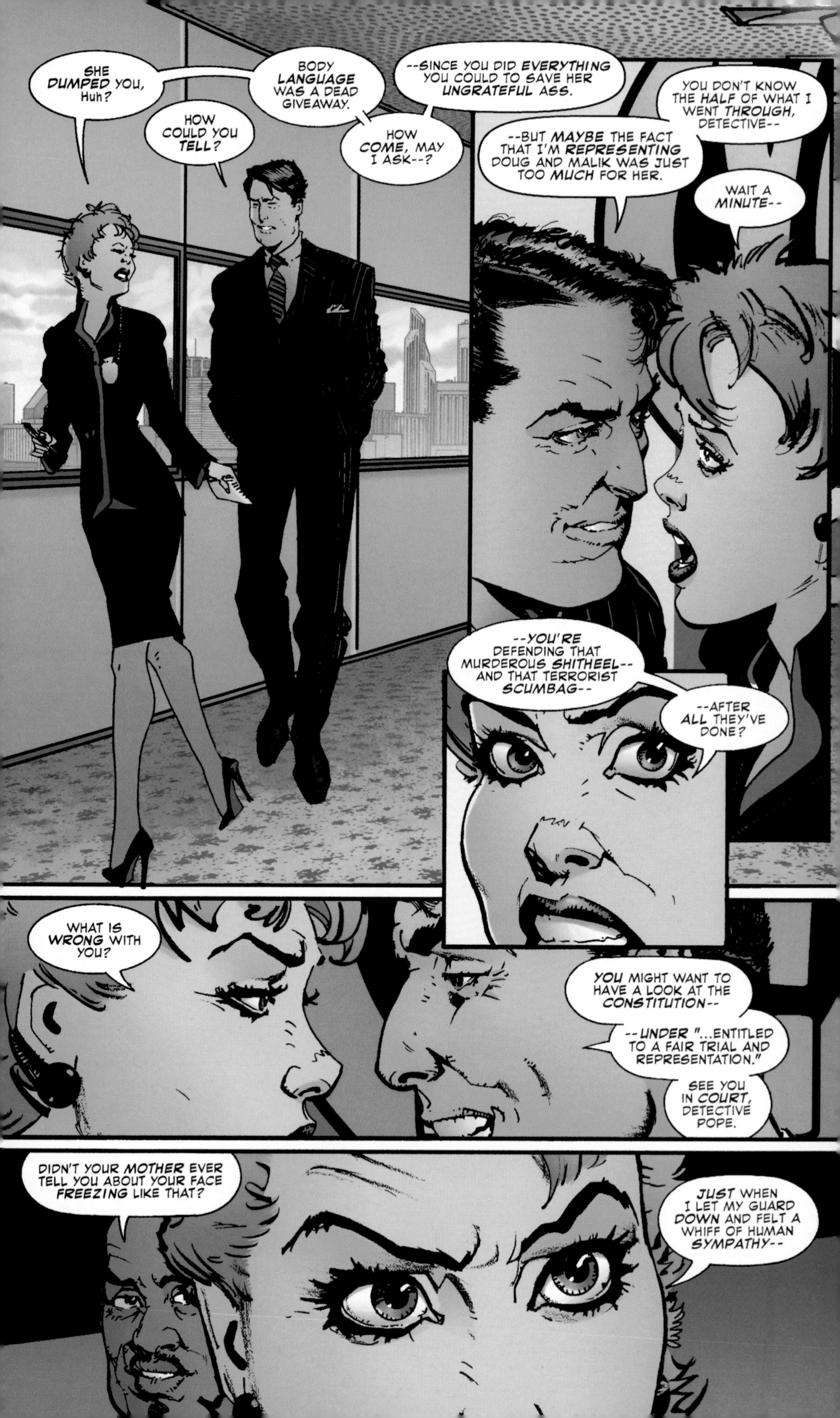
SHE DUMPED YOU, Huh?
HOW COULD YOU TELL?
BODY LANGUAGE WAS A DEAD GIVEAWAY.
HOW COME, MAY I ASK--?
--SINCE YOU DID EVERYTHING YOU COULD TO SAVE HER UNGRATEFUL ASS.
YOU DON'T KNOW THE HALF OF WHAT I WENT THROUGH, DETECTIVE--
--BUT MAYBE THE FACT THAT I'M REPRESENTING DOUG AND MALIK WAS JUST TOO MUCH FOR HER.
WAIT A MINUTE--
--YOU'RE DEFENDING THAT MURDEROUS SHITHEEL-- AND THAT TERRORIST SCUMBAG--
--AFTER ALL THEY'VE DONE?
WHAT IS WRONG WITH YOU?
YOU MIGHT WANT TO HAVE A LOOK AT THE CONSTITUTION--
--UNDER "...ENTITLED TO A FAIR TRIAL AND REPRESENTATION."
SEE YOU IN COURT, DETECTIVE POPE.
DIDN'T YOUR MOTHER EVER TELL YOU ABOUT YOUR FACE FREEZING LIKE THAT?
JUST WHEN I LET MY GUARD DOWN AND FELT A WHIFF OF HUMAN SYMPATHY--

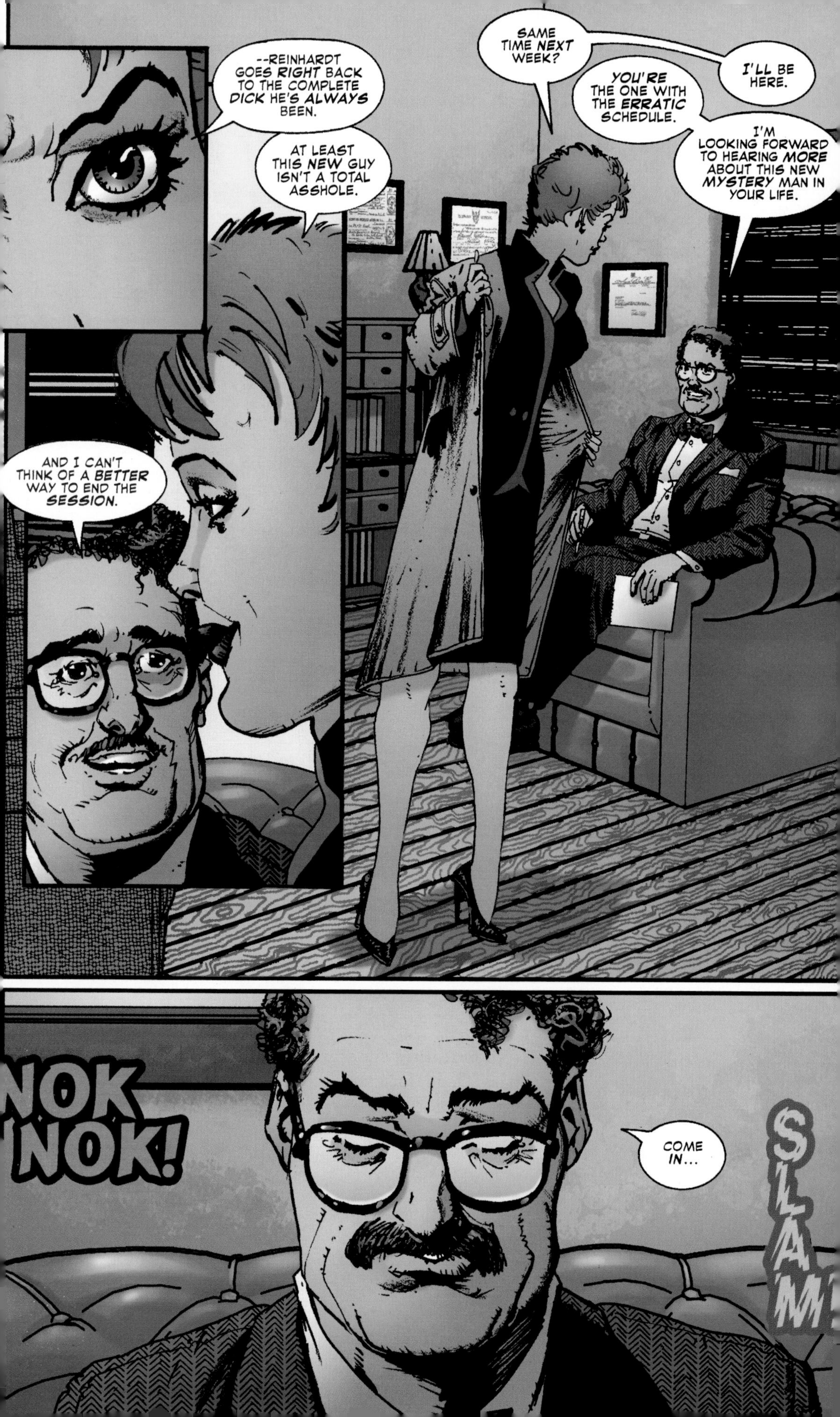
--REINHARDT GOES RIGHT BACK TO THE COMPLETE DICK HE'S ALWAYS BEEN.
AT LEAST THIS NEW GUY ISN'T A TOTAL ASSHOLE.
AND I CAN'T THINK OF A BETTER WAY TO END THE SESSION.
SAME TIME NEXT WEEK?
I'LL BE HERE.
YOU'RE THE ONE WITH THE ERRATIC SCHEDULE.
I'M LOOKING FORWARD TO HEARING MORE ABOUT THIS NEW MYSTERY MAN IN YOUR LIFE.
NOK NOK!
COME IN...
SLAM

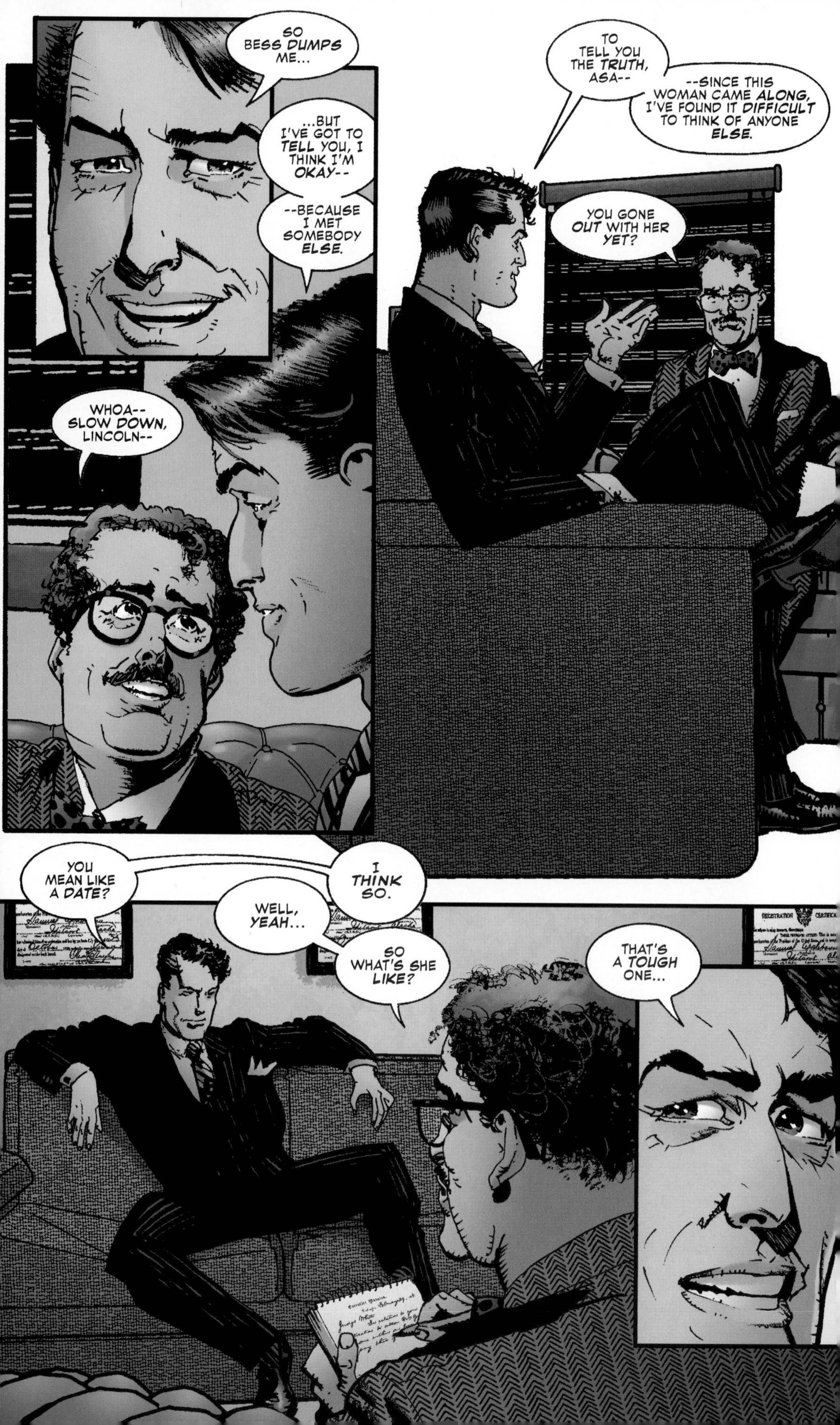
SO BESS DUMPS ME...
...BUT I'VE GOT TO TELL YOU, I THINK I'M OKAY--
--BECAUSE I MET SOMEBODY ELSE.
WHOA-- SLOW DOWN, LINCOLN--
TO TELL YOU THE TRUTH, ASA--
--SINCE THIS WOMAN CAME ALONG, I'VE FOUND IT DIFFICULT TO THINK OF ANYONE ELSE.
YOU GONE OUT WITH HER YET?
YOU MEAN LIKE A DATE?
I THINK SO.
WELL, YEAH...
SO WHAT'S SHE LIKE?
THAT'S A TOUGH ONE...

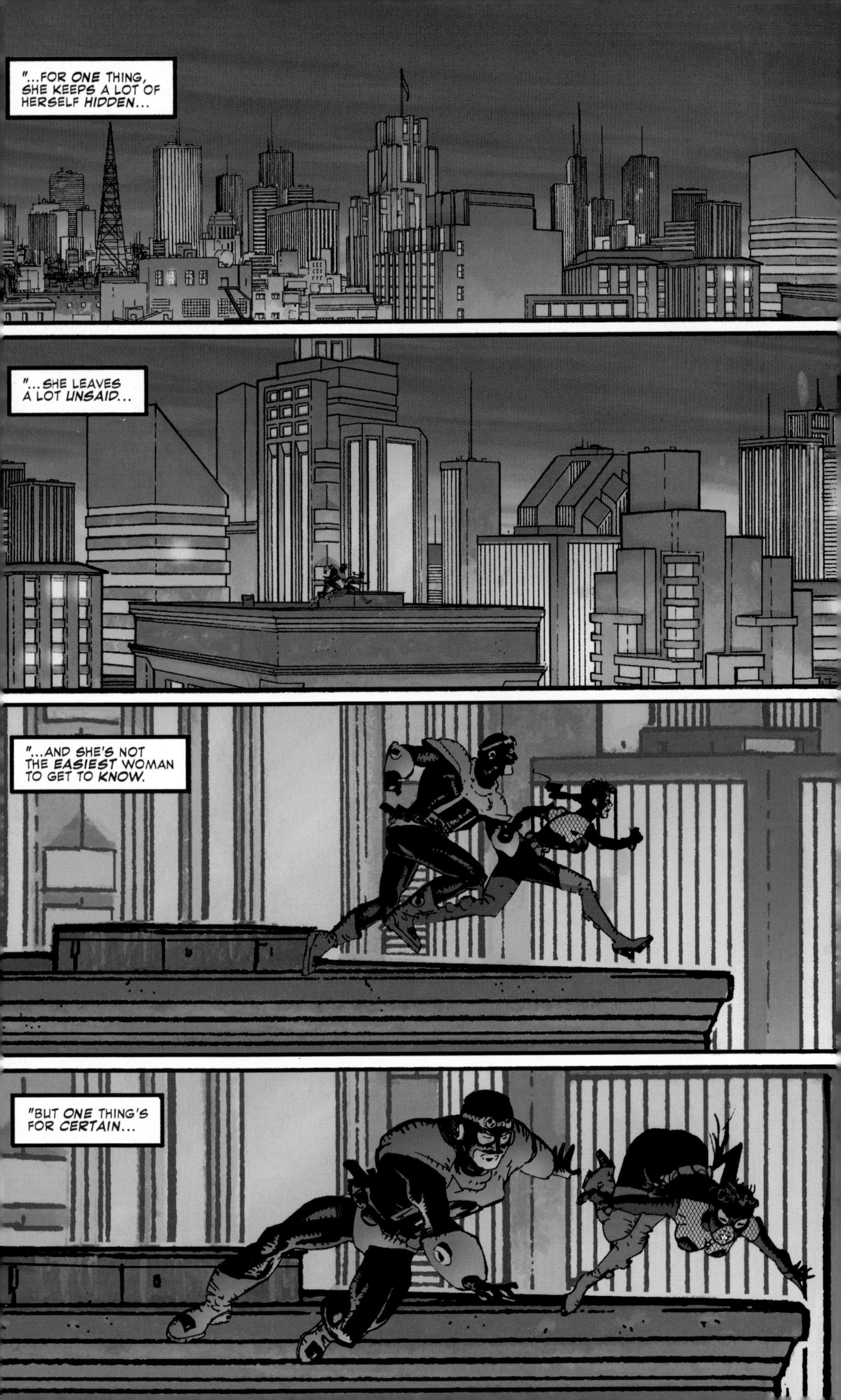
"...FOR ONE THING, SHE KEEPS A LOT OF HERSELF HIDDEN...
"...SHE LEAVES A LOT UNSAID...
"...AND SHE'S NOT THE EASIEST WOMAN TO GET TO KNOW.
"BUT ONE THING'S FOR CERTAIN...